EMBATTLED PARADISE

EMBATTLED PARADISE

The American Family

in an

Age of Uncertainty

ARLENE SKOLNICK

Basic Books
A Member of Perseus Books, L.L.C.

Library of Congress Cataloging in Publication Data
Skolnick, Arlene S., 1933–
    Embattled paradise: the American family in an age of
uncertainty / Arlene Skolnick.
        p. cm.
    Includes bibliographical references and index.
    1. Family—United States—History—20th century.
2. United States—Social conditions—1945-   I. Title
    HQ535.S56 1991
    306.85'0973'09045—dc20   91-70056
                                               CIP

Designed by Ellen Levine

98 99 00 LP 10 9 8 7 6

To Jerry, Mike, and Alex

C O N T E N T S

ACKNOWLEDGMENTS

This book grew out of many years of conversation, discussion, and debate with more people than I can name here. And since this is a "synthetic" work, I have also depended on the writings of many strangers whose ideas have helped shape or flesh out the story I tell. In the end, of course, I am to blame for any misstatements or misunderstandings that appear here.

I am especially grateful to the friends and colleagues who read drafts of chapters and offered suggestions for improvement. They include Karla Hackstaff, Anne Machung, Judith Stacey, Celeste MacLeod, and Marilyn Little. I owe particular thanks to Lillian Rubin, who gave a close reading of the whole manuscript at a critical stage in the writing.

I have been fortunate to live in a community that has many bright, creative people thinking and writing about family issues. In particular, the Berkeley Women's Research group helped me launch this project by hearing out my early ideas and pointing out what needed to be done to shape them into a book. Aside from the feedback during monthly meetings, I have been helped by conversations with Kristin Luker, Nancy Chodorow, Annette Lawson, Mary Ann Mason, Carol Stack, Ruth Rosen, Robert Post, Pat McBrown, and Ann Swidler. Then too, there are the ongoing informal seminars over the dinner table (usually theirs) of Hank and Lillian Rubin, who have been more than "just friends."

I'm grateful to two other old friends whose ideas have helped to shape my thinking about family matters—William J. Goode and Lenore Weitzman. Among the other friends and colleagues with whom I've shared ideas over the years, I'd like to mention Katherine Newman, Pauline Boss, Barbara Laslett, Tamara Hareven, Francesca Cancian, and Matilda Riley. Also Andrew Cherlin and Frank Furstenburg, in their writings and in person, have helped to shape my assessments of the changing American family.

I am indebted to the Institute of Human Development and its directors—John Clausen, Paul Mussen, Guy Swanson, and Joe Campos—for their support, encouragement, and intellectual stimulation over the years. The Family Dynamics seminar, organized by Guy Swanson and Phil Cowan, has provided an ongoing forum for discussing and debating the interplay among self, family, and society. Glen Elder's work with the IHD longitudinal data and his writings on historical change and the life course have had a strong influence on my own thinking. I have also benefited from the conversations and writings of other institute colleagues: Diana Baumrind, Don Hanson, Carol Huffine, Vicki Johnson, Dorothy Field, and Eliane Aertz.

Further, the longitudinal data at the Institute, a unique treasure chest of information on four generations in the lives of over two hundred American families, provide much of the empirical grounding for the arguments I make here. I do not deal in any detail with the lives of the study members in this book, but immersion in the IHD data has given me a basis for judging the validity of broad claims about the state of American character and culture and of the American family.

Early on in the writing I realized that I had to deal not just with the demographic and social "facts" of family life but with the family as a highly charged topic of cultural and political discourse in America. My approach to these issues has been informed by the work of two sociological colleagues who did not have a direct role in this book but whose work has informed it—Bennett Berger and Herbert Gans. Representing a skeptical, pragmatic brand of sociology, both work the problematic borderland between American cultural myth and social reality.

The people at Basic Books were enormously supportive and helpful from start to finish. I am grateful to my original editor, Judy Greissman, the birth mother of the book, and to Steve Fraser, who adopted it as his own. Steve's sharp critical eye perceived the statue in the marble of the original manuscript; Linda Carbone helped to carve it out. Thanks also go to Janet Halverson for designing a beautiful cover that catches the spirit of the book, and to Tina Barney for the photograph on the cover.

I would also like to thank my own extended and nuclear families for embodying the best kind of family values—love, concern, and just being there when I needed them. I especially want to thank my mother, Rosalie Silberstein, and my mother-in-law, Gladys Skolnick. Although my father, Harold Silberstein, and father-in-law, Bill Skolnick, are no longer around to read this, I want to acknowledge my love for them, and to memorialize them. My brother, Richard Silberstein, and his wife, Alice Liftin, are very special people, who began as relatives and have matured into best friends.

My husband, Jerry, and I each grew up in large extended families. Not all of our aunts and uncles and cousins remain, and those who do are too numerous to mention, but I want to start with the Silbersteins, especially with the matriarch of the clan, Aunt Frieda, a model nonagenarian and, in her own way, a feminist; and also to mention cousins Elaine, Shirley, Gladys, and Stanley, and their spouses and children, now all grown up. Not many remain of the Chaikens, but it's been good to have Aunt Molly and it's been fun to be with Norman and Arlene.

Jerry also has a huge and warmly inviting extended family. I want especially to acknowledge his aunts and uncles, Fanny, Ruthie, Roz and Ralph, Adele and Jack, and Uncle Jack, and their children and children's children. Jerry's cousin, Allen Hyman (a surrogate brother, actually), and his wife, Valerie, and their sons have grown closer and dearer to us as the years have passed.

I want especially to thank my own sons, Michael and Alexander, for their love and support: Alex's gifted guitar playing furnished a lovely background to my struggles with my writing; Michael pitched in with research assistance at a crucial time, tracking down references and helping to order my notes and bibliography. And I want to thank Jerry for putting up with the book's intrusive presence in our lives for more time than either of us at first suspected it would take to finish it, for his prodding and helpful criticism of several drafts, and above all for his loving companionship.

Finally, I would like to thank Vicky Goldberg, whose wonderful biography of Margaret Bourke-White supplied me with the phrase I knew had to be, from the moment I read it, the title of this book.

P R O L O G U E

"Who Killed Ozzie and Harriet?"

It is January 1990. I am watching a documentary produced by the San Francisco NBC affiliate and narrated by Sylvia Chase, one of my favorite newspersons. The show is called "Who Killed Ozzie and Harriet?" and cheerful scenes in black and white from the old television series are spliced into longer, full-color, not so cheerful scenes from contemporary family life.

The Nelson family is in the kitchen, admiring a fish one of the boys has caught.

A California suburb, 1990: A young mother arrives home from her job as her husband gets ready to drive to his. He's been on duty at home. He quickly tells her what's been happening with the children, what needs to be done around the house—a ritual they call the "handoff." Both parents work full-time at different shifts; they're not happy with the lack of time together, they explain, but it is the only way they can afford to live in a neighborhood with good schools.

Ozzie and the boys are tossing a ball back and forth on the front lawn; Harriet looks on smiling.

A California city; Two sisters, about nine and eleven, tell how scary it is to come home to an empty house while their parents are at work.

"I want my mother to be there waiting with a quilt and hot choco-
late," says the older girl.

Ozzie and Harriet and the boys are in the kitchen, sharing a birthday cake.

These alternating images do with pictures what most commentators
on the family do with words: portray change by contrasting a lost,
golden Past with an unhappy Present. Without sensationalizing its
subject, this program illustrates the nostalgia that pervades most discussions of the changes in American family life since the 1950s. There
was, of course, a disclaimer at the beginning of the program—Ozzie
and Harriet were only what television *told* us the family was like in
the 1950s; nevertheless, those intercut scenes of the happy Nelsons
and various contemporary families talking about their problems told
their own story, a tale of loss and decline.

Some social critics purvey a much darker brand of nostalgia. Advancing an almost apocalyptic vision of American society, they prof-
fer "the breakdown of the family" as part of a more general
disintegration of American character and culture. In contrast, the
television show presented a variety of families trying hard to carry
out the ordinary tasks of family life under new and difficult conditions. But nostalgia in any form induces at best a passive, bittersweet
mood of yearning—at worst, a sense of helplessness and despair.

In this book I take quite a different approach to making sense of
the changes in the American family since the 1950s. I argue not with
the *facts* of change—the revolution in sexual manners and morals and
the sharp rise in divorce, single-parent families, and women working
outside the home—but with what to make of them. I take issue with
those doomsayers who proclaim the decline of the family, as well as
with the dwindling band of family scholars who argue that the family
is in better shape than ever. I argue that the family can be a cherished
value, a durable institution, and "in trouble"—all at the same time.
The family is a place of enduring bonds and fragile relationships, of
the deepest love and the most intractable conflicts, of the most intense passions and the routine tedium of everyday life. It is a shelter
from the workings of a harsh economy, and it is battered by forces
beyond its control.

Embattled Paradise grows out of almost two decades of research and
writing on the family. My career in family studies began when I was
living with my husband and young sons in Berkeley in the late 1960s
and early 1970s. A member of the so-called silent generation, I had

made my first contribution to the baby boom during its waning years, after earning a Ph.D. in social and clinical psychology. Just as I was ready to settle down to a life combining work and family, I found myself at the epicenter of a decade of cultural and political upheavals.

An exhilarating and bewildering laboratory of social movements and experiments bubbled up around us and across the continent: the New Left, feminism, communes, the sexual revolution, cohabitation, the gay movement, and the beginning of the divorce revolution. Our second son was born in 1968, the calamitous year that has served as the title for several books, and that many Americans consider the worst year of the century. Trying to make sense of our lives in the context of what was happening around us, my husband—a sociologist and law professor who had previously co-authored a family law case-book, and who had spent the latter half of 1968 writing a report published as *The Politics of Protest*—and I decided to put together a book of readings on the family that we titled *Family in Transition*. (I became a "family sociologist" by following that book with a full-blown textbook on the family, *The Intimate Environment*, and by focusing my research on marriage and family matters.)

As we searched the literature for articles to print in *Family in Transition*, we were surprised and disappointed. Most writings on the family at that time not only had little to say about the vast and significant changes we saw taking place but seemed to deny that such things could ever happen. From the lofty theoretical perch of "functionalism" and "social equilibrium," the family as it had been in the 1950s was, it was said, a universal, changeless institution. But of course it wasn't. Changes were happening all around us.

Fortunately, we were able eventually to find old and new articles that did suggest alternative ways of thinking about family matters. Since those days, there has been a tremendous outpouring of research and writing on family life past and present. Many older assumptions about the family have been shown to have little or no foundation. Yet much public debate and discussion often continues to rest on such questionable beliefs.

Specifically, much discourse about the contemporary crisis of the family suffers from the following flaws.

Lack of a historical context. History is the best antidote to nostalgia. The image of a warm, secure, stable family life in past times that serves as a backdrop to most discussions of family change is deeply at odds with the findings of recent research in the history of the

family. Nostalgia devotees, in particular, seem unaware of the disruptive impact of high mortality rates on families in past times, or of
how close to the margin of survival most people lived before the
twentieth century. Further, this is not the first time Americans have
faced change in the most intimate aspects of life. Far from revealing
some lost era of family stability and harmony, the study of past family
life reveals a heritage of change and crisis.

*Using the family patterns of the 1950s as the last stand of the "traditional
family" or as a baseline for measuring change.* The 1950s were a unique
interlude in the history of the American family, unlike any other
decade in the twentieth century. Far from being the golden age of
American family life, even the happiest families—and especially the
women in them—were haunted by contradictory demands and expectations. The upheavals of the following decades grew directly out
of those contradictions.

*Lumping together a host of changes and social problems into one big "crisis
of the family."* The notion of family crisis is a conceptual black hole—
muddled and misleading. Popular discussions of the family "crisis"
can include any or all of the following: divorce, single-parent families, working wives and mothers, high rates of poverty among children, the concept of women's equality, low birthrates and childlessness, abortion, teenage pregnancy, sex before marriage, latchkey
children, alcoholism and drug abuse, family violence, child abuse, gay
couples, and alternative or nontraditional families.

Practically any problem affecting children, men, and women can
be considered a problem of the family—but it may not be useful to
think of it that way. Some troubles, such as family violence, poverty,
and racial conflict, were around well before the 1960s. Others—
mothers in the work force, abortion—are considered problems only by
people holding certain values. Some could be alleviated through shifts
in public and private policy. Putting all these issues in one basket labeled
"the family crisis" or "the disintegration of the family" impedes clear
thinking and postpones sorely needed adjustments to family change,
such as child care and parental leave. Blaming social problems on the
family is often a way of deflecting attention away from defects in American *society*, especially its economy.

*Ignoring the structural roots of recent family change, and assuming we
could return to "traditional" family patterns if only we (read women) had
the will and strength of character to do so.* The upheavals of the 1960s
and 1970s were part of a lengthy and challenging process of assimilating old dreams to new lives and new circumstances. The changes

they have wrought in gender roles and family life are rooted in long-term economic, demographic, political, and cultural trends. There is little likelihood that these will be reversed.

Assuming Americans are in flight from marriage and family. Despite all the changes of recent years, home and family endure as central values for Americans. But in a fast-changing postindustrial society, close emotional bonds become more precious yet more fragile and vulnerable to strain. Further, for Americans outside the highest income brackets, economic stagnation and a downward trend in real income have impeded the realization of family goals; postponing marriage and children, for example, has become a matter of economic necessity for large numbers of young Americans. Nevertheless, people continue to find in family ties their deepest source of happiness and meaning in life.

New conditions, old rhetoric. In blaming recent shifts in family life on such moral and psychological failings as narcissism and pathological individualism, some social critics not only ignore major transformations in the social and economic context of family life but clothe their concerns in an all too familiar discourse. The rhetoric of family crisis has persisted as a theme in our culture for more than a century. So has the more general belief that modern society itself is in a state of crisis, and that we are becoming a nation of rootless and alienated individuals. Whenever significant social change takes place, the old themes resurface to express the anxieties that change evokes.

A few final points: first, I use the term *the family* rather than *family life* or *families*; I am aware that this term tends to conjure up a stereotypical image of a mother, father, and two children, rather than an array of diverse families. Nevertheless, I want to reclaim *the family* and use it in the same way one might speak of *the economy*—as an important aspect of social life, not a particular kind of economic enterprise.

Second, when I focus on the family of the middle class, it is not because I am unaware of the dissimilarities and distinctiveness of American families by race, class, region, religion, and gender preference. Rather, it is because the mainstream middle-class family has defined the norms of family life in America. Traditionally, variations from this pattern, such as single parenthood, have been considered unfortunate deviations. One source of the present sense of crisis is that the middle class has been engaging in practices formerly considered deviant. Mothers work outside the home, unmarried couples live together, single women give birth or adopt children. Paradoxically, however, the middle class has also been America's most revolutionary class insofar as the family is concerned. Our major periods of family crisis have occurred when the middle class has redefined the meaning of family. Since the 1960s, America has been living through one of those times.

Finally, some thoughts about family as image and idea. After watching "Who Killed Ozzie and Harriet?" I found myself with mixed feelings. Despite my unease with the device of juxtaposing idealized fictional images with real families talking about their problems, I was nevertheless moved by the contrast. As advertisers and politicians know, images of home and family carry a deep emotional resonance that is not defused by their being used to sell something, or by our knowledge that they are not realistic. Familiar images often become transformed into a kind of reality.

By generating unrealistically high expectations for family life, idealized portraits of family happiness can sow seeds of discontent. Yet there is a positive side to sentimental and overly harmonious visions of family relations. In a fascinating essay on "I Remember Mama," a popular TV series of the early 1950s often taken at the time to be a realistic account of a Norwegian-American family, the historian George Lipsitz described how the show served as a source of consolation and hope for people whose own family lives had been far less happy. This included the actors who played in it, many in the audience who watched it, and the writers who created an ideal family out of what their own lives were not. Perhaps, as Lipsitz suggests, "If our own personal pasts cannot be venerated as moral guides for the present, we must choose another from history or art and embrace it as our own."[1] It is precisely this tension between the culturally promised family and everyday life, between the old dreams and the new realities, that is central to understanding our hopes and concerns about the family in late-twentieth-century America.

Berkeley, California
May 1991

INTRODUCTION

A Cultural Earthquake

[We] also need, as much as anything else, language adequate to the times we live in. We need to see how we live now and we can only see with words and images which leave us no escape into nostalgia for another time and place.
—Michael Ignatieff
The Needs of Strangers

In 1962, *Look* magazine invited a number of scholars, scientists, and political leaders to predict what America would be like twenty-five years into the future.[1] Most of the forecasters saw the America of 1987 as streamlined, clean, orderly, prosperous—a high-tech world of 500-mile-an-hour jet-powered carplanes and automated kitchens that would cook meals and clean up in minutes. Along with predictions of such techno-logical wonders were several descriptions of family life.

"Linda (the wife)," described a profile of a typical family, "runs her home with extreme good taste and manages her children with serene authority. But she does not try to run or manage her husband." An-other article imagined a mother's calendar on a typical day: "Clothes disposer repairman here. Shop: Buy baked ham pills, scotch and soda capsules. Pay radar bill. Have the Whites and Hammonds over for capsules. Take Bob's jet to hangar for grease job. Go to hypnotist for headache therapy."

Looking backward from the future these writers were trying to describe, we learn more about the "structure of feelings"[2] of that era—its distinctive mindset—than about the realities of our own. Their boundless faith in science and technology, and in a future that promised more of everything, now seems quaint. They imagined that the technology of 1987 would transform the material landscape of everyday life, but the future family they saw was unchanged, as if preserved in a time capsule.

Although the calendar indicated that the 1960s had begun, 1962 was still part of the era historians have called the American celebration, the American high, the proud decades[3]—the years when America's victory in World War II thrust the nation into an era of unprecedented prosperity and power in the world. The *Look* piece was among the last of a string of similar books and articles. In 1955, the editors of *Fortune* magazine had published "The Fabulous Future: America in 1980." The distinguished contributors to that article also predicted a stable, even, more uniformly prosperous and nearly classless America.

It seemed as if the nation had reached a final stage of historical development, that it was a "completed society."[4] The stability and legitimacy of major institutions went largely unquestioned. "All the problems are solved," complained a college editor in 1957; there seemed to be little to write about.[5] The only possible improvements would be those wrought by the kinds of technological wizardry described by the writers in *Look*. "Pockets of poverty" and other difficulties remained to be mopped up, but major social change—"the kind that is painful and agonizing and that forces individuals and generations into a sense of radical disjunction between traditional ways and contemporary realities—would henceforth be confined to developing nations, like Tunisia."[6]

The central symbol of the nearly perfected America of the 1950s was the suburban family. Suburbia meant more than physical comfort; it embodied a long-held American dream of a happy, secure family life.[7] The leading television situation comedies of the time—"Father Knows Best," "Leave It to Beaver," "The Adventures of Ozzie and Harriet"—portrayed cheerful, well-off, white suburban families, "orderly lives lived without major trauma or disturbance."[8]

Television images, then as now, did not portray the way most Americans actually lived. These were idealized families in idealized settings, successfully masquerading as "normal," "healthy," "typical," "average." Years later, Billy Gray, the actor who played Bud in "Father Knows

Best," said he felt "ashamed" he had ever had anything to do with the show. It was all "totally false," he said, and had caused many Americans to feel inadequate, because they thought that was the way life was supposed to be and that their own lives failed to measure up.[9]

Contrary to the homogeneous, idealized family portrayed in the sitcoms, the most distinctive feature of American family life has always been its diversity. Searching for the "normal American family" in the late 1950s, one researcher found "the most astonishing variance in its structure and function."[10] Families differed by income, by social class, by ethnicity and religion, by neighborhood and region, by number of members, by relations with kin, by patterns of authority and affection, by life-style, by the balance of happiness and unhappiness.

Yet, those smiling television families incarnated a symbolism deeply rooted in American culture; anthropologists have shown that this "sentimental model" defines family life even for those whose daily lives and cultural traditions differ radically from it.[11] Further, television's families did reflect a set of social trends affecting a sizable chunk of the population. The young adults of the time were rushing into marriage at a younger age than any other generation in American history, and producing a record crop of babies. With the mass migration to the suburbs, for the first time a majority of families joined the homeowner class.

To many social scientists as well as TV producers, America was "a middle class society in which some people were simply more middle class than others."[12] Sociological theorists saw the suburban family as the most highly developed version of a timeless social unit. The nuclear family, wrote one anthropologist, was "a biological phenomenon—as rooted in organs and physiological structures as insect societies."[13]

Little wonder, then, that the writers of the *Look* article projected Ozzie and Harriet's family unchanged into a stable, streamlined future. In 1962 there seemed no reason to doubt that the next twenty-five years would continue to bring social stability and economic progress. No one predicted assassinations, urban riots, student protests, a lost war, economic stagnation. Least likely of all was the prospect of revolutionary change in the most intimate aspects of American life—the family, sexual mores, the roles of women and men.

Ten years after the "American high" had reached its peak, the hopes and expectations of the 1950s lay in ruins. Instead of the social stability that had been expected, the two decades that followed were among the most turbulent periods of American history, comparable only to the Civil War era. To a greater extent than in any earlier

period, the upheaval was as much about cultural and sexual standards as public issues.

Between 1965 and 1975, the land of togetherness became the land
of swinging singles, open marriage, creative divorce, encounter
groups, communes, alternative life-styles, women's liberation, the
Woodstock Nation, and "the greening of America." A land where
teenage girls wore girdles even to gym class became a land of mini-
skirts, bralessness, topless bathing suits, and nude beaches.

Middle-class norms that once seemed carved in stone were crumbling away. In the 1950s, observes the anthropologist Lionel Tiger,
there was a "broad embargo on visual and aural information about
virtually anything between people's legs. Movies could not depict two
humans in the same bed unless one acrobat maintained a foot on the
floor."[14] A leading director got into trouble with censors for using
the word *virgin* in a movie; homosexuality, out-of-wedlock childbearing, and abortion were dark and dirty secrets.

But by the early 1970s, sexual mores had been transformed. Abortion became legal; four-letter words became a staple of Hollywood
films; homosexuals came out of the closet, marched in the streets,
and ran for political office; unwed girls and women began to keep
their babies; unwed middle-class couples openly moved in together,
a practice known in its formerly nonrespectable days among the lower
class as "shacking up." During the same years, apart from these and
other changes in morality, the leading statistical indicators of family
life were revealing equally dramatic departures from the trends of
the 1950s: skyrocketing divorce rates, a surge of women into the
workplace, rising rates of single motherhood, and so on. The solid
American family of Mom, Dad, and the kids was becoming fragmented into a bewildering array of life-styles. It was as if, said the
president of the Population Association of America, an "earthquake
had shuddered through the American family."[15]

By the late 1970s, the mood of the country had shifted once again.
A decade of revolt and liberation had spawned an inevitable backlash. The passion for change and experiment had burned itself out.
But apart from social and cultural change, the decade was marked by
a series of events that undid the assumptions about progress, prosperity, and American power in the world that had dominated both
the 1950s and the 1960s.

After Watergate, Vietnam, energy crises, inflation, and economic
stagnation, nostalgia settled like a haze on American political and
cultural life. Instead of looking forward to the automated utopia of

a "fabulous future," Americans hungered for the stability, order, and tradition of a lost golden age. But even as the image of a Norman Rockwell America became a cultural ideal and "old-fashioned" became a term of high praise, a deepening sense of decay, disintegration, and crisis hung over the present. Somehow, the family seemed to be at the center of it all, or at least it supplied us with a language for talking about the feeling that things were falling apart. In his now-notorious "malaise" speech, President Carter captured the national mood. Supposedly addressing the energy crisis, he lamented that "in a nation that was proud of hard work, strong families, close-knit communities and faith in God, too many of us now tend to worship self-indulgence and consumption."[16]

The election of 1980 marked a turning of the cultural as well as the political tides. A "new politics of old values" swept Ronald Reagan into the presidency.[17] The "liberated," "greened" America of the 1960s and 1970s had become a land of sexual fear, television evangelists, and antidrug and antipornography crusades. Underneath it all was a profound collective yearning for enduring emotional bonds and a fear that the social fabric had become dangerously frayed. Reagan came to power promising to restore all that had been lost since "the proud decades": American might abroad, the traditional family at home.

Despite the nostalgia for traditional moral codes and family values that dominated the culture and political rhetoric of the Reagan era, social reality did not turn back. The intact nuclear family may have returned to the top of the television charts—"The Cosby Show" and "Family Ties" supplying the same rewards as "Father Knows Best" and "Ozzie and Harriet"—but the celebration of traditional family values masked the radical changes that had taken place in family life and household economics. By the end of the 1980s it was clear that the New Right's dream of restoring the family forms, affluence, and dominance of the 1950s "American high" had failed.

WHAT HAPPENED TO THE AMERICAN FAMILY?

How can we make sense of these changes? What happened to the stable, two-parent, breadwinner/housewife families of the 1950s? How could such drastic changes have happened so quickly? Why did the return of traditional values and the election of a socially conservative president pledged to restoring the traditional family fail to turn back the clock on family change? Finally, what language should we use to describe the transformation of the American family?

Since the early 1970s, public conversation about family change has been dominated by a bleak rhetoric of loss and decline. The American family has "broken down," "fallen apart," "collapsed"; it is "in crisis" or, at the very least, "in trouble." Some believe the family is dying, if not already dead. One sociologist predicted that if present trends continue, not a single family would be left in America by the end of the century.[18]

In stark contrast, a number of scholars of the family have argued that the decline of the family is a myth. Taking issue with the "alarmists and doomsayers who predict the disintegration of the American family,"[19] the optimists point to demographic and survey data showing that despite evidence of change, the vast majority of Americans remain deeply committed to marriage and family. Far from rejecting family bonds, most Americans claim to find in them their deepest single source of satisfaction and meaning in life. This optimistic side of the debate has been presented to the general public in the sociologist Mary Jo Bane's *Here to Stay* (1976) and the political analyst Ben Wattenberg's *The Good News Is the Bad News Is Wrong* (1984) among other books. In *Middletown Families* (1981), Theodore Caplow and his team of sociological researchers offered the strongest statement: returning to "Middletown" (actually Muncie, Indiana), the town that the sociologists Robert and Helen Lynd had studied and made famous in the 1920s and 1930s, they discovered "increased family solidarity, a smaller generation gap, close marital communication, more religion and less mobility."[20]

Despite these reassurances, pessimism about the family has continued to deepen. Indeed, by the late 1980s, the optimists themselves were becoming an endangered species.[21] The issue was no longer whether the family had a future; the breakdown of the family seemed firmly at the center of a broad syndrome of cultural decline. There was a widespread nervousness that something had recently gone wrong with the hearts and minds of individual Americans—a loss of moral fiber, a debilitating preoccupation with the self.

Moral decay was a pervasive image in the ideology of the religious New Right conservatives who helped propel Ronald Reagan into the White House. "History has proven over and over again," said one conservative activist, "that a country can be destroyed by moral decay from within. . . . Why do you suppose Rome crumbled?" A Moral Majority preacher warned that God destroyed Sodom and Gomorrah for the very things going on in America today.[22]

But the theme of moral decay was not confined to New Right religious activists. Critics across the political spectrum complained that
individualism, hedonism, feminism, and a new therapeutic ethic was
eating away at the social fabric. Left and liberal social critics offered
commentary that read remarkably like sermons of the religious right.
"There is neat irony," observed the writer Ellen Willis in 1979, "in
the fact that leftists are now romanticizing the family and blaming
capitalism for its collapse, while ten years ago they were trashing the
family and blaming capitalism for its persistence."[23]

Christopher Lasch's *The Culture of Narcissism* (1979) is the prime
example of the genre—the "quintessential Doomsday book," as one
critic observed.[24] Lasch's narcissistic America is a nightmarish social
landscape with scarcely a single redeeming virtue. Consumer capitalism and mass culture, according to Lasch, have destroyed the paternal authority of the classical Victorian bourgeois family. The
enfeebled modern family has created a new weak and dependent
character type, incapable of emotional attachment, craving intimacy
but fearful of commitment: "Our society . . . has made deep and lasting friendships, love affairs and marriages increasingly difficult to
achieve. As social life becomes more and more warlike and barbaric,
personal relationships, which ostensibly provide relief from these
conditions, take on the character of combat."[25]

Comparing the pervasive assumption of family decline with indicators of its tenacity, one is reminded of Macauley's statement that
we have heard nothing but despair and seen nothing but progress.
Resolving this paradox is the central task of this book. I see an element of truth in both positions, yet neither is helpful in addressing
the very real problems that beset the family. Both the despair and
the progress are real, but neither side has captured the complexities
and ambiguities of recent social and cultural change.

The major flaw of the pessimists is their ahistorical nostalgia. They
suffer from what the historian Peter Laslett calls the "world we have
lost syndrome"[26]—the tendency to contrast an idealized Past, when
families were presumably strong, stable, and caring, with a decadent,
fallen Present. Although this genre of writing seems to be about history, it avoids detailed descriptions of family life in any particular
time or place. Whether the golden age is located in the 1950s, the
Victorian era, or the preindustrial past, its portrayal in these writings
bears approximately the same relation to the historical record as a
Disneyland setting bears to its historical counterpart.

Ironically, this nostalgia for the lost family has blossomed at a time
when the social history of the family has emerged as an intellectual

growth industry. We have learned more in the past two decades about family life in past times than we have in the preceding two centuries. Looking in detail at the family in specific times and places, historians have located no golden age of family harmony and stability. Every family pattern, it seems, has its own costs and benefits, its own tensions and internal contradictions, its own concerns about the gap between ideal and real.

One recent survey notes that Americans have been worrying about the family for over three hundred years: "Within decades of the Puritans' arrival in Massachusetts Bay Colony, Puritan jeremiads were already decrying the increasing fragility of marriage, the growing selfishness and irresponsibility of parents and the increasing rebelliousness of children."[27] The "crisis of the family" it seems, is a national tradition, and not just in America: historians of the family in other countries have made much the same discovery.[28] The facts, as opposed to fantasies, about pre-twentieth-century family life portray not a world we have lost but one we have in many ways escaped—a world of high mortality rates and rampant disease, in which vast numbers of people barely subsisted.[29]

Nor were the 1950s the golden age of family life. It was in part the tensions and discontents simmering underneath the seemingly bland surface of life in that decade that fueled the cultural revolts of the 1960s. And the social critics of the time denounced the suburbs and the suburban family as fiercely as their later counterparts denounced narcissism and individualism, blaming them for "many of the country's real and alleged ills, from destroying its farmland to emasculating its husbands."[30]

In any event, the family patterns of the baby-boom era were a response to the historical circumstances of that particular period. Further, in evaluating the changes that took place since the 1960s, it is important to realize that the 1950s family was not as traditional as most people assume it to have been. In fact, the decade stands out as an unusual one for twentieth-century family life, whose historical trends have been falling birth rates, rising divorce rates, and later ages of marriage.[31] The family patterns of the 1950s are as much in need of explanation as are the departures from them that have occurred since then.

But realizing that there never was a golden past we can return to only makes it more difficult to assess the sense of strain and crisis that change has brought. The sheer speed of the changes has been disorienting, leaving all of us with a sense of loss and bewilderment. Those most committed to the traditional order have seen their deeply held values

and assumptions swept away; those who hoped that change would repair an unjust social system have seen those hopes frustrated.

Women have gained the freedom both to have children and to
pursue careers, but society and institutions have not adapted to a
world where women are in the workplace to stay. Large numbers of
women have lost the economic security of traditional lifelong marriage, without the earning capacity to support themselves and their
children. Men have felt the ground shift under their own definitions
of male roles as women have challenged traditional notions of gender; men have lost the legitimacy, if not the reality, of their traditional domination over women.

And if the cultural revolution were not enough to contend with,
Americans in the 1970s also had to face an even greater threat to
their accustomed way of life: a declining economy and a declining
place in the world. The fall of Vietnam and later events in Iran
seemed to signify the decline of the American empire. For the first
time in history, American parents had to face the prospect of their
children having a lower standard of living than themselves. For the
first time in a generation, middle-class young adults could no longer
count on the basic ingredients of middle-class life—a good job and a
single-family home. Little wonder that religious conservatives were
ready to believe that God was no longer willing to shed his grace on
America and that apocalyptic thinking spread throughout the land.

The lamentations of the pessimistic social critics also spoke to the
sense of dislocation provoked by all this change and, by naming and
packaging that mood, amplified it still further. Their work became
an integral part of the cultural climate of their time. Thus millions
of people, ambivalent about the changing mores and family patterns,
uncertain about the present, with no clear vision of a better future,
resonate to denunciations of a corrupt present and join with the
critics in blaming our current troubles on the loss of an idealized
past. These works have an emotional resonance lacking in the literal
works of the optimists. For people dreaming of somehow restoring a
golden age of family happiness, it is cold comfort to be told that such
an age never existed.

Nevertheless, the lure of nostalgia blinds us to the facts of social
change and impedes us from coming to grips with the problems created by that change. To blame moral decay or therapeutic culture for
our ills creates an illusion. It misleads us into believing that through
a combination of individual acts of will, moral fortitude, and regres-
sive social policies, we can restore an imaginary past.

In the end, however, these works are self-refuting. They have touched a nerve in large numbers of people precisely because they echo our widespread yearnings for moral order, for intimate connection to others, for meaning in life beyond material success, for involvement in community life. Paradoxically, the very success of these works belies their central message about the corruption of American character and culture.

BEYOND NOSTALGIA
AND MORAL PANIC

How, then, can we make sense of the shifts in family life over the past several decades? We need a more complex and historically grounded account of the changes than we now have. The central argument I am advancing here is that the key to understanding the recent changes is not to be found in moral decay or in some deep flaw in the American character. Rather, because of the demographic, economic, and social changes that have transformed America and other advanced industrial countries in the twentieth century, we confront unprecedented circumstances. We live in a world unique in human history, a world our ancestors could hardly have imagined.

These changes have altered basic aspects of the human condition— from the facts of life and death, to the length and stages of the individual life course, to the kind of work we do, to the way we think and feel. The changes in our hearts and minds are responses to large-scale social change, rather than a fall from moral grace. Thus, family arrangements that made sense in 1800 or 1900 or even 1950 have little relevance for how we live today.

This is not the first time Americans have had to come to grips with unsettling new realities. As the historian Page Smith points out, "future shock" has been part of the American experience since the Pilgrims landed.[32] Yet in certain eras in our history, future shock has imposed a greater than usual strain on American consciousness. In such times, rapid and far reaching economic and social change has ushered in a period of cultural confusion and personal stress; there has been an uncomfortable mismatch between cultural norms and images and the ways people are actually living their lives.[33] These dislocations show up early in the family, as the behavior of large numbers of husbands and wives, parents and children, departs from expectations.

SOURCES OF
SOCIAL TRANSFORMATION

The changes in larger society, as well as their reverberations in the family, call into question basic assumptions about the nature of American society, its family arrangements, and Americans them-selves. A "cultural struggle" ensues as people debate the meaning of change.[34] One of these periods of cultural upheaval occurred in the early decades of the nineteenth century; a second occurred in the decades just before and after the turn of the twentieth century. For the last thirty years, we have been living through another such wave of social change.

Three related structural changes seem to have set the current cycle of family change in motion: first, the shift into a "postindustrial" information and service economy; second, a demographic revolution that not only created mass longevity but reshaped the individual and family life course, creating life stages and circumstances unknown to earlier generations; third, a process I call "psychological gentrifica-tion," which involves an introspective approach to experience, a greater sense of one's own individuality and subjectivity, a concern with self-fulfillment and self-development. This is the change misdi-agnosed as narcissism.

The Postindustrial Revolution

To most Americans, the "traditional" family consists of a breadwinner-father and a mother who stays home to care for the children and the household. When New Right politicians and preach-ers speak of the biblical, Christian, or Judeo-Christian family, this is the family pattern they have in mind.[35] Yet in historical and inter-national perspective, the breadwinner/housewife form of family is, as the sociologist Kingsley Davis observes, an uncommon and short-lived arrangement—an "aberration that arose in a particular stage of de-velopment and tends to recur in countries now undergoing devel-opment."[36]

The breadwinner family is actually the first form of the modern family, associated with the early stages of the Industrial Revolution. For most of human history, work was a household enterprise in which all family members took part. The shift of the workplace from the home that came with industry had a profound effect on gender as well as parent and child roles.

If the early stages of modernization helped to create the breadwinner/housewife family, the later stages helped to undo it. Davis has tracked the rise and fall of the breadwinner system in the United States and other countries at various stages of industrialism. With the onset of industrialization, the new family pattern develops slowly, eventually reaching a climax in which few wives are employed, then declines as a steadily growing number of married women find white-collar jobs as file clerks, secretaries, teachers, and the like. In America, the breadwinner system peaked in 1890.

Since 1945 the United States, along with other highly advanced societies, has been shifting from a goods-producing to a service-producing economy, from the factory to the office, from blue-collar work to white-collar work. The term "postindustrial society" is often used to describe this shift. Yet, as a number of writers have suggested, the changes seem more a continuation of industrial society—a high-tech era based on an increasingly complex division of labor, the further application of science and technology to increase productivity. If the steam engine, the steel plant, and the automobile assembly line symbolize the old order, the computer, VCR, satellite broadcasting, CAT scanners, and genetic engineering symbolize the new.[37] One could also argue that the invention of the typewriter marks the onset of the postindustrial era, symbolizing the beginning of the service and information economy and the coming feminization of the work force.

The historical shift of women into the workplace has been going on for a century, but did not reach a critical mass until the 1970s. The long-term impact of postindustrialism on family life was magnified by the effects of inflation. The shift in the economy was reducing the number of high-paying blue-collar jobs for auto and steel workers, and creating a demand for the low-paying pink-collar jobs like typist and file clerk. Also, since the mid-1960s, the costs of food, housing, education, and other goods and services have risen faster than the average male breadwinner's income. Despite their lower pay, married women's contributions to the family income became critical to maintaining living standards in both middle- and working-class families.

It was this quiet revolution of women's steady march into the workplace that set the stage for the feminist revival of the 1970s. There is no evidence that feminist ideas led the mass of married women to work in the first place.[38] Nevertheless, the impact of both the feminist movement and the new realities of working women has shifted the cultural ideal of marriage in a more egalitarian or symmetrical direction. At the moment, we are in a painful period of "cultural lag"[39] or "stalled revolution."[40] Women have changed, but social arrangements—and men—have not kept pace.

The postindustrial shift of women into the workplace has led to other changes in family life: it has increased the "opportunity costs" of pregnancy and child rearing—that is, the money lost when women leave their jobs to bear and raise children—fostering lower fertility rates. There is also some evidence that the increasing employment of women makes divorce more likely, by reducing a woman's dependence on her husband's income, making it easier for her to leave an unhappy marriage.[41]

Finally, the shift to a service and information economy has had effects on family life besides those linked to gender. For young people, the coming of the postindustrial society has made adolescence and the transition to adulthood more complex and problematic, exacerbating a dilemma that arose in the nineteenth century with the decline of the family economy. A greater amount of schooling is now necessary not only to maintain middle-class status but even to find jobs in the manufacturing sector. Until the 1970s, there was a supply of moderately well-paying jobs that did not require a high school diploma. High school graduates could find an array of decent jobs open to them. More schooling was necessary for a middle-class career, but there were alternative paths to making a living.

The high-tech postindustrial economy has changed all that. Today all roads to a successful livelihood lead through the classroom. Recent decades have seen a plummeting demand for unskilled labor and a sharp decline in the kind of well-paying blue-collar job that used to form the backbone of the American economy. A young working-class man who in the 1950s could have found an unskilled job paying enough to support a family now faces radically curtailed economic prospects. These vast changes in the economy led to shifts in family behavior that paralleled those due to cultural change— later marriage, lower fertility, women flooding into the workplace. For many people, these choices reflected economic pressures, not new values.

The Life-Course Revolution

The breadwinner/housewife family was a response not only to nineteenth-century working conditions but to nineteenth-century demographic circumstances. Because people lived shorter lives and had more children, a woman could expect to live her entire life with children in the home. Today, the average woman can expect to live more than thirty-three years after her last child has left the house. The traditional nuclear unit of parents and small children exists for only a small proportion of the life of an individual or a family. Shifts in the length and patterning of the life course have made the conditions of modern existence unimaginably different from those that existed only a century ago.

Nostalgic images of family stability in past times typically leave out the terrible facts of high mortality rates in infancy and early adulthood. Before the twentieth century, death was as much a hovering presence in the home as divorce is today. While the death of a baby or small child was almost a typical experience of parents down to the early decades of the twentieth century, the loss of a father or mother was also a common event of childhood and adolescence. The biography of almost any Victorian conveys the vulnerability of even the upper classes to untimely death.

In historical perspective, these changes have been remarkably sudden. Only in the twentieth century could a majority of people expect to live out the normal life course of growing up, marrying, having children, and surviving with one's spouse until age fifty.[42] The changes in life chances between the 1920s and the 1950s have been as rapid as in the years between 1880 and 1920.[43]

In advanced societies today, death strikes few youngsters and few adults between their twenties and fifties. Couples in enduring marriages will spend most of their married life together without having young children in the home. The shrinking of the active parental phase of the life course is also one of the reasons women have entered the work force in increasing numbers since the 1950s. Domesticity is not enough to fill a life span of almost eighty years. Little wonder then that marriage has become more of a personal and sexual relationship than it was in the past.

The emergence of old age as an expectable part of the life course is, as Ronald Blyth points out, one of the essential ways we differ from our ancestors; today's elders are among the first generations in which the mass of the population, not just the hardy few, survive long enough to experience the aging process, that "destruction of the physical self" so familiar to us now.[44] People over eighty-five are the fastest-growing age group today. But for much of old age, people are not *old* in the traditional sense but healthy and active.

Our lives have become have not just longer but more complicated. Stages of life that scarcely existed a hundred years ago have become part of the average person's experience: adolescence, middle age, empty nest, retirement. Also, in recent years, the life course has grown more fluid; people experience more transitions than earlier generations did, not just because of rising divorce rates but because of changes in the workplace. In an age of rapidly changing technology and market conditions, few employees can count on being "organization" men or women the way people did in the 1950s.

Ironically, the demographic and social changes that lengthened and reshaped the life course were desired themselves, yet are responsible for some of the major problems besetting family life today. Before mass longevity, the aged were not a problem population because there were so few of them. Mixed-up adolescents were rare when adult work began in childhood and formal education ended, if it ever began, in grade school. Identity was not a problem when a person's place in society was decided at birth. In the past, middle-aged men and women were not sandwiched between the needs of their adolescent children and their aging parents; nor when life expectancy was forty-nine or fifty did they have to confront the issue of what to do with the rest of their lives. Even though the "woman question" was an issue during most of the nineteenth century, women then did not confront the reality that the active phase of mothering would usually involve only a small portion of their lives.

All of this possibility for change created new sources of stress. Transitions can be problematic periods in which both individual identities and family relations have to be redefined and renegotiated. The emergence of a focus on the self and the idea of development as applied to adults is not just a fantasy of pop psychology. The popularity of books like Gail Sheehy's *Passages* reflects genuine changes in the structure of individual experience across the life course.[45] The emergence of a heightened sense of self is a natural by-product of this more complicated life course.

Psychological Gentrification

The third major transformation is in part a product of the changes in the nature of work and in the shape of the life course. But it is also a product of other social and cultural changes, especially rising levels of education and increases in the standard of living and leisure time. In the past, few jobs required learning or personal development. Working hours were long—about fifty-three hours a week at the turn of the century—and there was little time for leisure or extended vacations. Thus men's lives were dominated by the job; women's, by domesticity.

The affluent, postindustrial society of the postwar era involved more than an increase in living standards. Despite persisting inequality, the decades since the end of World War II were years of remarkable progress for masses of Americans. The democratization that began in the 1940s when the G.I. Bill opened up educational opportunity and the possibilities of home ownership eventually led to "the democratization of personhood"—the opportunity for large numbers of ordinary people to "take themselves seriously . . . to make a sustained project of the ordinary self."[46]

At a time when jeremiads about the decline of the American mind appear on the best-seller lists, it is easy to forget that during the postwar decades higher education became a reality for the first time to millions of Americans. In 1940 only 15 percent of young people between eighteen and twenty-two went to college; a college education was one of those rarely crossed boundaries separating the upper middle class from those below them. By the middle of the 1960s nearly half of young Americans went to college. By the end of the decade the number of college students was four times what it had been in the 1940s.[47]

The explosion of education was due not only to the demand of a new middle class for what it saw as key to success for its children; it was also due to the need of a postindustrial economy for a more educated work force. However pragmatic and instrumental the motivation for increased education, rising educational levels have had a profound influence on American culture. Middle-class Americans became, as the sociologist Todd Gitlin observes, "cultural omnivores," traveling abroad, going to concerts, museums, and theaters, joining book clubs, in growing numbers.[48] Everyday life in America has become "internationalized," as Americans become more familiar with and appreciative of other cultures. "We have grown from a nation of meat-and-potato eaters to a nation of sushi samplers," observes Walter Mead, "and we like it that way."[49]

Another result of this increasing cosmopolitanism is that avant-garde ideas that had once shocked the bourgeoisie in earlier generations, from cubist painting to bohemian sexual mores to Freudian psychology, diffused to college students in the 1960s and then to the middle-class masses in the 1970s. This diffusion can be clearly seen in the comparison of the results of national surveys conducted in 1957 and 1976 by the University of Michigan's Institute of Social Research. Aimed at assessing the state of American mental health, the studies delved into a wide range of questions concerning satisfactions and dissatisfactions with self, family relations, and work.

Comparisons of the two surveys reveal striking insights into the recent changes in American culture. In *The Inner American*, Joseph Veroff, Elizabeth Douvan, and Richard Kulka suggest that a "psychological revolution" took place between 1957 and 1976. Over the course of two decades, Americans had become more introspective, more attentive to inner experience, more willing to admit to marital and personal problems than in the past, and yet more satisfied with their marriages. Above all, they became more attentive to the emotional quality of relationships, not just in the family but at work as well. Increasingly, people wanted friendly, warm relationships at work and intimacy and closeness in the family.[50]

Paradoxically, the new emphasis on warmth and intimacy can place new burdens on family relationships and create discontents that didn't exist when family life was a matter of conformity to social roles and rituals. But the results of this study, carried out at the height of the so-called Me Decade, show no evidence that we have become a nation of narcissistic, unattached individuals. Family ties were shown to be even more important than in the past, especially for men. Despite high divorce rates and a willingness to admit marital problems, the study found an overwhelming preference for being married, and many more men and women were happy about their marriages than they had been in 1957.[51]

The Michigan studies provide clear documentation for the process of psychological gentrification. The habit of introspection, the psychological approach to life and preoccupation with warmth and intimacy was not new in the 1970s. In the 1950s, however, it was found almost exclusively among the most highly educated. Twenty years later this way of looking at the self and the world had become "common coin."[52]

CONCLUSION

As a result of all the changes I discussed in this chapter, the realities of life in late-twentieth-century America and other advanced societies are unlike those faced by any earlier generation. No other people ever lived longer or healthier lives, or exercised so much choice about life's central dramas: work, marriage, parenthood. Many of the troubles and anxieties confronting the American family today arise out of benefits few of us would undo if we could—lower mortality rates, reliable birth control, mass education, the democratization of American life.

The metaphor of an earthquake, often invoked to describe the social and cultural upheavals of the 1960s and 1970s, turns out to be a fairly good model of what actually did happen during those years. No other natural cataclysm—hurricanes, tornadoes, floods—strikes less randomly than earthquakes; they occur at fairly regular intervals, along clearly detectable fault lines.

The seismic forces at work in the social and cultural earthquake were, on the one side, locked-in cultural norms about family structure, gender roles, and sexuality and, on the other, a set of long-term changes that include the demographic, economic, and structural trends I have discussed. For example, the sexual revolution of the 1960s was also a product of a long trend away from Victorian sexual restrictions; premarital sex had been increasing gradually since the early decades of the twentieth century. As a result of these trends, social reality was increasingly at odds with the prevailing assumptions that "all brides are virgins, all marriages are first marriages, all wives are housewives."

The reality of everyday experience was at odds not only with the rigidity of middle-class norms but also with the cultural images of family happiness that were supposed to result from holding on to those norms. All during the silent 1950s, these discontents were simmering below the surface. In the 1960s and 1970s the upheavals of the Vietnam War and racial tensions called established cultural norms into question. Pressure continued to build up along the fault line, the trends reaching what the sociologist Jessie Bernard calls "tipping points."[53] Behavior that had formerly been practiced only by a minority approached, or became, majority behavior. In a time of political turbulence, the two sides of the fault line jolted apart. We are still digging out the rubble, but there is no way of going back to where we were before.

C H A P T E R 1

Sentimental Journeys: Making and Remaking the Modern Family

To study the history of the American family is to conduct a rescue mission into the dreamland of our national self-concept. No subject is more closely bound up with our sense of a difficult present—and our nostalgia for a happier past.
                                                                —John Demos
                  "Myths and Realities in the History of American Family Life"

Joseph White and Minna Bourke fell in love in the summer of 1897 and married the following June. During their engagement, Joseph wrote to Minna every day, describing his philosophy of life and their plans for the future, especially their shared ideal of "making a home as perfect as possible." As part of their design for a perfected family life, they agreed they would have intercourse only when they wanted to have a child, a practice many doctors recommended at the time. Nevertheless, Minna enjoyed the sexual side of marriage, and taught her children that sex was "beautiful."

For the three children they eventually had, the perfect home that Minna and Joseph tried to create became a "kind of embattled paradise." It was hard to live up their parents' exacting standards: "The chief lesson the family taught was the lesson of how to be good. Hard on its heels came the lesson that being good was not enough; you could always do, could always be better."[1]

One of Minna's daughters, Margaret Bourke-White, led a very different life from her mother's. She became a world-famous photogra-
pher, renowned for her courage and daring as well as for her brilliant
images. Like many professional women of her day, she struggled to
reconcile her work and personal life. For Margaret, with her demanding career, it ultimately proved impossible. She experienced
two divorces and never had the child she hoped for.

Minna and her daughter spanned one of the largest generational
divides in American history. Minna was one of the last Victorians;
Margaret was clearly a twentieth-century woman. She came of age in
the 1920s, the decade that witnessed a revolt against Victorianism.
People began to think differently, act differently, and even look different—especially women, with their bobbed hair, painted faces, and
drastically shortened skirts.

It was Margaret and her generation, the young people of the 1920s,
not the counterculture youth of the 1960s, who staged the major sexual revolution of the twentieth century. Rising divorce rates, falling
birthrates, changing roles for women, as well as the new sexual mortality, led many people to believe that the family was in a terminal
crisis. In retrospect, it is clear that the young people of the 1920s
were not abandoning the family but revising it and adapting it to
new circumstances. Indeed, the new "companionship" or "companionate" model of marriage and family life—emphasizing affection,
friendship, and happiness—was in many ways an elaboration of Victorian themes.[2] Margaret was her mother's daughter after all.

The dramatic changes in family life that took place in the 1920s
were not without precedent. At the beginning of the nineteenth century, an even more wrenching era of family crisis and reorganization
had produced the Victorian model of the family. Paradoxically, the
nineteenth-century version of the family now widely viewed as "traditional" was in fact the first incarnation of the modern family. The
rapid changes in family life since the 1950s are just the latest episode
in a long history of family transformations.

An understanding of this history is essential to making sense of the
current family situation, especially since debate and discussion about
contemporary family life are often based on assumptions about the
past grounded more in nostalgia than in historical evidence. In the
1980s, for example, many Americans fell in love with the Victorian
era. "Where twenty years ago, a love of things Victorian was considered dubious taste at best," reported the *New York Times* in June 1987,
"in this year of the anniversary of her accession to the throne, Vic-

toria's influence is rampant." It can be found, the article went on to note, in Laura Ashley dresses, brass beds and ceiling fans, period-inspired McDonald's, suburban subdivisions boasting of " 'neo-Victorian flair,' " and "young professionals in search of cherub-laden wall brackets and historically correct paint colors."[3]

The new appreciation for things Victorian was more than a change in tastes. In an era reeling from rapid social change, Victorian artifacts and images spoke to widespread yearnings for stability and order, coziness and safety. Meanwhile, social critics of the right and left upheld the moral superiority of the Victorian bourgeois family over its degenerate late-twentieth-century counterpart.[4] In England and America, conservative politicians denounced the permissiveness of the 1960s and 1970s, and called for a return to the lost values and virtues of the nineteenth century.

The actual study of nineteenth-century family life, however, does not support this idea of the Victorian era as a world we have tragically lost and should attempt to restore.[5] The majority of the population who were not middle class lived in ways that did not correspond to the prevailing images of comfortable domesticity. Those who could afford the middle-class domestic ideal discovered there were problems inherent in it. Indeed, some of the dilemmas and tensions besetting us today have their roots in the nineteenth-century bourgeois family: the yearning for intimacy in marriage versus the barriers of gender difference and inequality, the intense emotional investment in children who must ultimately leave home to make their way in the world.

Perhaps most troublesome of all, the Victorians bequeathed to us utopian expectations about the perfectibility of family life. They told themselves that the home could become a place of individual fulfillment and family happiness and, at the same time, the foundation of the social order. This was a radically new idea in the history of the family, and one whose consequences are with us still. Indeed, the persistent gap between social reality and cultural images has been responsible for a recurrent sense of crisis about the family that has haunted American society for the past century and a half.

BOURGEOIS REVOLUTIONS

The Victorian conception of the family emerged in the United States in the years between the American Revolution and the Civil War.

Although *Victorian* originally referred to English culture during the reign of Queen Victoria (1837–1901), the term is also applied to American middle-class life in the nineteenth century and, more broadly, to that in other Western European cultures. For example, Freud's Viennese patients and the Norwegian characters in Ibsen's plays were Victorians.

In both its Victorian and twentieth-century versions, the modern family pattern differed sharply from the "traditional" family that had previously prevailed. A series of related changes, summed up by the term *modernization*,* is closely linked to these transformations in family life. Briefly, modernization includes the shift from an agrarian society with high birth and death rates and child labor, to an urban industrial society with low birth and death rates, the rise of political democracy, the growth of science and technology, and the spread of mass schooling and literacy. In response to these shifts in the larger society, individuals and families also changed. While the core nuclear structure of the family remained constant, gender relations, family roles and functions, the emotional quality of family relationships, and the cultural meaning of family life shifted markedly.

In this chapter, I will sketch the main contours of these changes. Obviously, a comprehensive review of the social history of the family is beyond the scope of this chapter. Nor would one be useful. My aim here is only to illuminate the major shifts in the emotional and symbolic meanings of family life. The middle-class family is at the center of the discussion. Its domestic ideals and practices have been culturally dominant in America, defining what is normal, natural, and moral. At the same time, the middle class has been at the forefront of family change, challenging and revising the norms of family life from the nineteenth century through the present. It has been, in short, America's "most revolutionary class."[7]

In talking about the middle class, it is important to remember that it is an elusive and extremely diverse social category, harboring contrasting visions of the good life.[8] Economically, it has ranged from

---

*The word *modernization* is widely used to describe the set of social, economic, and political changes that transformed European society since the Renaissance. The current use of the term does not imply an evolutionary process that applies to all societies, as the "modernization theories" of the 1950s and 1960s assumed.

  Most historians no longer regard modernization as the "cause" of changes in family life. Industrialization and urbanization may have set the stage for changes in family life, but the ultimate outcome is not determined by those factors. Cultural values, individual preferences, and family strategies influence family arrangements.[6]

wealthy merchants and leading professionals to people at the edges of poverty. Its ranks have included the crude and the cultured, the public-spirited as well as those who confine their sympathies to the family circle, cosmopolitans and provincials, the smug and self-satisfied as well as reformers, radicals, and bohemians. Indeed, the fiercest critics of middle-class culture and family life have come from the middle class itself. "What nineteenth century bourgeois had in common," observes the historian Peter Gay, "was the negative quality of being neither aristocrats nor laborers, and of being uneasy in their middle class skins."[9] His observation still holds true.

The concepts of home and family constructed by the white middle class in the nineteenth century became the core of what came to be thought of as the American way of life and the American dream. The same has been true in other Western European countries: in England, Sweden, and other industrial societies, an expanding middle class defined its beliefs and practices as both human nature and the essence of the national culture. Thus, the middle-class ideal became the image and definition of family in America, even though the reality of actual family arrangements was far more diverse.

Some aspects of the family model created by the American middle class in the nineteenth century were foreshadowed in earlier times and places. For example, what the historian Lawrence Stone calls "the closed domesticated nuclear family"—held together by strong emotional attachments and valuing privacy, domesticity, and comfort—emerged in Dutch merchant families in the seventeenth century, in the English upper classes in the eighteenth century, and in the middle class in the nineteenth century; it did not become common in the working class until the decades following World War II.

The same is true of other aspects of middle-class family life, such as the suburban home. The physical embodiment of the closed, domesticated nuclear family ideal, the first suburbs were invented by the wealthy merchant elite of late-eighteenth-century London. From the nineteenth century to the present, the suburban way of life came to be available to more and more of an expanding middle class and eventually, after World War II, to the working class as well.[10]

Elaborating on this theme, Michael Young and Peter Willmott have argued in *The Symmetrical Family* that the history of industrial countries has been like a slow march, with the rich at the head of the marching column and the poor in the rear. The image applies most clearly to possessions. Since the beginning of industrialization, products that were first available only to the rich—from cutlery and cotton clothing to carpeting and television sets—over time became available to the working class and even the poor. The same principle applies to less tangible things, like legal rights, education, and family styles. To be sure, the working class has not come to resemble the middle class in every way, but the image of the slow march fits many aspects of change in family and personal life.

THE EUROPEAN ORIGINS OF
THE AMERICAN FAMILY

The cultural roots of the dominant American notions of family patterns lie in England and northwestern Europe, a region in which family practices have been more individualistic and "modern" than those of other cultural traditions. In the 1960s the demographer J. Hajnal described a distinct Western European marriage pattern, dating at least from the Reformation of the sixteenth century. Found in England, Scotland, the Netherlands, and northern France, its two central features were a late average age of marriage for both sexes (often twenty-five years or more for women) and a sizable proportion of adults who never married—especially women, as many as 15 percent of whom stayed single.[11]

The Western pattern of marriage was selective in two senses: one could choose whether as well as whom to marry, although the parents' consent was needed for the marriage partner. The relative freedom of choice has been linked to a tendency toward less gender inequality in Western societies. The Western family pattern also featured separate nuclear family households, with fairly weak links with kin except for those in the three-generation nuclear family of grandparents, parents, children, aunts, and uncles.

Thus, the widespread notion that the coming of modern industrial society broke up the three-generation extended family and led to the rise of the isolated nuclear family is mistaken. In 1963 William J. Goode anticipated the recent findings when he argued that "the classical family of Western nostalgia"—the large household of parents, grandparents, and kids living happily together—had never existed as a typical family pattern. Indeed, Goode argued that the nuclear family structure may have set the stage for economic development and modernization.[12] Recent research on the family has confirmed this contention. Further, far from breaking up extended families, the coming of industrial society seems to have, until recent decades, fostered the tendency for kin to live together and to cooperate economically.[13]

While the core features of the modern family—nuclear family households and the idea of companionate marriage—can be traced back to the Middle Ages, other aspects of family life, such as family structure, ideology, gender relations, family roles and functions, the emotional quality of family relationships, and above all, the cultural meaning of family life, changed markedly in the context of modernization.

FAMILY LIFE IN EARLY AMERICA

The history of the American family before the eighteenth century generally coincides with the premodern pattern just described, although it has been shaped by unique circumstances: the frontier, economic opportunity, immigration. In early colonial America, as in Europe before the eighteenth century, paternal authority formed the core of the "well-ordered family."

Although obedience and harmony were the ideal family virtues, their absence was often lamented. The family was "a little commonwealth—a lively representation" of the whole. The father was head of the family, just as the king was head of the state—indeed, "the principle of fatherhood lay right at the heart of most political thinking during this period."[14] The father was also the economic head of the family; the vast majority of Americans were farmers, and other businesses were also family enterprises and so included not only parents and their children but apprentices, servants, unrelated youths, and others. Authority, not affection, was clearly the guiding principle in the family.

Another difference between the premodern and modern family was that in past times, death was omnipresent in everyday family life. Childbirth was often lethal for mother and child. Almost half of all children died before reaching adulthood, most in early childhood. Half of those who survived died before reaching fifty. Since many parents of minor children died, orphans were a constant problem for the community. Furthermore, only a third of marriages lasted more than ten years.[15]

What might be most striking about the colonial family to a time traveler from the nineteenth or twentieth century, apart from the high death rates, would be the blurring of boundaries between public and private. Colonial Americans had far less awareness of the family as a distinct entity than would later generations of Americans. Family life was enmeshed with community. Neighbors and servants as well as community authorities were expected to oversee and intervene in the intimate affairs of individuals and families.

Family matters that Victorian and contemporary Americans would have considered private—marital conflict, adultery, unruly children, drunkenness—were the direct concern of the community. Children might be taken away from parents whose child-rearing practices were found wanting. And children commonly served as apprentices in other people's homes, an arrangement common in premodern Europe as well.

Colonial America, like other premodern societies, lacked an elaborated concept of childhood. Moreover, in Puritan America children were seen as inherently corrupt beings, having come into the world with original sin. A central task for parents was to "break the will" of their children and vanquish their naturally evil propensities. Physical punishment and humiliation were considered legitimate expressions of parental authority. Children were expected to submit, not understand: "Obedience is absolutely essential to proper family government.... Neither is it enough that a child should yield to your arguments and persuasion. It is essential that he submit to your authority."[16] In a hierarchical, patriarchal society, no less was demanded of adults.

If children were less bound to their parents' households than in modern times, married couples were far more tightly held together. Although colonial Americans believed in the ideal of companionate marriage, social order and family stability counted far more. For example, a woman who complained to a court that she could not live with an abusive husband would typically be ordered to return home. The authorities did not allow the individual autonomy or privacy that the companionate ideal implies, nor did they weigh individual happiness or unhappiness in making their decisions: "in supporting the interests of stability and patriarchy, community goals and pressures played havoc with people's lives. Colonial marriages were expected to fulfill private needs as well as social obligations, and they suffered from their cross-purposes."[17]

THE PURSUIT OF SENTIMENT

By the middle of the eighteenth century, a number of changes—population growth, an increasingly diverse and commercial economy, and political and religious conflict—had loosened the tightly bound culture of early colonial America. Free land was a major catapult to change, enabling individuals and families to escape the constraints of community, and young people to strike out on their own. New world conditions also granted women a greater degree of autonomy and independence than their European sisters had. As the grip of the community over family life eased, families came to be seen as separate, private units, and individuals as separate from both the community and the family. At the same time, emotional relationships within the family were becoming more intense.

In England and Europe as well, most family historians see the eighteenth century as a watershed era in the making of the modern family. Edward Shorter has written of a "surge of sentiment" in family relations among family members generally, but the evidence is clearest for the upper ranks of society.[18] Lawrence Stone, in his study of family life in the English gentry and upper middle classes, writes of the rise of "affective individualism" in the eighteenth century—a far-reaching shift away from patriarchal authority, formality, and emotional distance in family relations, and toward both individual autonomy and intense emotional bonds between husbands and wives, parents and children.[19] Rudolph Trumbach finds a marked shift toward more egalitarian relations and more intense emotional attachments among family members of the English aristocracy.[20] Trumbach and Stone have found evidence of permissive, even "Spockian," child-rearing practices and of companionate, relatively egalitarian relations between men and women. Alan Macfarlane, who traces modern English family patterns back to 1300, finds a general shift in the eighteenth century toward a more passionate and erotic form of love—he calls it "instituted irrationality"—as the basis for marriage.[21]

But historians differ about the quality of emotional relations in families before the eighteenth century. Whether or not, as Stone and Shorter contend, coldness and indifference in family relations were the rule in past centuries, the historical shift was not so much in feelings themselves as in their cultural meaning and importance. There may have been loving families earlier, but it was not until the eighteenth century that the loving family became a model to emulate. Charles Taylor speaks of this shift as "the moral consecration of sen-

timent."[22] It is reflected in today's assumptions that loving feelings are at the very center of family life, that they are a crucial part
of what makes life worth living, and that their absence is a terrible
defect.

The second half of the eighteenth century witnessed the rise of this
new set of ideas and practices. As families became more private and
domestic, a shift that involved alterations in the material setting of
family life as well as in feelings, houses began to be transformed into
"homes"—places of intimacy, comfort, and privacy. The increased
availability of consumer goods raised the standard of living. Meals,
for example, became elaborate, leisurely domestic rituals, as knives
and forks, glasses, and equipment for making tea and coffee spread
from the rich to ordinary folk.[23]

The spread of tea drinking to the "common sort" marked a significant shift in life-style, touching off a debate in "respectable society"
that would be echoed many times in the future as new consumer
goods made their way from the rich to the masses. Some argued that
tea drinking would corrupt the poor, leading them to squander their
time and money; others argued that laborers were entitled to some
leisure time.

After 1750, the Enlightenment ideas associated with the American
Revolution came to be intertwined with concepts of family life. "The
pursuit of happiness" became an "inalienable right" enshrined in the
Declaration of Independence.[24] The intimate links between the political and the personal could be seen in the figure of Tom Paine, whose
pamphlet "Common Sense" helped to ignite the revolution. Paine
also published "Reflections on Unhappy Marriage," which stressed
the importance of love and affection in marriage: "God made us all
in pairs: each of us has his mate somewhere or other; and 'tis our
duty to find each other out since no creature was ever intended to
be miserable."[25]

Indeed, the journal that Paine edited contained many articles on
marriage as well as politics, and one frequent contributor also ran
an eighteenth century version of "Dear Abby." This linking of family
matters and public issues reflected more than Paine's own preoccu-
pations. As the literary historian Jay Fleigelman has argued, there
were deep ideological connections between domestic and political
life. In a society in revolt against patriarchal authority, father and
son could no longer serve as the most fundamental human relationship. Instead, the new paradigm for human relations became man
and wife: "The point of the Revolution would not be simply to dis-

solve an intolerable union but to establish a more glorious one founded on the most primary of social unions—the voluntary marriage contract, . . .—'friendship made perfect.' "[26]

Not surprisingly, enlightenment and republican ideas began to be applied to women. In 1792 one woman wrote a letter to a woman's magazine objecting to the word *obey* in the marriage service: "Marriage ought never to be considered as a contract between superior and an inferior, but a reciprocal union of interest . . . where all differences are accommodated by conference."[27] But such ideas, whether in public or private life, were a distinctly minority view. The republican ethos would not yet alter women's legal position. Women could not vote or own property in their own names. Patriarchal ideas continued to hold sway over women and the family, if less so in society at large. This gap between rhetoric about equality and women's inferior status created another persistent "American dilemma," alongside that of race. As the historian Linda Kerber observes, it is possible "to read the subsequent political history of women in America as the story of women's efforts to accomplish for themselves what the revolution failed to do."[28]

Ideas about children and parent-child relationships also changed during this period. John Locke's political writings had influenced the American Revolution, but his writings on child psychology were even more widely read. Locke, along with Rousseau, developed ideas about childhood that were in keeping with the sensibilities of affective individualism. Both saw childhood as a distinct stage of development with a distinct set of needs.

Locke and Rousseau, along with the growing body of advice-to-parents literature that popularized their ideas, stressed the need for gentle, loving parents. Locke portrayed children as easily impressionable beings whose minds were blank slates. Rousseau saw them as naturally sociable beings with a built-in capacity to develop. Obedience as simple submission to authority was no longer regarded as a virtue.

The new ideals were not uniformly accepted. Phillip Greven has identified three distinct Protestant "temperaments" in early America based on patterns of child rearing and attitudes toward the self, religion, and sexuality that persist to this day. The "Evangelical temperament" believed in original sin, felt hostility toward the self, and supported the practice of "spare the rod and spoil the child." "Genteels" were Lockian if not Spockian in their child rearing, "at ease with themselves, their desires, their pleasures." "Moderates," anx-

iously and ambivalently "caught between the poles of duty and desire," sought a middle road.[29]

By the end of the eighteenth century, American family values and
practices had shifted in significant ways from colonial times. Many
aspects of the new family pattern would not become common beyond
the middle class until the twentieth century; indeed, it was only several decades into this century that a majority of the population could
be counted as middle class.[30] Nevertheless, American culture had been
transformed; the ideas surrounding the American Revolution had
bequeathed a heritage of individualism that would remain in tension
with the Puritan communitarianism of the early settlers.

SEPARATE SPHERES

The ideological changes associated with the political revolutions of
the eighteenth century were half of a dual revolution that transformed the lives of most Western men and women and created the
modern age. The other half was the complex of social, economic, and
demographic changes associated with the shift from a largely rural,
agricultural society to an urban industrial one. By 1820 America was
on the other side of the dividing line between the older way of life
and the newer one.

These changes led to a profound alteration in the function and
cultural meaning of family life, as well as in the relations between
family and society. They separated home and work, and transformed
men's, women's, and children's roles both inside and outside the family. Instead of an economic enterprise, in which the family worked
side by side with hired hands, servants, or apprentices, the family
came to be defined as a man who went out to work and a woman
who stayed home to keep house and care for the children.

In the decades before the Civil War, the new household functions
and the new roles within the family were elaborated in a compelling
and pervasive belief system known as the ideology of "separate
spheres" or the "cult of domesticity." The glorification of motherhood and the notion that "women's place is in the home"—ideas that
influence thinking about family life to this day—were born in this
era. With men leaving home to go work, the contrast between the
home and the outside world came to be seen as a contrast between
Woman and Man. Domestic tasks became spiritualized and "pastor-
alized"; they were no longer work but woman's God-given mission.[31]

Clergymen, fiction writers, and journalists developed a "cult of true womanhood," celebrating women's purity, piety, and submissiveness.[32] Home—women's sphere—was an emotional and spiritual refuge, a place where the True Woman would comfort, educate, and civilize men and children. The man's sphere of work and public life was defined in opposition to woman's: a place of greed, cutthroat competition, moral corruption. These conceptions of family and gender relations served to reverse some of the liberalizing trends of the eighteenth century. A more restrictive and repressive ideology of gender roles and sexuality was grafted onto the companionate ideal. Patriarchal notions reemerged and notions of child rearing swung back to sterner discipline.

Historians suggest that the ideology of gender spheres was a response to anxieties generated in a period of chaotic change. Lawrence Stone attributes the revival of patriarchy and puritanism to the same reasons that originally had led to Puritanism: "a sense of political and social crisis, a fear that the structure of social hierarchy and political order were in danger."[33] The sociologists Neil Smelser and Sydney Halpern agree that the more tightly bound family culture of the Victorians was part of a quest for stability, the outcome of the cultural struggle to come to terms with the family's new structural attributes. Along with Stone, they argue that Victorian prudishness may be understood as a form of social control in a time of rapid change, "an exercise in over-control of a new institution that was unfamiliar and appeared to be dangerously fragile."[34]

Alfred Lord Tennyson expressed the spirit of the new domesticity and the danger lurking behind it in an 1849 poem, "The Princess":

> Man for the field and woman for the hearth:
> Man for the sword and for the needle she:
> Man with the head and woman with the heart:
> Man to command and woman to obey;
> All else confusion.[35]

A more saccharine version of domestic themes appeared in the new mass media that proliferated during the second quarter of the nineteenth century: novels, tracts, newspaper articles, and ladies' magazines. Middle-class women and Protestant clergymen became the custodians of femininity and domesticity. Excluded from the materialistic, competitive world outside the home, they upheld the softer values banished from that world. This sentimental imagery, one writer

has argued, "asserts that the values a society's activity denies are precisely the ones it cherishes. . . . [It] provides a way to protest a power
to which one has already capitulated."[36]

This opposition between home and society at large was one of the
most significant aspects of Victorian culture; instead of the community regulating and repairing moral defects in families, now it was
the burden of the family to compensate for the moral defects of the
larger society. This shift had profound implications; it encouraged
the belief that the perfection of the society could be realized through
perfection in the home.

The separation of home and work undid the economic foundations
of family cohesiveness, yet increased its psychological importance as
the only place where emotional security and release could be found.
The home came to be seen as both the mainstay of the social order
and a precarious enterprise in need of constant shoring up. Thus,
any challenge to the prevailing ideology provoked an angry response.
In effect, women were held hostage to values that men both cherished
and violated in their daily lives.

> In a society where values changed frequently, where fortunes rose
> and fell with frightening rapidity, where social and economic mo-
> bility provided instability as well as hope, one thing at least re-
> mained the same—a true woman was a true woman. . . . If anyone,
> male or female, dared to tamper with the complex of virtues which
> made up True Womanhood, he was damned immediately as an en-
> emy of God, of Civilization, and of the Republic.[37]

Not surprisingly, the image of the True woman contrasted with the
reality of women's lives. Ironically, the glorification of the home undermined the economic significance of women's work there. Running
a middle-class household in the nineteenth century was hard work,
but it was not recognized as such. Nor was the fact that many housewives inside and outside the middle class also took part in their husbands' enterprises. Since the home was described in spiritual terms,
women's household tasks were seen as a moral responsibility, not as
an economic contribution to the family.[38]

The ideology of separate spheres also masked the fact that considerable numbers of women did work for wages outside the home. In
the early 1800s, when manufacturing began to expand, the ideology
of separate spheres had not yet been elaborated. Both men and
women, married and single, were encouraged to join the growing

labor force. Married women could sew or do other work for wages at home, while single women worked in factories as "mill girls." After the economic depression and the growing ideology of separate spheres in the 1830s, fewer women worked for wages.[39] Immigrant and black women continued to do so, but notions about domesticity and gender placed them beyond the pale of respectable society. The only acceptable occupation for middle-class wives was taking in boarders, a widespread practice until the beginning of the twentieth century.[40]

The cult of domesticity sharpened class differences and at the same time encouraged working-class men and women to aspire to the ideal of the woman as full-time homemaker. Indeed, over the course of the nineteenth century, lower-class families preferred to send children, rather than wives, out to work to supplement the family income. By 1890 only about 2 percent of married women were employed outside the home.[41]

PRIVATE LIVES

The elaborate facade of middle-class Victorian ideology did not accurately reflect the reality of middle-class lives.[42] Constrained Victorian notions of gender and sexuality might undoubtedly have fit the lives of many people in the nineteenth century; for others, they were goals to strive for that might seem forever out of reach; for still others, they were contested terrain. As Peter Gay, Carl Degler, and others have argued, Victorian bourgeois culture was more complex, ambivalent, and diverse than we generally realize.

Victorian sexuality, for example, was marked not by consensus and moral certainty about traditional values but by battles over conflicting values and behavior and a spectacular gap between publicly pronounced virtues and privately practiced vices. "There was no golden age of sexual propriety," observes Jeffrey Weeks, "and the search for it in the mythologised past tells us more about present confusions than past glories."[43]

The facade of Victorian ideology also concealed notions of self and personality that contradict stereotypes of Victorian character and culture. Victorian character is often portrayed as the polar opposite of twentieth-century "personality."[44] One represents Duty and the identity of the self with its social role, and the other represents the Self and its idiosyncrasies, which stand at some distance from its roles.

There is increasing evidence, however, that middle- to upper-middle class Victorians understood and valued the concept of a true or real self separate from social roles, and suffered the agonies of identity crises. Middle-class courtship, for example, was often based on intimacy and self-disclosure—the sharing of the couple's interior lives, the probing of personality with all its flaws and weaknesses. Even sentimental glorifications of domesticity contained notions of a true self that could be expressed and nurtured only in the loving home:

> there at least you are beloved; ... there you are understood; ... there your errors will meet ever with gentle forgiveness; ... there your troubles will be smiled away; ... there you may unburden your soul fearless of harsh, unsympathizing ears, and ... there you may be entirely and joyfully—yourself.[45]

Historians who have studied nineteenth-century marriage portray it differently. Some have found evidence that the companionate ideal of marriage was widespread, and that many married couples were indeed deeply loving companions. Some argue that married women's closest emotional bonds were with other women, not their husbands. Some stress that patriarchy and the doctrine of separate spheres undercut the possibilities of companionate marriage as well as of women's equality in public life. Helena Wall argues that although the idea of companionate marriage promised women a kind of equality in the home, the "crippling legal and economic disabilities of women ... made the idea of companionate marriage something of an oxymoron."[46]

It seems likely, however, that rather than being mutually exclusive, patriarchy and marital companionship can coexist uneasily, as they do today. Even relationships based on extreme inequality, such as a slave and her mistress, do not entirely preclude the possibility of some kind of friendship. Despite women's legal disabilities and the ideology of gender difference, a variety of historical evidence suggests that many nineteenth-century couples did share profoundly intimate emotional relationships with each other, especially during courtship. Patriarchy may have undermined companionate marriage, but the experience of romantic love during courtship, and the empathy and merging of selves it encouraged, may well have played a role in undermining patriarchal attitudes.[47]

Over time companionate aspects of the family ideal came to be increasingly important, not just in the decision to marry but within marriage itself. The historian Robert Griswold's study of California divorce litigation from 1850 to 1890 reveals both trends:

> These records reveal that the companionate ideal did, indeed, affect the lives of rural men and women from all social classes. [They] make it clear that men and women from all social classes conceived of family relations in affective terms, placed a premium on emotional fulfillment within the family, considered women's opinions worthy of respect and consideration, emphasized male kindness and accommodation, and assumed that children were special members of the household in need of love and affection.[48]

Along with the shift in gender roles and relations, urban industrial society also led to a profound change in the conditions of child development. Modern parents bear few children and provide lengthy and attentive care without expecting a material return, defining their commitment in emotional and moral terms.

The shift in parents' perception of their offspring was from the "economically useful child" to the child who is "economically useless" but "emotionally priceless."[49] Looked at economically, the rise of modern society involves a reversal in the flow of wealth in the family: in agrarian society, wealth flows from children to parents; in modern societies, the flow is from parents to children.[50] This transformation in the value of children was a long-term trend that was not completed for lower-class families until the virtual end of child labor in the twentieth century.

Along with the increasing emotional value of children, the nineteenth-century middle-class family pioneered family limitation and the use of birth control. The need to control fertility may have been one source of the notorious prudery of the Victorians,[51] although, as we have seen, not all Victorians fit the passionless stereotype.[52] Middle-class families chose to rear a small number of children carefully, rather than raising large families for current or future economic support.

PARADOXES OF PERFECTION

"It is hard," observes John Demos, "to avoid seeing the nineteenth century as a time of troubles—not to say tragedy—in the history of the family."[53] The price paid for inflexible ideas of femininity, masculinity, virtue, and domestic perfection was often a heavy burden of failure, guilt, and neurosis. To be sure, many middle-class men and women did find the happiness they sought in domestic life. Yet the failure of family life to live up to idealized images and extravagant expectations contributed to the sense of family crisis that has taken a variety of forms and haunted our culture ever since.

In many ways, the domestic ideology of the nineteenth century portrayed the family as a utopian society, much like the communes that sprang up during the same period.[54] Descriptions of both the commune and the home stressed the themes of retreat, conscious design, and perfectionism. Further, the perfection of the home was the key to the redemption of the larger society. This idea of the family as the key to both personal happiness and the improvement of the larger society had major consequences. Since the majority of Americans were not members of the comfortable white Anglo-Saxon middle class and did not follow the family code in all its details, the makings of a crisis of the family were at hand.

By the middle of the century, critics were complaining about divorce, desertion, male drunkenness, and women's restlessness as homemakers. Further, young people had emerged as a major social problem. In the earlier, family-based economy, young people began to work alongside adults (not necessarily their own parents) at early ages, on farms, as apprentices in workshops, as servants. Their integration into adult life was gradual. The transformation to industrialism led to increasing unemployment among youth. "Idle youth" became a national issue that threatened the social order. Public school systems emerged in response.[55] Persistent concern over youth and the family led to the beginnings of organized child development studies and social science.

Although lower-class and immigrant families were often the main objects of social reform, middle-class families had their own problems. There were both rewards and costs to male and female roles as they were defined during the Victorian era. Each sex faced demands that were burdensome and at times contradictory. Gender differences became an increasingly significant and worrisome aspect of culture and personal identity.

Women's roles in particular were beset by a number of strains and contradictions. For one thing, women were caught between social and economic pressures to marry and their high expectations for companionship and love. Stripped to its bare economic essentials, the job description for a wife was disturbing: in return for sharing a man's income, she had to devote herself to running his home and "had to have sex with him on demand, bear and raise as many chil- dren as he engendered, keep him in good humor, and obey him on pain of violent punishment, if he chose."[56] And in a society where divorce was a rarity, this was not a job she could quit.

Most marriages probably did not fit the image of such stark ex- changes; as we have seen, significant numbers of couples were indeed loving friends. Nevertheless, nineteenth-century women were aware of the tension between love and economics in the choice of a mar- riage partner. Love did not always coincide with what parents con- sidered a good match. A frequent theme in Victorian autobiographies and novels is a hero or heroine who, like Romeo and Juliet, fights for love against the incomprehension of parents and society.

The transition to marriage was often difficult for women in Vic- torian America. In the early nineteenth century, Alexis de Tocque- ville noted the contrast between the independence of young women before marriage and their extreme dependence afterward.[57] Women expected this loss and often suffered great anxiety as they ap- proached the end of courtship and the beginning of marital respon- sibilities. What historians of the Victorian era describe as a "marriage trauma" involved more than regrets over the loss of liberty; the pros- pect of childbirth was often frightening at a time of high death rates for both mother and child.[58]

Victorian notions of domesticity and gender subjected married women to contradictory demands. If, as the Victorians believed, the home was the foundation of the republic, it was the responsibility of the morally upright woman to create the perfect home that would reform and redeem the larger society. Mothers were responsible for raising morally sound, successful children. They were also cast in the role of motherly nurturers of their husbands. But the morally superior, strong Mother was also expected to be the weak, dependent, intellectually inferior Wife and Lady who submitted to male author- ity. The evidence suggests that these conflicting demands exacted a high toll on these women. Rather than complain directly, they often developed hysterias, neurasthenias, headaches, pains, and a host of "women's diseases."[59]

Similarly, the emphasis on loving, peaceful, happy homes created great expectations for family life that were difficult to fulfill. "It is a duty to exclude everything permanently disagreeable from the fam- ily," wrote Catherine Sedgwick in 1845, "for home should resemble heaven in happiness as well as love."[60] If the home was to become a sanctuary of love and happiness, an Edenic retreat from the world, it was the woman who had the heavy, if not impossible, task of making it so.

Nevertheless, she tried. One study of memoirs of nineteenth-century bourgeois childhoods contrasts warm and loving portrayals of saintly mothers and more ambivalent portraits of father. Often described as "house tyrants," "powder kegs," or "volcanoes who might erupt at any time," fathers were both respected and feared. When their mood shifted from playfulness and affection to anger and melancholy, darkening the family atmosphere, their wives tried to make it light again. One woman wrote in her memoirs that it took time to get conversation going around the dining table, because the wife and children had to determine "what nuance the father's disposition had."[61]

The advent of urban industrial society also made male roles problematic. The shift of work out of the home, the erosion of early patterns of patriarchy, and the emergence of new concepts of womanhood raised questions about what it meant to be man. The father/ husband was no longer the boss of the family enterprise but a breadwinner who carried the burden of supporting the entire family; his success or failure determined the family's economic well-being and its standing in the community. Moreover, a man's sense of himself as a man was tied up with his occupational success.

Yet by relying on work to validate their manliness, men were treading on "psychically dangerous ground."[62] The ups and downs of industrial economies did not provide continuous employment or economic security. The failure of businesses—especially new businesses—was common, as was downward mobility.

Sexuality for Victorian men was also marked by contradiction. Aggressive sexuality was seen as the core of manliness, yet the middleclass Christian man was expected to exercise control over sex, both before and after marriage. Masturbation was believed to be not only a sin, but a cause of insanity and death. Adolescent boys were often put to bed with elaborate devices said to prevent involuntary sin, and patent medicines promised to cure masturbatory impulses.[63]

Nevertheless, most people conceded that male sexuality could not be contained within the prescribed limits. A double standard was tacitly accepted and prostitution flourished, enabling middle-class men to indulge their sexual appetites with lower-class women, thus preserving "civilized morality." One cost of this practice was the spread of venereal disease from red-light districts to respectable households.[64] Another was a psychological effect Freud observed: im potence among middle-class men. Some could no longer be aroused by the women they loved and respected, but only by partners they saw as debased: "Where such men love they have no desire and where they desire they cannot love."[65]

Victorian gender ideology, with its extreme differentiation of sex roles, also unsettled man's place in the home. As Stephanie Coontz observes, "by giving women sole responsibility for cleanliness, godliness, culture and manners, the domestic architects had constructed people that manly men could hardly bear to be around."[66] The home was both man's castle and woman's sphere. One masculine response to the nineteenth-century gender arrangements was a flight from domesticity, in fantasy as well as in reality.

In *Love and Death in the American Novel*, Leslie Fiedler argues that the theme of male escape from marriage and responsiblity has dominated American literature from Rip Van Winkle to Huckleberry Finn and Tom Sawyer to the present.[67] The historical record reveals that this motif carried over into reality, as considerable numbers of men dropped out of family roles. Divorce rates rose after the middle of century, but official figures do not reveal the much larger number of marriages that ended through separation or the "poor man's divorce"—desertion.

Demos points to the rise of tramps and hoboes, men who dropped out of work and family roles: "Demoralized and destitute wanderers, their numbers mounting into the hundreds of thousands, tramps can be fairly characterized as men who had run away from their wives. . . . Their presence was mute testimony to the strains that tugged through the core of American family life."[68]

THE INVENTION OF ADOLESCENCE

The social transformations of the nineteenth century also brought new complications to relationships between parents and children. As I mentioned earlier, in contrast to agrarian parents, those in urban industrial societies bore fewer children and bestowed on them more emotional and economic resources. This represents "one of the most radical shifts in the parent-child relationship in human history," a pattern that "knew no precedent except in the rearing of royal princes."[69] Nineteenth-century culture supported this new mode of parent-child relations through the sentimental idealization of child-hood, as in the novels of Dickens, as well as in legal and institutional change, such as the provision of mass schooling and the passage of laws against child labor.

But children in lower-class families continued to work. And middle-class children in the nineteenth century reaped not only the benefits of the new protected childhood but also its costs. Instead of joining the adult world early, the transition to adulthood became longer, lonelier, and more problematic. Identity was no longer received at birth but something that had to be worked out in the course of one's youth.

Having to raise a child for a future that was essentially unknowable made parenthood far more uncertain and anxious than it had been in earlier eras. Starting in the 1820s, the search for guidance in child rearing became a cultural obsession. Parental anxiety heightened around the time the child left home.

Middle-class families had to confront the emotional contradiction they embodied: affectional bonds between parents and children had become deeper and stronger, while children remained dependent on their parents longer than in the past. At the same time, young people were expected to be more autonomous and independent of their parents once reaching adulthood. The new conditions of growing up seem to have led to a rise in family conflict and the intensifying of adolescent problems.[70] Not until the Victorian era did adolescence emerge as a new stage of development between childhood and adulthood.

For parents, the new arrangements brought both increased responsibility and lessened control. As middle-class parents concentrated financial and emotional resources in caring for and educating a small number of children, their offspring came to represent the family's emotional future. In their adult lives the children would reward or betray the hopes and sacrifices of the parents.

The possibilities of both upward and downward mobility were great during this period,[71] which also heightened the sense of individual and parental responsibility for success or failure. The story of heartbroken parents was a popular theme in nineteenth-century domestic literature, in the stories of lives that were ruined because a beloved son or daughter had fallen from virtue and was now only, in the words of a popular song of the 1890s, a "picture that is turned to the wall."

FROM VICTORIANISM TO
THE JAZZ AGE

Between the 1880s and World War I, the pace of social, economic, and technological change began to quicken. The country had become more urban, more industrial, and more of a modern consumer society. As farming declined, waged and salaried employment increased. A "second industrial revolution" led to an astonishing increase in productivity. To be sure, poverty persisted, but living standards rose and a larger proportion of the society was becoming middle class. An astonishing range of inventions and discoveries appeared during these years, including electricity, X rays, anesthesia, the telegraph, the telephone, the bicycle, the automobile, radio, the movies.

The middle-class young people, especially women, who came of age during those years were increasingly likely to question what they saw as suffocating Victorian assumptions about sexuality, gender, and decorum. At the same time, America itself was being transformed from an agrarian, small-town culture to one in which the cities were becoming a dominant influence.

The sense of cultural dislocation began well before the 1920s. The divorce rate had been climbing steadily since the Civil War, from a total of 7,000 in 1860, to 56,000 in 1900, to 100,000 in 1914.[72] Over the same period, birthrates of the white middle class declined, leading President Theodore Roosevelt to warn in 1903 that Americans were committing "race suicide." Politicians, preachers, academics, and journalists lamented the breakdown of the family. "We are unsettled to the roots our being," declared Walter Lippman in 1914. "There isn't a human relation, whether of parent or child, husband and wife, worker and employer, that doesn't move in a strange direction."[73]

World War I served as a catalyst for metamorphoses that had been in progress for decades; the soldiers had left in the twilight of the Victorian era and returned to find themselves in the twentieth century. The horse and buggy had given way to the automobile. People of the 1920s looked and acted in ways that seem closer to the 1990s than the 1890s. In a major cultural upheaval—arguably *the* major cultural revolution of the twentieth century—these years witnessed a momentous break with Victorian sexual norms and gender roles.

The upheaval had been preceded by transformation in the conditions of everyday life. White-collar work expanded with the ascendancy of the large corporation and opened new opportunities for women. Improvements in health care and living conditions reduced mortality rates and extended the life span by over six years between 1900 and 1920: from forty-eight to fifty-five for women, and from forty-six to fifty-four for men. Also, by the early 1900s there had already been a shift from a leisure class to mass leisure. Between the 1860s and the 1920s the work week shrank from six to five days, and the working day from twelve to eight hours.[74]

New consumer products, or products that had formerly been luxuries, became widely available, producing a "democratization of convenience."[75] These included food in tin cans, iceboxes, out-of-season produce. A clothing revolution produced stylish clothes at moderate prices, making class distinctions less obvious. Automobile ownership soared in the 1920s, and mass production made cars affordable even for some of the working class. The invention of the flush toilet and the indoor bathroom transformed everyday life at the most private and primal level. At first found only in luxury hotels and mansions, these amenities were common in American homes after 1900.

A number of studies of the period have noted the remarkable parallel between economic expansiveness and an expansion of "personal life"[76]—a concern with inner experience and the self, love and intimacy, psychological development and the stages of life. Aristocrats and artists had always been concerned with personal life, but in the nineteenth and twentieth centuries this awareness spread to large segments of the population. It was in the 1920s, for example, that Freud became a household name among the educated middle class. But the interest in the new psychology was not confined to psychoanalytic ideas; John Watson's behaviorism, which informed theories of child rearing for two decades, was probably even more influential.

The First Sexual Revolution

To the older generation of Victorians, the most striking aspect of 1920s culture was the preoccupation with sex. In the Roaring Twenties, a sexual revolution overlapped with the last stages of this century's first wave of feminism. Women's roles had been in ferment for several generations. The flappers who symbolized the 1920s—with their "bobbed hair and powdered noses, with fringed skirts just above the knees and hose rolled below, with a cigarette in one hand and a man in the other"[77]—were the latest version of a series of New Women who had begun to appear after the Civil War.

The middle-class New Woman, along with the rising numbers of working-class "working girls," stood for a kind of autonomy and individuality that challenged traditional Victorian gender roles. Their growing numbers filled the ranks of a variety of reform movements, giving particular strength to the suffrage movement, which won the vote for women in 1920—a century after it had begun.

Although most women did not fit the image of the flapper, she symbolized a major shift in the meaning of sexuality—the separation of sex from reproduction and toward the modern idea that sexual expression is central to individual happiness.[78] The young people who came of age after World War I rebelled against their parents' Victorian code of sexual purity. *Flaming Youth*, a popular lurid film of the decade, gave the name to a generation. As would happen in the 1960s, it was the behavior of young women who changed most dramatically, shocking feminists from the first wave of the women's movement as well as the mainstream of the older generation. Daughters of respectable families turned themselves into the brazen figure of the flapper, committing acts that would have been unthinkable— if not illegal—before the war: they painted their faces, bobbed their hair, smoked, drank, wore their skirts above their knees, talked about sex, and danced to the raucous beat of jazz.

The flapper's short skirt was probably the single biggest change in women's clothing in all of Western history. Through centuries of changing styles, women's legs had always remained hidden. In the Victorian era, skirts touched the floor, and legs could not even be mentioned in polite company. As late as 1918, women greeted returning soldiers in skirts not much shorter.

Behind these fashions lay a shift to a new conception of women's nature, and of the relations between men and women. Changes in the social landscape were making Victorian notions of separate spheres obsolete. Instead, the new era focused on the camaraderie of young men and women, and the opposition of youth to age. In the emerging culture of college youth, brought to the center of national attention by the new national media, sex was the central symbol of the generational divide. "We do all the things that our mothers, fathers, aunts and uncles do not sanction, and we do them knowingly," wrote a student in the Ohio University *Lantern* in 1922.[79]

Young people below college age were also beginning to lead a more modern life: both young men and women attended high school, spent time after school with friends of both sexes, dated without chaperones, and made romance and sexual attraction a central part of courtship. When "Middletown" was studied in the 1920s, it was in the midst of a generation gap brought about by these changes. The automobile and the movies were transforming everyday life and creating new tensions between parents and children. The car and the new practice of dating freed young people from the watchful eyes of their parents. The emerging car culture overthrew previous social rules, for example, that a high school boy does not need much spending money and that parents ought always to know where their children are.

For the older generation at the time, the strange ways of young people were deeply worrying; passionate discussions and debate in the public media reflected widespread personal concern about what was happening to the nation's youth. In a 1922 letter to his brother William Howard Taft, former President and then Chief Justice of the Supreme Court, Horace Taft wrote:

> You get into deep water when you discuss the seriousness of the younger generation. There *are* those who live in simple homes and have old fashioned ambitions, etc. but the automobile & the movies & jazz life have invaded homes that are far from wealthy. That is the main trouble. A boy does not have to be rich nowadays to have the distractions and temptations that we used to connect in our minds with the small circle of very rich.[80]

The Kinsey reports of the late 1940s verified that sexual behavior and attitudes had changed dramatically in the 1920s. Women born in the first decade of the twentieth century differed more from earlier generations than later generations would differ from them. While 14 percent of women born before 1900 reported having premarital intercourse, 36 percent of those born between 1900 and 1910 reported doing so.[81]

The changes were greatest for the college-educated. The new generation of college-educated women supported themselves in newly expanding female occupations, such as teaching and nursing. Although more than half of them married, compared to their less educated counterparts they married later and bore fewer children. Before 1900 college-educated women were less likely than other women their age to have sex before marriage; after the turn of the century, their sexual activity rose. "That stratum of women who were most expected to do something with their lives, who had in earlier generations stood out for their high-minded ideals, stood out in the

1920s for their confrontations with smoking, drinking, and staying out at night."[82]

Male sexual patterns changed, too, not by an increase in premarital sex but by a change in their typical partners. Although chastity for both sexes has been the official standard in Western society for at least two thousand years, the real norm has been the double standard that accepts sexual activity for unmarried men but condemns it for unmarried women. In most times and places, only a minority of men have been virgins at marriage.[83] Prostitutes, along with "bad" or lower-class women, have traditionally filled the sexual gap created by the double standard. But this age-old pattern changed with the emergence of modern sexual norms in the 1920s. Men born after 1900, Kinsey found, had a dramatically reduced rate of sex with prostitutes compared to their fathers' and grandfathers' generations.[84]

But rates of intercourse are only one indicator of broader changes in sexual meanings and practices. The major contribution of the 1920s to the sexual culture of the twentieth century was the invention of "dating" and "petting." In the nineteenth century, young men and women rarely socialized except in large groups in public, pairing off only as a step toward marriage. A somewhat more modern pattern of courtship was the practice of young men "calling on" young middle-class women in their homes. The couple would remain in the parlor or on the porch, with the parents nearby if not in the same room.

By the middle of the 1920s, the new system of dating had almost completely replaced the practice of "calling." Courtship became increasingly "a private act conducted in a public world," away from family supervision and control.[85] Further, unlike earlier forms of courtship, dating did not necessarily imply a serious interest in marriage.

In their newfound privacy, the dating couples of the 1920s evolved new patterns of sexual play. Necking and petting became part of a new code of sexual behavior that staked out a middle ground between erotic yearning and the no-sex-at-all Victorian standard prescribed by parents and other adults. Although the new autonomy and sexuality of the young was as shocking to adult sensibilities as the sexual revolution of the 1960s was in its day, what looked like the overthrow of standards was actually a new sexual code with its own strict etiquette.

The new code granted recognition to female sexual desire, but it did not do away with the double standard. There were still two kinds

of women. The line that separated the two categories was not between sexual activity and no sexual activity, but between those who
followed the rules and those who went further and faster than the
rules allowed.

Love and Marriage

Contrary to fears at the time, the revolution of youth in the 1920s
was not a revolt against the family. In fact, the family was becoming
a more central part of life, as expectations for happiness and fulfillment through marriage reached new heights. The "glorification of
sex" was an aspect of "the sexualization of marriage."[86] The new ideal
of companionate marriage emphasized the sexual side of marriage
as part of a more intimate personal relationship between husband
and wife. Dating and petting permitted young people to explore their
compatibility with a variety of partners.

In fact, marriage was more popular than ever in the 1920s. Young
women were attending college and working in record numbers, yet
the average age of marriage was dropping. To the disappointment of
many radicals and feminists, the unleashing of female passion had
made marriage more attractive to women. Jane Addams, for example,
was dismayed by the new values of young women. She perceived that
the breakdown of "sex taboos" was related to "new standards of marriage."[87] But she was disappointed in the young women of the 1920s
who were turning their backs on social idealism in favor of freedom
and personal fulfillment. She had seen large numbers of their counterparts in her own generation remain celibate all their lives without
any difficulty.

Despite the fact that couples were marrying younger and having
more sex, birthrates dropped in the 1920s. People were healthier and
better nourished, childbirth was safer, and income levels rose, but
fertility rates were not influenced by these trends. The rationale for
the high birthrates of the past no longer existed. Parents could reasonably expect to see their babies live to adulthood, so they no longer
needed to endure "extra" pregnancies and birth as insurance against
infant and child mortality.

The small modern family of two or three children had been begun
by upper-middle-class whites in the middle of the nineteenth century.
White working-class families soon picked up the trend. Meanwhile,
through the first decades of the twentieth century, the traditionally

high fertility rate of farm families, immigrants, and blacks continued. As a result, diversity in family size peaked around the turn of the century. After 1920, all groups moved closer to the two-child norm.[88]

Ultimately, the new pattern of marriage was not so much a rejection of Victorian marriage as an extension of its central themes. "It was the nineteenth-century emphasis on affection, companionship, and mutual respect and regard," observes Robert Griswold, "that built the foundation for the later developments: romance, expression, playfulness, sexual gratification, all these well-known desiderata of twentieth-century marriages depended upon and grew directly from the moral assumptions of the nineteenth-century family."[89]

The 1920s, then, were a transitional period for American family life. The Victorian ideology of family, invented by the nineteenth-century middle class, was undergoing dramatic revision by its twentieth-century counterparts. The pattern of companionate family life in the 1920s had not solved the problems of reconciling women's roles in work and family, the broader issues of gender equality, or the paradoxical growth in both the fragility and the emotional centrality of marriage. But new ideas about birth control, marriage, child care, and housekeeping were under debate.

The cultural ferment of the 1920s ended with the Great Depression. Feminism, flappers, and debates about women's careers seemed irrelevant in the struggle for economic survival. With one out of four men unemployed, public opinion turned with a vengeance against women who seemed to be taking jobs away from men and their families. In fact, millions of single and married women went to work to support themselves or their families. In the end, however, the Depression, and later the war, reinforced traditional notions of women's place and stirred nostalgic longings that would eventually be realized in the postwar baby-boom family.

CONCLUSION

Looking backward over the past several centuries of American and Western European family life reveals both striking continuity and massive change. It is also clear, as the historian Michael Anderson observes, that "almost no generation has got by without debate over family crisis; most problems of our time have also been problems in the past."[90] Rather than argue whether the family lives of people in other eras were more truly dutiful and virtuous than our own, it may be more useful to think of American families in different historical eras as if they were different cultures. The Victorian family, despite the current nostalgia for it, was not the ideal model of family life we yearn for, nor were the versions of family life that preceded it. It seems unlikely that those whose hearts are warmed by the thought of a communal, patriarchal colonial family seamlessly woven into the social fabric would be willing to return to that world as it appears in the historical record and sacrifice the sense of home as a place of intimacy, privacy, and comfort.[91]

These different cultural orders, and the different meanings ascribed to family life in them, are responses to the social, political, and economic contexts in which they are embedded. It seems clear, for example, that living near the margins of subsistence focuses a family's energies around staying alive in the short run.[92] Adults have the first claims on food, infants the last. Children must take on productive roles at an early age.

Even if we were to locate some golden age of family life, we could not now return to the seventeenth- or nineteenth-century circumstances that led to it. Americans have traditionally assigned a primary causal role to the family, holding that families are the building blocks of society, that changes in the family will affect everything else. Obviously, what goes on in families affects what goes on elsewhere in society. Yet looking at the historical record, the causal arrow pointing the other way—from the larger society to the family—stands out clearly and powerfully. "On the checkerboard of social institutions," observes John Demos, "the family seems to display a markedly reactive character. Time and again it receives influences from without, rebuffs them, modifies them, adapts to them."[93] In short, families are not passive objects of social change; to paraphrase Marx, families also make history, but they do not make it "just as they please."

In the end, perhaps the main lesson to be learned from the historical study of the family is the pointlessness of both nostalgia and simple notions of progress. Every family arrangement brings both costs and benefits. Some families emerge from changes as haves, others as have-nots. Gains in autonomy for some family members are losses of control and power for others. Families are "responses to historical and cultural predicaments,"[94] and each such response invites new predicaments.

C H A P T E R   2

"Trying Out the Dream": The Family in the 1950s

Rarely has an era strived so hard, in the midst of immense social change, to define the normal and the seemingly immutable. —Thomas Hine
Populuxe: The Look and Life of America in the '50's and '60's

If I had to choose one image of the decade, I would say that the fifties were one big closet. —Benita Eisler
Private Lives: Men and Women of the Fifties

"You know, I get a really funny feeling every time I curl up on the sofa and tune into those 'Leave It to Beaver' reruns," says a thirty-nine-year-old San Francisco bachelor. A veteran of the Berkeley student revolt of the 1960s, he had lived in a commune whose members had once debated the slogan "Smash monogamy." "There's June, Ward, Wally and the Beaver," he goes on, "leading a domestic life so innocent, so comfortable, that I find myself thinking, why the hell did we make things so complicated? Can't we take some of that, that security? Isn't there some way to take what we have now—our careers, our beliefs, our sophistication—and still go back home again?"[1]

He is not alone in his tastes. A 1987 survey carried out for *Rolling Stone* magazine, based on a national sample of eighteen- to forty-four-year-olds, asked its respondents to list the television shows with values

they wanted their children to learn; they named "Father Knows Best"
and "Leave It to Beaver" along with their counterparts from the 1980s,
"The Cosby Show" and "Family Ties."[2]

The nostalgia for the 1950s began as the 1960s ended and has
persisted ever since. Nor is it confined to popular culture. Writing
in *Commentary* in 1969, John Mander proclaimed the 1950s the "happiest, most stable period the western world has known since 1914."[3]
Yet this view of "the fifties"—shorthand for the period from the late
1940s through the early 1960s—as a golden age tells us more about
the discontents of our own era than about the experience of people
living through those years.

True, it was a fortunate time in American history. Winning a world
war, the country entered an era of peace, prosperity, and international dominance. The long-held dream of a fulfilling family life in
a comfortable home seemed at last to be coming true for millions of
people; not everyone was affluent or middle class, but it was assumed
that those left out would eventually get their share. In many ways, it
was a time of remarkable democratization as America was trying out
the dream, in Paul Wilkes's phrase.

But not everyone views the 1950s with nostalgia. It was, as one
commentator observed, "an era of suppressed individuality, of national paranoia, and of largely unrecognized discrimination against
minorities, women, the poor, foreigners, homosexuals, and indeed
most of those who dared to be different—the era that came to an
end with the onset of the '60s was a time bomb waiting to explode."[4]

These contrasting visions of the 1950s began during the decade
itself. Indeed, far from portraying the era as a golden age, novels,
popular culture, and intellectual social critics painted bleak portraits
of the time, presenting Americans with what the historian Warren
Susman has called "a dual collective representation of themselves"[5]—
and the family was central to both representations. On the one hand,
images of happy suburban families smiled out of TV sets and magazine pages; on the other, a nightmare vision of American family life
filled the works of America's leading playwrights, as Eugene O'Neill,
Arthur Miller, Tennessee Williams, and Edward Albee portrayed dis-
integrating families and rotting marriages. Experts and the mass media across the land warned about dominating mothers and weak
fathers, the spreading menace of juvenile delinquency, a failing educational system, and the corruption of youth by movies, radio, television, and comic books.

Most surprising, in light of today's nostalgia for the 1950s, was the fierce denunciation of the postwar suburbs that reached its peak in the middle of the decade. Journalists, novelists, and social commentators unleashed a barrage of criticism, creating a "myth of suburbia" that blamed the new suburbs for a host of social ills, from undermining the family to weakening the American character.

Above all, it was a time of paradox. American power was at its peak, but Americans felt menaced as never before by threats from foreign enemies and internal subversion. An era that revered and symbolized normality and stability, it was a time of mass migrations and social and cultural change. At a time of exaggerated sex roles and a narrowing of women's options, social critics denounced the homogenization of sex roles and women's excessive power. And at a time when millions of Americans had been lifted out of poverty, social critics warned that affluence and suburbia were destroying American character and culture.

In this chapter, I will examine both the imagery and the realities of family life during this complex period as a necessary prelude to understanding the social changes of the 1960s and 1970s. First, the 1950s family remains the baseline from which current changes in family life are frequently measured. Second, we cannot understand the cultural revolution of the 1960s and early 1970s without a clear picture of what it was revolting against. Much of the energy that fueled the revolt came from discontents that seethed unexpressed during the 1950s. Yet at the same time, the revolts may be viewed as a continuation of the search for the good life that characterized the 1950s. The vision of a perfected family life in harmony with nature linked the postwar suburbs to the Victorian past as well as to the communes of the counterculture.

Finally, some trends that began in the 1950s still govern American life. It was the decade in which America first entered the postindustrial age; white-collar workers outnumbered blue-collar workers for the first time; the suburb replaced the city and the farm as the habitat of the typical American family; and uneasiness with cultural and social change fastened on the family as the symbol and source of all that was right—and wrong—with America.

THE DEVIANT DECADE

Ironically, the era that stands for stable, traditional family patterns was unlike that of any earlier time.[6] Studies by demographers and others have led to a surprising conclusion: far from being the last era of family normality from which current trends are a deviation, it is the family patterns of the 1950s that are deviant.

The young adults who came of age during and after World War II differed not only from their baby-boom offspring but also from their own parents and grandparents. Born between 1920 and 1940, they have been called "the lucky generation": though they had known Depression and war as children and adolescents, they entered adulthood at a time of expanding opportunity and increasing affluence. Today's young adults may have departed from the high marriage and birth rates and moderate divorce rates that prevailed in the 1950s, but it is their behavior rather than their parents' that is consistent with the long-term trends. As one study summed it up, "had the 1940's and 1950's not happened, today's young adults would appear to be behaving normally."[7]

The 1950s were marked by a remarkable set of circumstances in the economy, in international relations, and in demographic trends. The social and cultural climate also fell out of line with long-term trends. It was a throwback to the Victorian cult of domesticity with its polarized sex roles and almost religious reverence for home and hearth. But the new suburban Victorianism was part of the "long amnesia"[8]—the years between 1930 and 1960 when earlier debates about the position of women seemed to have been forgotten, and traditional conceptions of gender roles dominated public and private life.

It's not the domesticity of the 1950s that is puzzling—the closed domesticated nuclear family had been at the center of bourgeois life for centuries—but the exaggerated form it assumed: a birthrate that approached that of India, the insistence that marriage and motherhood take up the whole of a woman's identity, and the increased emphasis on gender difference.

For middle-class women, especially, the return to "tradition" in fact marked a turning away from choices made by their counterparts in earlier generations. Since the nineteenth century, American women had a reputation for markedly more freedom and independence than women in other countries. Educational opportunity also opened earlier to American women. By the first half of the twentieth century, men and women were attending college in roughly equal proportions. This educational parity was lost by women who reached adulthood in the postwar years. Data from a Berkeley longitudinal study indicate that in comparison to their fathers, three times as many men who came of age in the 1940s and 1950s graduated from college. The women of that era, by contrast, barely achieved the same proportion of college degrees as their mothers had. In close to half the marriages of the study members, husbands had more education than their wives.[9]

The extreme domesticity of those women who did attend college in the 1950s also departed from middle-class tradition. In the early decades of the century, most women went to college with the idea of pursuing demanding occupations like law, medicine, or journalism. In 1930 half of all professionals were women.[10] But in the 1950s, most women who attended college had no career plans, and dropped out in large numbers to marry. College was the place for a young woman to find a husband and to acquire the polish to carry off the role of the doctor's or lawyer's or organization man's gracious wife.

With the shift in middle-class women's domestic ideals and the rise in living standards, middle-class and working-class family patterns converged for the first time. The working class could afford middle-class comforts, and the upper middle class acquired a taste for fertility and domesticity. Traditionally, there had been an inverse correlation between social class and birth rates—or, as the old saying put it, "the rich get richer and the poor get children." In the 1950s the poor still had large families, but those at the upper end of the income scale were reversing the traditional pattern by having three, four, or five children.

Despite the rhetoric and reality of domesticity, however, millions of women entered the workplace during the 1950s. Women's participation in the labor force, which had begun around the turn of the century, continued to grow.[11] The increase came largely from middle-class married women, especially those over thirty-five. Rather than pursuing careers, most of these women worked part-time in pink-collar occupations such as clerical work, and their work was largely in the service of family goals—to help pay for the mortgage or put the kids through school. Nevertheless, an important cultural line had been crossed. During the 1950s, the meanings that had been implied by a married woman's working—lower-class status or a husband in dire financial straits—quietly faded away.

Thus, in ways large and small, the decade ushered in a way of life based on family and gender arrangements that were deeply contradictory and that flew in the face of long-term historical trends. The appearance of private traditionalism and public calm was deceptive. "It was as if the whole period was a front . . . the topsoil that protected the seed of rebellion that was germinating below."[12]

AFTER SCARCITY

To understand family life in the 1950s, we must consider the most remarkable single fact about America at that time: its unprecedented prosperity. Although most American families did not attain the lush affluence depicted in magazine advertisements—a spacious home on a tree-lined street, two late-model cars—the decades following World War II did witness a significant rise in their standard of living. Between the late 1940s and the early 1970s, America enjoyed the longest economic boom in history, hailed as the onset of the American century.

Of course, economics alone cannot explain the baby boom and the return of domesticity but it did set the stage for the family patterns of the 1950s. After fifteen years of Depression and war, the new prosperity set off a mood of celebration and hope. At the start of the 1940s, millions of Americans still faced seemingly endless unemployment. A 1942 poll found that only 32 percent of Americans believed their children would have more opportunity than they had had.[13]

By the late 1940s, it was as if, as one writer put it, "milk and honey [had] appeared suddenly to a people who had been trudging across an economic Sinai for a decade and a half."[14] For the first time ever, a majority of the population was on the comfortable side of the poverty line. By the mid-1950s, 60 percent of Americans had attained a middle-class standard of living, in contrast to only 31 percent in the last year of prosperity before the Great Depression.[15] The American dream of upward mobility seemed to be coming true. The average American man's job placed him several rungs higher on the economic ladder than his father had been. *Life* magazine told of young men just out of college or the army who had their choice of well-paying jobs that would make their parents proud.[16] Instead of a pyramid-shaped distribution of income, with most people on the bottom, America's income structure bulged out in the middle and came to resemble a football.

A factory worker recalled the changes that followed the war:

I think that one of the important things that came out of World War II was the arrival of the working class at a new status level in this society.... Most of the people that I worked with lived in rented houses and close to slum conditions. By the fifties everybody in that kind of world expected that they would live in a suburban house—

one they owned. The war integrated into the mainstream a whole chunk of society that had been living in the edge.[17]

But critics pointed out that the distribution of wealth had not changed from what it had been in earlier decades; substantial num- bers of Americans were in fact left out of the feast. "Most Americans never had it so good," observed the economist Robert Lekachman, but "possibly 15 to 20 percent have it as bad as ever."[18] As Michael Harrington put it, poverty had become "socially invisible," until the following decade, when it was "discovered" by policy makers and the public.[19]

Also invisible was the vast number of Americans who lived above the poverty line but below the level of affluence portrayed in the mass media. Typically, television and advertising presented a white nuclear family, headed by a single, white-collar breadwinner and liv- ing on a tree-lined suburban street, with two cars in the garage. This image left out people of color, ethnics, and others who lived in city neighborhoods, single or divorced people, and working mothers, as well as middle Americans of the white working class and lower mid- dle class.

Middletown Revisited

Remarkably, Americans in every income category *were* better off than they and their families had been before the war. In the 1920s, when Robert and Helen Lynd studied "Middletown," they found a wide gulf, a "watershed," separating what they called the "business" from the "working" classes. By *business class*, the Lynds meant the 25 per- cent of the Middletown families in which the men wore suits and ties to work, worked with people or paper, and kept their hands clean. *Working-class* men wore blue collars, worked with "things," and got their hands dirty. Which side of the watershed one was born on, they observed, was "the most significant single cultural factor tending to influence what one does all day long throughout one's life."[20]

When the Lynds returned to Middletown in 1935 to study the ef- fects of the Depression, they found that the economic crisis had pushed the two main classes even farther apart. While business-class families of the 1920s and 1930s lived at a level of material comfort not very different from that of today, in 1935 many working-class families lived in homes that were dirty, uncomfortable places, with no running hot water, central heating, bathtubs, showers, or indoor toilets. Some families had some of these amenities; few had all.

In the 1970s a new research team went back to study Middletown for the third time. They found graphic evidence of the changes in American life brought about by the postwar boom, even though the economy by that time had started to decline. The watershed between the classes had eroded considerably. Although inequality of occupational status or prestige remained—and, in fact, had increased over the years—most of the differences in living standards and life-styles observed by the Lynds had disappeared.[21]

Working-class life had changed the most dramatically. Middletown people in the 1970s, like Americans generally, were not only better off financially than their counterparts in the 1920s and 1930s but healthier and more educated, and had more leisure time. The long period of affluence had democratized and enriched American cultural life. Although a chorus of critics railed at the "empty values" of television and other mass media, and such symbols of tawdry consumerism as cars with tailfins, there was more to the good times of the 1950s than consumer goods.

Psychological Gentrification

Before the war, a college degree, along with the presence of servants in the home, marked the boundary between the business and the working classes. As late as the 1920s, fewer than 17 percent of young people even graduated from high school.[22] After the war, the G.I. Bill of Rights opened the doors of higher education to the sons of factory workers and truck drivers, establishing education as a basic right of citizenship. The number of people who had access to higher education doubled between 1950 and 1965. In the election of 1952, voters whose education had been limited to grade school outnumbered by 3 to 1 those who had been to college for any length of time; by 1972 the latter outnumbered the former 2 to 1.[23]

Education was only one part of the cultural expansion and psychological gentrification that began in the 1950s. Museums, theaters, symphony orchestras, and dance companies spread across the country. Long-playing records improved the quality of music available in the home; Americans spent more on tickets to classical concerts than to baseball games.

Quality paperbacks made good books cheaply available; the "paperbacking of America" democratized reading.[24] Though critics had warned that television would destroy interest in the printed word, book sales doubled during the 1950s.[25] The Lynds had observed in their original studies that "Middletown is not a book-buying city"; by 1977, according to Caplow and his colleagues, "it was emphatically a book-buying city,"[26] and the books Middletowners were buying were not by and large trashy.

Middle-class Americans also used their newfound prosperity to travel. With the arrival of paid vacations, interstate highways, and cheap gas, Americans in the 1950s began to explore their own country as never before. They also traveled outside it in record numbers. Before World War II, foreign travel had been limited to those at the top of the economic scale; only a tiny minority of Americans had ever visited Europe. Suddenly more and more Americans could afford to make trips outside the country.

Better housing, along with shorter working hours and other advances in material well-being in the postwar era, had a profound effect on the quality of working-class family life. The portraits of life in the new suburbs studied by Herbert Gans and Bennett Berger in the 1950s and early 1960s contrast sharply with the grim images of working-class family life presented by the Lynds in their first study of Middletown.[27] The Lynds saw the typical working-class marriage as a bleak, frustrating relationship lacking in communication, emotional support, and sexual satisfaction. Both men and women seemed exhausted much of the time. The ever-present threat and frequent reality of unemployment disrupted families and saddled men with the feeling of failure in their efforts to support their families. Sexual relations were troubled by fear of pregnancy and lack of information about birth control; wives did not dare discuss the matter with husbands but instead tried to avoid sex. These constraints on marital sex may have contributed to the high rates of prostitution in Middletown during the 1920s.

THE MYTH OF SUBURBIA

Just as the long-held dream of a comfortable life began to come true for large numbers of people, many journalists, academics, and social critics cast a cold eye on postwar American society, especially the burgeoning middle class and the new suburbs. The new affluence made many people uneasy. Western culture has been marked by a strange animosity toward economic progress and material well-being. Every time the standard of living has increased for some segment of the population, or new consumer goods have become available, strong feelings of disappointment, even hostility, have surfaced. "Along with appreciation, infatuation, and even addiction," Hirschman observes, "affluence seems to produce its own backlash."[28]

Far from being a product of the post–World War II era or, indeed, of the twentieth century, both the consumer society and the moralistic recoiling from it first emerged prior to 1800.[29] The manufacturing industries that began the Industrial Revolution produced articles for everyday use, luxury products for their time—cloth, buckles, buttons, mirrors, cards, toys, cutlery, beauty products, clothes—which were bought by a growing segment of the population that was neither rich nor poor.

In the nineteenth century, as the flow of new, mass-produced goods and objects increased, so did the denunciations and lamentations of what would come to be called *consumerism*. Here, for example, is Flaubert in 1854, denouncing the new wave of consumer goods that appeared with a period of economic expansion: "We must shout against cheap gloves, against the mackintosh, against cheap stoves, against fake cloth, against fake luxury . . . ! Industry has developed ugliness in gigantic proportions."[30]

The attack on the suburbs that were springing up all over the country grew out of a more general critique of postwar American culture. Appearing in 1950, *The Lonely Crowd* by the sociologist David Riesman and his associates, was the first and most influential statement of themes that would dominate discussions of American society in the 1950s and later—namely, that the character structure of Americans had been radically transformed.[31] Six years after Riesman's book, William Whyte's *The Organization Man*, the other leading work in this genre, made similar observations.[32]

To Riesman, Whyte, and other social critics, the growth of the mass-produced suburbs was one part of a new social order that was destroying individualism and autonomy and turning Americans into a herd of conformists. A bureaucratized, consumer society had shifted Americans from a "psychology of scarcity" and "inner direction" to a "psychology of abundance" and "other direction." The "inner-directed" individual, typified by nineteenth-century entrepreneurs and pioneers, was guided by a moral "gyroscope"; the postwar "organization man" and suburbanite was guided by psychological "radar."

Sensitive to the changing fashions and opinions of others, the other-directed person was guided by no firm principle, only by a need to be liked by, and to be like, others. Reisman saw *both* inner and other direction as forms of conformity; his ideal was the autonomous individual not guided by either a gyroscope or radar. Most of his readers, however, took him to mean that other-direction represented conformity and a decline from the good old days of inner direction.

While both books dealt with the suburbs as a prime symbol of a new era in American culture, Whyte's chapters on "The New Suburbia" became the starting point for a wave of more extreme attacks aimed specifically at the suburbs. Basing his discussion on a study of the new town of Park Forest, Illinois, Whyte argued that the traditional values of individualism and self-reliance were declining, to be replaced by a new "social ethic"—the notion that "belongingness" was the ultimate need of the individual. The attack on suburbia took off where the more complex and nuanced works by Riesman and Whyte left off. With works such as *The Crack in the Picture Window* and *The Split Level Trap*, journalists, fiction writers, and social critics had created by the mid-1950s what Bennett Berger called "the myth of suburbia."[33]

To speak of a myth of suburbia is not to deny that massive migration did take place to new housing developments on the outskirts of the cities. The creation of the suburbs was one of the most dramatic transformations of the physical and social landscape ever. In response to a severe housing crisis after the war, the government provided easy credit and builders found ways to mass-produce homes on undeveloped land. The result was an unprecedented housing boom. By the end of the decade, the new suburbia contained more than a quarter of the American population.[34]

To be sure, serious criticisms can be made about the suburban trend in the postwar era. The flight of the white middle class from the city and its problems intensified those problems, while the growth of the suburbs imposed heavy costs on the disadvantaged. American society was becoming divided between angry, despairing inner cities and the surrounding suburbs. Eventually, suburban sprawl spoiled the country landscapes that people had fled the city for in the first place. There were many shortcomings in the suburban developments themselves—a lack of public facilities and services, the isolation of women and children, and the relative lack of activities for teenagers. But the myth of suburbia had little to do with such matters. Rather, it told of dire effects the suburbs had on the hearts and minds of those who lived in them.

Suburbanites, according to the critics, were lonely and alienated yet deprived of privacy, caught up in a frenzied, never-ending round of neighbor and group activities. Living in identical houses, they had lost their individuality and turned into mass-produced replicas of one another. "All dwellings are the same shape," complained one critic, "all dwellers are squeezed into the same shape."[35] A classic tale of the time was of the man who came home late one night, mistook his neighbor's house for his own, got into bed with his neighbor's wife—and didn't realize his mistake until the next morning.

Much of the criticism took aim at the presumed dangers of suburbia for families and children; it turned families into matriarchies with overbearing wives, emasculated husbands, overinvolved mothers, absent fathers, spoiled and delinquent children. Mental illness, drunkenness, and adultery were rampant. "Each suburban family is somehow a broken home, consisting of a father who appears as an overnight guest, a put-upon housewife with too much to do, and children necessarily brought up in a kind of communism."[36]

In many ways, the myth of suburbia resembled an "urban legend." Like the story of the misguided suburban husband, these are tales told as true stories, often based on fact but exaggerated as they spread. Among urban legends are the tales about mice in soft-drink bottles, Kentucky fried rats, and babies left on car roofs as unwitting parents drive off, as well as stories of Halloween sadism and satanic rituals involving child abuse.[37] Urban legends have been explained as a response to strain and uneasiness brought about by changes in existing social arrangements. They "often depict a clash between modern conditions and some aspects of a traditional life style."[38]

Living in Levittown

A number of sociological studies were carried out against the background of this mythology. Berger studied a working-class suburb in Milpitas, California, and Herbert Gans studied a newly built Levittown on the outskirts of Philadelphia. What these and other studies showed was that there was no such thing as "suburbia," only specific suburban developments reflecting the characteristics, especially the class cultures, of the people who came to live in them.

Berger's Milpitas automobile workers, for example, did not resemble, or come to resemble, the well-educated middle-management organization men who lived in William Whyte's Forest Park. Berger did not dispute what Whyte claimed to have found, but did object to generalizations based on a few studies of upper-middle-class suburbs. Suburbia did not transform the Milpitas families into Republicans, churchgoers, or party givers. Like other working-class people at the time, they were Democrats and they socialized mostly with the extended family. Unlike their organization-men counterparts, they did not hope to get ahead on their jobs or to move to a better house: "Most of them viewed their new suburban homes as paradise permanently gained."[39]

Herbert Gans's study of the mainly lower-middle-class Levittown—the name that symbolized the new postwar suburbs—cast similar doubt on the transforming power of suburbia as well as on other aspects of the myth. Already one of the nation's largest homebuilders in the early 1940s, Abraham Levitt and Sons pioneered in the postwar application of mass-production techniques to the building of houses. In 1958, motivated by "hair-raising stories" about life in the first two Levittowns, Gans and his family moved into a new one being built outside Philadelphia to see if "any of the evils described by the critics actually existed."[40]

After two years, Gans found little evidence to support the stereotypes. Levittowns were basically "old communities on new land," places whose cultures were shaped by the kinds of people who lived in them.[41] People's lives were changed somewhat by living in a raw new community at some distance from the city, but their basic values, ambitions, and way of life had not changed. Further, the majority of Levittowners were pleased with their move; they enjoyed their new homes, found friends in the community, did not experience the malaise or boredom ascribed to suburbanites in the myth. To be sure, some people were lonely, socially isolated, or depressed. But for many people who had been socially lonely before, moving to Levittown proved a godsend. Some, especially women, missed the family they had left behind in the city. Levittowners talked to their relatives frequently on the telephone and visited them often, but Gans found not one who wanted to move back to the city to be closer to family.

He saw much evidence of the togetherness the magazines were celebrating, which the families had moved to Levittown to find. Parents and children did more things together than they had before the move. Surprisingly, commuting to and from Levittown did not produce much of the father absence the critics railed against—certainly no more than for men in similar jobs elsewhere.[42] Also surprising was the finding that most men spent no more time than before traveling to work, and some even had shorter commutes. Most of the fathers

in Levittown were involved with their children and spent a good deal
of their spare time in projects around their homes.

Married life did not seem to be different in Levittown than in any
other setting: some married couples were very happy, some very unhappy. The majority of marriages seemed to be the same mixture of
"bliss and bickering" found elsewhere. Malaise, to the extent it existed, was a female, not a suburban, problem. Many women complained of the monotony of housework and the difficulties of caring
for young children—a common problem in the baby-boom era, when
many couples had two or three babies in rapid succession. Gans observed:

> Much of the popular talk about an emerging matriarchy strikes me
> as a misreading of the trend toward greater equality between the
> sexes—a middle-class value which is also being adopted by many
> working-class women these days.... Public concern about matriar-
> chy is natural—at least among men, ... those who must relinquish
> power usually phrase their complaints as social criticism.[43]

Despite the careful observations of Berger, Gans, and other researchers who examined life in the suburbs, the myth of suburbia
lived on. Attacking the suburbs was as much a part of the culture of
the 1950s as were the sunny images of happy suburban families on
television; suburb bashing was part of the dark side of America's dual
collective representation of itself.

Suburbia as Scapegoat

In the end, the myth of suburbia raises more questions about its
creators and the large numbers of people who resonated to it than
about the complex realities of the suburbs themselves. Trying to make
sense of the myth, Bennett Berger and other critics suggest that mass
suburbanization coincided with, and seemed to embody, the major
changes of the postwar era: the new affluence and social mobility,
the rising marriage and birth rates, the political conservatism, the
revival of religion, the growth of the mass media.[44]

As Berger observed, the idea of the suburb was somehow able to
arouse intense yet contrasting emotions in different ideological segments of the population. "Suburbia" was a safe and convenient way
of talking about America and American culture in general, both to

those who celebrated it and those who criticized it.[45] A striking example of the suburban home as a symbol of the American way of life
occurred in the famous "kitchen debate" between Vice President
Nixon and Nikita Khrushchev. Visiting an American exhibition in
Moscow in 1959, Nixon pointed to a model of a ranch-style house,
complete with furniture and appliances, as proof of American superiority.[46]

For liberal and left-wing social critics, "suburbia" stood for com-
placency, conformity, mass culture, consumerism. It replaced the
outmoded "bourgeois" as a term of rebuke. In a conservative time,
disillusioned with the left-wing politics of the 1930s, social critics
turned their wrath away from their classic targets—corporate greed
and power, the maldistribution of wealth, political corruption—and
aimed it at the suburbs.

They uncritically accepted the popular notion of America as a homogeneous, affluent society and ignored the millions of poor people
in what Michael Harrington called "the other America," the disen-
franchised blacks, the first stirrings of the civil rights movement, the
constraints of women's roles. Thus, unlike political or economic criticism, the essentially cultural critique of suburbia "threatens no entrenched interests, and contains no direct implications for agitation
or concerted action."[47]

Ironically, critics who did not define themselves as conservatives
were hostile to what was actually a democratization of American life.
Their attack on the tastes and living styles of suburbanites—Whyte's
complaint about "the pink lampshade in the picture window"; Dwight
Macdonald's criticism of "middlebrow culture," as typified by the
Book-of-the-Month Club, "threatening to engulf everything in its
spreading ooze"[48]—brought the critics' views closer to those of traditional conservatives, whose hostility to modern society and its vul-
gar masses was often expressed in cultural terms.

What was there about patios, barbecues, the Book-of-the-Month
Club, and picture windows, with or without pink lampshades, to merit
such contempt? Why throw satirical stones at other people's houses,
even if they did look like "little boxes," as a popular song once put
it? Pointing at mass consumption as the main culprit of postwar
America's problems was a flawed practice for many reasons. As the
historian Jackson Lears observes, the tendency to see America as a
homogenized mass of manipulated consumers who defined themselves in terms of cars and washing machines was in fact to make
consumption a major, and strangely apolitical, category of analysis.[49]

The focus on taste and style amounted to telling other people how to live their lives. In his preface to *The Levittowners*, Gans describes his vision of sociology as a "democratic method of inquiry" that "assumes people have some right to be what they are."[50] The critics of suburbia did not agree. Although the target was new, their attack on suburbia and American culture was a variation on an older theme, a pessimistic discourse against modernity that has become an inherent part of modern culture itself.[51]

Obsessed with the psychological and moral shortcomings of the burgeoning middle class, the postwar social critics ignored the diversity of America's class, ethnic, and regional subcultures as well as the problems that would later become glaringly obvious. They attacked the affluent society not for the hardships of the poor or for race and gender inequality, but because middle-class Americans no longer seemed to embody the mythical virtues of eighteenth-century yeomen or nineteenth-century entrepreneurs.

Nevertheless, despite their analytic flaws, the social critics of the 1950s kept open a channel of dissent in a time of political constraint and repression. There was ultimately a political message in the apolitical myth of suburbia; the official dogma of the "American celebration" declared that America had become a nearly perfect, completed society, but the critics said, "No, not really, not yet." In so doing, they watered the seeds of dissent and rebellion that lay dormant under the smooth surface of postwar America.

COMING HOME

In an oblique and displaced way, the social critics were expressing discontent with a family pattern and ideology at odds with mid-twentieth-century postindustrial society and economic realities. To most people at the time, however, the American baby-boom family pattern represented normality. Sociological theories portrayed the middle-class family of the 1950s as the most evolved version of a timeless, universal nuclear family, its division into gender and generational roles "functional" to the psychological needs of family members and to those of the larger society. Today, however, postwar family patterns, especially the high fertility rates, are a demographic mystery.

Why did the postwar generation rush into marriage and parenthood? The issue is not the centrality of home and family in American life—those had always been core American values. They had been no less central in the 1920s, when issues much like today's were widely discussed: combining work and family duties, the fifty-fifty marriage, child care, and so on. Rather, what needs to be explained is the "orgy of domesticity" that took place in the late 1940s and 1950s and ran counter to historical trends.[52] It was not just that a neo-Victorian version of separate spheres allowed women no other role than that of wife and mother, despite the fact that women were entering the workplace in increasing numbers. There was also a sort of McCarthyism of marriage and the family toward anyone who deviated from the prevailing family patterns: the unmarried adult, the working woman, the childless couple, the "effeminate" male.

There is, as the sociologist Andrew Cherlin points out, no simple, single-factor explanation for the unprecedented embrace of marriage and parenthood in America in the postwar years.[53] None of the many explanations offered can account for all the aspects of the baby-boom family pattern.

The most obvious explanation is that after the war, people were hungry for a return to hearth and home and a "normal" family life. "Janet White," mother of six baby-boom children, recently recalled, "After all that devastation, you just wanted to have a bunch of kids, gather everybody around the fireplace, and hug them. And you didn't have to worry that there wouldn't be enough money to support them, or enough room in the house."[54]

But the trend toward earlier marriage and larger families had been evident before the war. Further, while birthrates often do go up after a war, the rise can be short-lived. Europeans responded to World War II with a small baby boom, nothing on the order of the American one. The war theory does not explain why the American baby boom continued as long as it did: it peaked not right after the war but in the 1950s, and high birthrates persisted into the 1960s. Some other factor had to be working to sustain the baby boom for almost two decades past the end of the war.

Further, the yearning for home and hearth is not an inevitable response to the end of war. The period right after World War I was a culturally rebellious era, more like the 1960s than the 1950s. For some observers, the unparalleled prosperity of the times explains the post–World War II domestic revival. It is hard to imagine the baby boom occurring in the absence of an expansive economy. Also, as the demographer Richard Easterlin has argued, because of low birthrates during the Depression, the supply of young workers was small, improving still more the economic prospects of young adults coming of age in the 1940s and 1950s.[55]

One of the puzzles about the domestic revival and its concomitant narrowing of women's roles is that it followed a wartime crisis in which women's roles had been radically altered. Millions of women entered the labor force as men went off to war. "Rosie the riveter," clad in overalls and bandanna and hard at work in a defense plant, looked out of countless posters, magazine illustrations, and newspaper photographs. She symbolized women's success at doing men's work. Almost 200,000 women joined the Wacs and the Waves; they also operated cranes in steel mills, greased locomotives, built ships, and cut down giant redwoods.[56] As women showed they could take on the kind of physical labor previously done only by men, it looked to many people as though a social revolution were in progress. The editor of the *Christian Science Monitor* wrote, "In the long years ahead, we will remember these short years of ordeal as a period when women rose to full stature."[57]

How, then, as one study recently asked, "did the strong figure of Rosie the riveter become transformed into the naive, dependent, childlike, self-abnegating model of femininity in the late forties and 1950s?"[58] In 1963, Betty Friedan supplied an answer: the postwar return to domesticity was nothing less than a conspiracy to revive the Victorian family and "trap women in the home."[59]

There is, in fact, a good deal of truth to the conspiracy theory. During the war, the Office of War Information had collaborated with advertisers and the mass media, especially women's magazines, to carry out a "womanpower" campaign to recruit women into the workplace. As the war wound down, these efforts were replaced by concerns about converting back to a peacetime society. Although there was no elaborate propaganda campaign to get women back home, the government agencies did suggest that a return to traditional women's roles was in order. Instead of trying to generate positive attitudes toward child-care centers, for example, women's magazines were advised to concentrate on the "new national problem of juvenile delinquency," assumed to be the fault of working mothers.[60]

In the intervening years, feminists and other scholars have come to tell a more complicated story about women's place in wartime America and the coming of the baby boom. Three decades of research, social change, and revisions in feminist scholarship have put the family patterns of the 1950s in a new light. Women no longer appear to have been simply passive victims of a propaganda cam-paign: effective advertising and propaganda work not by injecting alien ideas but by striking responsive chords, appealing to wishes and fears that are widely shared. The yearning for home and family in the immediate postwar era had deeper roots than media manipula-tion could have provided.

Recent research suggests that the roots of postwar domesticity were fed by the psychosocial effects of Depression and war. The Depres-sion was, as the sociologist Glen Elder found, a profoundly "alien" experience for the Americans who lived through it.[61] The encounter with economic insecurity, the loss of a father's income and role as breadwinner, and the subsequent shifts in family life and gender roles were all seen as tragic deviations from normality. For the men who found themselves out of work, the Depression was psychologically devastating: a historic crisis that threatened the very basis of the male role, that of family provider.[62] The ironic result is that what might have been a shift toward a more symmetrical division of labor in the family ended up reinforcing traditional gender roles.

The apparent challenge to tradition in World War II had a similar ironic outcome. From our vantage point, the transition from Rosie the riveter to the polarized gender roles of the 1950s no longer seems abrupt. We now realize that women's wartime experience was ambiv-alent and complex. Rosie and her sisters confronted many of the same problems in the workplace that their counterparts in the 1970s and 1980s would have to face: sex-segregated jobs, less pay for the same work, sexual harassment, shortage of child care, a double shift of work and home responsibilities.

Further, Rosie the riveter was not as much of a challenge to tradi-tional gender roles as she at first seemed. "Beneath her begrimed exterior," concludes one study, "she remained very much a tradi-tional woman."[63] The media usually portrayed women's war work as a temporary sacrifice, motivated by patriotism and the desire to bring their loved ones home sooner. One 1944 ad showed a mother in overalls leaving for work on a bicycle; next to her is a little girl dressed the same way. The caption, in large letters, reads: "Mother, when will you stay home again?" The text underneath reads: "Someday mother will stay home again, doing the job she likes best—making a home for you and Daddy, when he gets back."[64]

In addition to the factors already mentioned, the cold war—which erupted into a full-scale war in Korea and flared up periodically dur-ing the 1950s—also contributed to the renewed emphasis on domes-

ticity. As the historian Elaine May suggests, cold war tensions between
the United States and the Soviet Union, and the menace of the atomic
bomb, encouraged the retreat into the home in a search for security
in a dangerous new world.[65] But the warlike atmosphere of those
years may have encouraged domesticity in a more direct way. All
during the 1950s, the nation was committed to a large peacetime
army. Getting married and having a child was a way for a young man
to avoid the draft. For those who served, being married was a way of
softening some of the rigors of military life. A married soldier, for
example, could live with his wife in an apartment instead of in the
barracks.[66]

Despite the pressure toward an intensified domesticity, the immediate postwar years, as the historian William Chafe points out, offered a major "moment of possibility" for social change.[67] Women,
like blacks, might have been able to expand on the gains they had
made during the war. The vast majority of women who had taken
war jobs, especially those over forty-five, wanted to continue working.
(Most women of childbearing age had left their jobs even before the
war ended, but they had never made up a majority of the work force.)

Some policy makers and editorial writers in those early postwar
years argued that it was unfair to tell women to go to work in a
national emergency, then simply dismiss them when jobs got scarce.
Some voices even called for more equality on the home front. A War
Department pamphlet called for family allowances, community laun-
dries, and child-care facilities, and even urged returning soldiers to
share the housework. "Family problems are produced by social
change," it argued, and "often can be solved only by further
changes."[68] But social change in the form of more equality between
the sexes would have required leadership from policy makers, organization, and a new vision of sex roles within the family. The spirit
of the times was otherwise.

THE FREUDIAN FIFTIES

The spirit of the postwar domesticity was two-sided. On one side
was the lure of a secure and fulfilling home life. On the other side
were the social and psychological costs of departing from the prevailing norms. "Togetherness" may have been "an instant joke among
the cynical,"[69] but it was just an updated version of the 1920s notion
of companionate marriage. Togetherness was the subject of an edi-

torial in the May 1954 issue of *McCall's* magazine. Summing up the new family pattern that had emerged over the past decade, the magazine noted that men and women were marrying and having babies at an earlier age and rearing larger families. The editorial also described the blessings that affluence had brought to millions of Americans. But the most significant change was that men, women, and children together were creating a "new and warmer way of life." The same issue featured an article about a paper-mill executive who not only shared the household chores with his wife but helped decorate the home and was very involved in the day-to-day care of his three young children.[70]

The pull toward home was matched by social pressures and institutional constraints. Working wives and child care were denounced as Communist ideas. As late as 1971, President Nixon vetoed a Child Development bill that would have provided child care, on the grounds that it would "commit the vast moral authority of the national government to the side of communal approaches to child rearing."[71]

Freudian ideas—as they were defined at the time—provided additional ideological support to the campaign against deviance in matters of family, gender roles, and sexuality. Freudian ideas about woman's biological nature were widely influential in popular culture. Normality for a woman meant finding fulfillment only in marital sexuality and mothering. Any inclination toward independence, interest in work outside the home, or dissatisfaction with the roles of wife and mother were seen as signs of neurosis and "penis envy."

In a curious way, an updated Freudian version of the idealized family of the Victorian era became the "normal" family of the postwar era. Like the nineteenth-century utopians who believed that society could be regenerated through the perfection of family life, postwar child-rearing experts and social scientists looked at the pathological family as the cause, and therefore the potential cure, of a host of social problems: poverty, crime, mental illness, and all forms of "deviance." And, as in the nineteenth century, the burden of molding the future of their children fell squarely on mothers.

The New Cult of Motherhood

In many ways, the psychological glorification of women's domestic roles in the postwar era made even more stringent demands on women than its Victorian cults of domesticity and motherhood had.

If a family was to be regarded as normal and healthy, its members were supposed to experience love, happiness, and fun.

In a 1954 study of American child-rearing manuals, the psychologist Martha Wolfenstein coined the term "fun morality" to describe this emphasis on good feelings.[72] Fun morality, she noted, contained a paradoxical demand—the obligation to have a good time. In a similar way, the version of Freudian theory being purveyed at the time insisted that the proof of healthy femininity was to be found in feelings of emotional fulfillment in carrying out the roles of wife and mother.

By prescribing inner states rather than behavior, the new psychological standards made parental success more elusive than in the past. Fun morality was truly a morality; surveys of middle-class mothers in the 1950s revealed widespread guilt and anxiety over child rearing.[73] In earlier eras, when infant and child mortality rates were high, mothers were concerned primarily with their child's survival. If your child was healthy, clean, and reasonably well behaved, you had little cause to look into his or her psyche—or your own. But in the 1950s, the mundane tasks of child rearing—feeding, bathing, toilet training—became embroiled in issues of personality development. "Checking the bread and milk a child eats and seeing that he or she chews it well are concrete labors mothers can complete," observes the historian Nancy Weiss; "[t]he permissive task of enjoying the child at the table, and considering the learning element in feeding, are ... less susceptible to being finished. These are tasks that linger, and ones of Sisyphean proportions."[74]

The task of postwar mothers was complicated still further by the contradictory advice offered them. The experts not only disagreed with one another and changed their messages over time but contradicted themselves. Even the kindly Dr. Spock is full of double binds. For example, in a detailed analysis of Spock's best-selling advice books, the historian Michael Zuckerman points out that while Dr. Spock tells mothers to relax and trust their instincts ("you know more than you think you do"), he also warns them that they have an "ominous power" to destroy their children's innocence and make them discontent forever.[75]

However contradictory and anxiety-inducing such child-rearing advice offered them, middle-class parents supplied a large market for it, as they had in the nineteenth century and continue to do today. Furthermore, they have acted on this advice. Research in the 1950s revealed that parents internalized expert advice, changing their practices as expert opinion shifted.[76]

Moreover, children may have internalized this advice as well. As the psychologist Jerome Kagan observes, non-Western cultures, and Western society before the seventeenth century, did not view parental love and proper child-rearing practices as sources of the child's personality. These beliefs can act as self-fulfilling prophecies: parents believe they will harm their children if they take a false step or fail to love their children enough; children and adolescents learn of these theories, and as adults attribute their unhappiness and psychological problems to a lack of love during childhood, instead of, as in the past, fate, or inborn temperament.[77]

Contradictory Male Roles

Men were not exempt from Freudian norms. The Victorian patriarch was held up as a model of masculinity, although few living examples of him seemed to exist. Nevertheless, psychoanalytically informed "experts" warned of the dire effects of the "passive" or "ineffectual" father. He and his partner in psychiatric crime, the dominant mother, were blamed for "everything from homosexuality to ingrown toenails."[78] Meanwhile, comic strips and television programs poked fun at emasculated, "henpecked" males like Dagwood Bumstead.

The ideology of the strong male was at odds with the ideology of togetherness. The literature on marriage and the family, as well as the women's magazines, were arguing that the strongest families and the happiest marriages were "democratic." Yet a film like *Rebel Without a Cause* could mock James Dean's "weak father" for wearing an apron and not standing up to his wife, thereby depriving his son of a "manly" role model. The contradiction could be seen in the 1954 *McCall's* issue proclaiming the new togetherness. While one article lauded the executive I discussed earlier who shared household chores and child care, another warned that: "For the sake of every member of the family, the family needs a head. This means Father, not Mother."[79]

For either sex, the single state was regarded almost as a contagious disease. A young man who remained single for too long opened himself up to charges of "emotional immaturity" or "latent homosexuality"—phrases that were part of the basic vocabulary of the 1950s. An influential book of the period argued that all bachelors over thirty should receive psychotherapy and that spinsters should be legally forbidden to teach schoolchildren on the grounds of emotional incompetence.[80]

Just as communism was the ultimate political evil, homosexuality was the ultimate crime against the family. In that hostile climate, most homosexuals remained in the closet. This had an ironic effect; with no visible group of men admitting their homosexuality, any man could be suspected of being a latent or hidden homosexual. It was, as Barbara Ehrenreich observes, "a diffuse possibility that haunted every man, a label that could be hurled against the man who was 'irresponsible' as well as the one who was overtly 'effeminate.' "[81]

The Secret Self

In sum, the 1950s experienced a far swing of the pendulum toward a culture of social constraint, of stern yet contradictory sexual morality, of tightly drawn roles and rules, of clearly marked boundaries—political, sexual, and familial—that one crossed only at great peril. It was what the anthropologist Mary Douglas called a "strong grid" or tightly bound culture. Such cultures often breed festering discontents, secret selves, and hidden lives.[82]

In a recent study of those who, like herself, were young adults in the 1950s, the writer Benita Eisler observes that the most characteristic generational trait she found in her interviewees was the presence of a hidden, "outsider" self lurking behind a bland outward appearance: "a collective discrepancy between the way we are and our protective coloration; the willed blandness in style, speech and dress; our propensity for and subsequent problem with role playing; our need for 'covers'—from gray flannel suits to marriages in which we would disappear."[83] The unprecedented upward mobility in the 1950s may have been part of the reason many of that generation felt like "outsiders." Many people in the middle class had not started out there.

Virtually every commentator on the culture of the 1950s eventually calls it a "paradox."

> It was an age of stable nuclear families and marital tension, of student conformity on the campus and youth rebellion on the screen and phonograph, of erotic arousal before the visual and sexual hesitancy before the actual, . . . of upward mobility and later doubts about the meaning and value of the age's own achievements.[84]

Of all the contradictions of the era, those afflicting women were the most palpable. Motherhood was glorified, yet women were deni-

grated. Sex discrimination flourished, yet women were regarded as
the privileged sex in America. Attitudes that today would be regarded
as embarrassingly sexist were taken for granted as part of everyday
life. Women were entering the workplace in increasing numbers, yet
work for women was denounced as unnatural.

The "paradox of the happy housewife" described the curious tendency of married women to rate their satisfaction with their lives and
their marriages as extremely high, while admitting to a large array of
specific complaints and symptoms of stress, depression, and anxiety.[85]
Large numbers of women did find contentment in marriage and domestic life, especially if their husbands were economically successful,
but, tellingly, most "happy housewives" did not want their daughters
to follow in their footsteps. A Gallup poll of 2,300 women in 1962
found that 96 percent reported themselves "very happy" or "extremely happy," and believed that women's subordination to men was
natural. But 90 percent of these same women hoped that their daughters would get more education than they had had, and would lead
different lives.[86] It was a message their daughters would heed.

CONCLUSION

American culture is not yet done with the 1950s. If middle-class family life was not the dystopia portrayed in the myth of suburbia, neither was it the domestic utopia portrayed by the Cleavers, the
Andersons, and Ozzie and Harriet. While the dark myth and the ills
it portrayed—matriarchy, conformity, frenzied sociability—have been
forgotten, the glowing images of an idealized family life survive,
planted deep in the national unconscious. As *Newsweek* recently
pointed out in a special edition on the twenty-first-century family,
"The television programs of the '50's and '60's validated a family style
during a period in which today's leaders—congressmen, corporate
executives, university professors, magazine editors—were growing up
or beginning to establish their own families."[87] The impact of this
idealized family was further magnified by the very size of the postwar
generation.

Despite the profound yearnings of this generation to go home again
to what seems to be the traditional family, the family pattern that
dominated the 1950s was both a response to its unique time and an
anachronism. By the end of the decade, the pendulum of social
change began, invisibly at first, to swing the other way. In the late

978046501924374   EMBATTLED PARADISE

1950s, people began to marry later and to have fewer children. The divorce rate began to rise. Neither the economy nor individual families could afford to keep women confined to the home. A new generation was coming of age. The educated middle class, which had invented the Victorian family ideal, the New Woman, the companionate family, and the new domesticity of the baby-boom era, was about to resume its historic role as innovator in family style by unveiling the latest and most revolutionary version yet of the modern family.

C H A P T E R   3

The "Burned-over" Decade: Public Disorder and Private Transformation in the 1960s

We are the people our parents warned us against.   —Graffiti in the 1960s

The sixties woke everybody up to everything that was going on in their minds. It wasn't so cut and dried. Up until then: "This is the way it is, folks, grow up, get married, get a job." The sixties said to all kinds of people: not necessarily.   —Paul Mazursky
                                                    Film Comment (August 1988)

Early in 1968, a sophomore at Barnard College named Linda Leclair became embroiled in a struggle with the school administration. Barnard wanted to expel her for what they saw as the intolerable offense of living off campus with her boyfriend, a Columbia University junior. After several months of debate and negotiation, the dispute was eventually resolved by a student-faculty committee. They recommended that Leclair remain a student at Barnard, but that she be denied the use of the cafeteria, the snack bar, and the recreation room.[1]

Momentous events dominated the headlines that year. The Vietnam War raged on, as did the protests against it. January saw the beginning of the four-week Tet offensive, the turning point in the war; it destroyed American hopes for a quick victory. In March, President Johnson announced he would not run for reelection. In early April, Martin Luther King, Jr., was assassinated, setting off the most widespread of a series of bloody ghetto revolts; since 1965, the sight of sections of American cities going up in flames had become almost commonplace on the evening news.

Despite these dramatic happenings, the battle between Linda Le-clair and Barnard set off a media blitz. It was covered on television, in *Time* and *Newsweek*, and in eleven different articles in the *New York Times*. The seventy-five-year-old mother of the publisher of the *Times* told her son she thought the story was being given excessive atten-tion. "Why not put sex in perspective?" she asked. "It went on in my day, too."[2]

But Linda Leclair's struggle with Barnard was more than a titillat-ing tale of a college sexual scandal. It was a landmark event that marked an abrupt shift in cultural generations. There have been few periods in American history, observes the journalist Frances Fitz-gerald, "in which the dominant sector—the white middle class—transformed itself as thoroughly as it did in the sixties and seventies: transformed itself quite deliberately, and from the inside out, chang-ing its costumes, its sexual mores, its family arrangements, and its religious patterns."[3]

Though the cultural revolutions of the period seemed shockingly sudden, they grew out of a series of quiet shifts in behavior and attitudes that had been taking place across the postwar years. Linda Leclair and other members of her generation were ratifying changes that had been under way since before the 1950s. As in the 1920s, given the accumulation of change in work, family, education, and culture, a generational shift was almost predictable.

Indeed, in many ways, the 1960s marked the resumption of cultural themes put aside since the 1920s. As I discussed in the introduction, that earlier decade witnessed not only the original—some would say the major—sexual revolution of the twentieth century but also fervent debate and discussion about women's rights, household divi-sion of labor, child care, and other issues surrounding women's changing roles. A new, smaller family emerged in the middle class, and a new style of marriage focused on companionship, sexual sat-isfaction, and personal fulfillment.

The Great Depression, however, ended this cultural ferment and sowed the seeds of a traditionalism that would last more than three decades. What happened in part in the 1960s and 1970s was the return of the repressed. It was precisely because the family, gender and sexual patterns of the 1950s were so at odds with twentieth-century realities that the revolt against them was so fierce, and their unraveling so traumatic.

Linda Leclair was obviously not the first American woman to have sex with her boyfriend, or even to move in with him. But, although an increasing number of young couples were living together out of wedlock at the time, premarital chastity was still the middle-class norm. As late as 1966, over half the respondents in a Roper poll had stated that *both* bride and groom should be virgins, the same proportion as in 1937.[4] A young woman who went "all the way" risked falling into the category of a "bad girl." If a respectable young woman was not a virgin on her wedding night, decency demanded hypocrisy: she should at least pay homage to "virtue" by keeping her mouth shut about it in public. Yet here was a daughter of the middle class openly proclaiming her right to control her sexuality and living arrangements.

Sex, conventional morality, and "traditional" family arrangements comprised one front in the cultural and political wars of the "sixties"—which loosely refers to the period from 1965 to 1975—along with the civil rights movement, the antiwar movement, the student movement, and the counterculture. The common denominator of all these upheavals—whether the challenge was to the Pentagon; to university administrations; to bureaucracy; to male or adult authority inside the family; to middle-class norms of respectability, deference, and demeanor; to rules of dress—was a revolt against power, dominance, and social hierarchies of all kinds that had pervaded everyday life in the 1950s.[5] The upheavals were not confined to the United States, although America was the focal point of protest and radical movements. Only a minority of those who were young in the 1960s joined protest movements or pursued a countercultural life-style. Yet there was, as one observer put it, an "epidemiology of dissent";[7] ideas started by small groups of students in Berkeley, Cambridge, or Ann Arbor would spread, in diluted form, to other colleges, to high schools, and through the media to the general public.

The culture wars of the 1960s have not yet been resolved, a social fact that has impeded coming to terms with the changes in family life that began in that era. In the late 1980s, the twentieth anniversary of the events in the late 1960s gave rise to a new wave of nostalgia and debate. Nehru jackets, tie-dyed shirts, headbands, and love beads surfaced as new youth fads. Long-smoldering political and cultural feuds flared up again. Some looked back to the 1960s as a lost golden age of idealism, political commitment, and intense moral concern. Others saw those years as a time when America lost its way; writing in *Newsweek*, the columnist George Will denounced the era as an age of "intellectual rubbish," "sandbox radicalism," and "almost unrelieved excess."[8]

Few of us can look back at the period without seeing it through the lenses of hindsight and nostalgia; our view of the time is colored by our knowledge of AIDS, the crack epidemic, economic decline, and the crisis of the family. But to make sense of what happened to family and personal life in the 1960s, we need to understand the atmosphere of that time, what life felt like to those who lived through it. Above all, we need to put the period in historical context.

In the early 1960s, with most families apparently fitting the image of breadwinner/housewife and children, the traditional family structure seemed an unquestionable fact of life. Yet many changes had slowly been in progress and were reaching "tipping points," so that many formerly deviant family patterns—working mothers, divorce, premarital sex—were not only becoming common but beginning to affect a majority of the population. Further, the rising educational demands of a postindustrial society were keeping young people in school longer, prolonging adolescence, and yet increasing the sophistication of the young, creating an undefined new stage of life.

In contrast, the young people who came of age between the late 1940s and the early 1960s entered adulthood quickly, in a closely linked set of steps: marrying, having children soon after, and settling into careers, all in their early twenties. Fueled by a booming economy and memories of Depression and wartime deprivation, the family—especially the middle class family—formed a pattern unlike any other in the twentieth century. There was an increasingly poor fit between this pattern and a changing social reality.

Sooner or later, Americans would be confronted with the need to rethink the sexual norms, gender asymmetry, and marital patterns of the 1950s. That rethinking seemed revolutionary rather than evolutionary because it took place in a time of protest, confrontation, and loud proclamations of hostility to the norms of middle-class adults by their own offspring.

FROM CONSENSUS TO
CONFRONTATION

At the very start of the 1960s, the historian Arthur Schlesinger, Jr., made an uncannily accurate prediction about the coming decade. In the January 1960 issue of *Esquire* magazine, he argued that America was on the threshold of a new mood in its national life. The torpor of the 1950s was ending. Americans had buried themselves in the private concerns of family, home, and career during two decades of crisis—depression, world war, cold war, and limited war in Korea. Now there were signs that the country was growing psychologically restless and spiritually discontent.

In fact, there had been a considerable amount of ferment stirring during the "torporous" 1950s.[9] The civil rights struggle, rock and roll, and the Beat counterculture were in place well before the 1960s. Schlesinger pointed to other symptoms of impending cultural shifts: the popularity of satire and "sick humor" purveyed by comics like Mort Sahl and Lenny Bruce, and best-selling books articulating dissatisfaction with the quality of American life, such as *The Lonely Crowd* and *The Organization Man*. Material comfort and leisure had not led to the fulfillment Americans had hoped for; there was a vague yearning for a new sense of national purpose. As Schlesinger put it: "It is an odd and baffled moment in our history ... as if increasing numbers of Americans were waiting for a trumpet to sound."[10]

The trumpet sounded with the election of President Kennedy. The first president to have been born in the twentieth century, Kennedy seemed to embody youth and change. As the first Catholic to serve as chief of state, he overturned a barrier that many had thought impregnable. America seemed more tolerant, more open to new possibilities.

"The beginning of a new political epoch," Schlesinger wrote, "is like the breaking of a dam. Problems which have collected in years of indifference, values which have suffered neglect, energies which have been denied full employment—all suddenly tumble as in a hopeless, swirling flood onto an arid plain."[11] Once the movement for reform began, it unleashed a chain reaction that spread from one group to another, one cause to another. The civil rights movement spawned the student movement, which spawned the antiwar movement. Women activists in these movements, unhappy with their treatment at the hands of the males who ran the show, started the women's liberation movement.

It was also a time of cultural effervescence. The underground counterculture of the 1950s exploded into popular mass movements, a
flowering of experiments in living, and a wave of creativity in the
arts. From the Beatles to pop artists, a new sensibility blurred the
boundaries between popular and high art.

In an uncertain time like our own, a time that seems to lack a sense
of moral and social cohesion and to be dominated by a sense of
fragmentation, when social critics of the left and the right denounce
individualism and the loss of communal frameworks, it is difficult to
capture the sense of suffocation many people experienced in a society that seemed all too certain and cohesive. Yet without understanding that "feeling of entrapment in an all-encompassing system that
fed the body but starved the soul,"[12] we cannot make sense of the
cultural revolution that followed and the excesses it encouraged.

In the 1950s, as I discussed in the last chapter, a number of sociologists and social critics explored the ideas of threats to individuality
in a world dominated by large-scale organizations. One of the characteristic themes of the period was the portrayal of the misfit, the
sociopath, the "rebel without a cause" not as villain but as hero.[13]
The appeal of this imagery prepared the way for the unconventional
quality of radical protest in the 1960s, and the willingness of young
people of the time to experiment with drugs and alternative life-
styles.

The image of the Establishment as an insane asylum, and of the
protester as inmate, turned a 1950s theme into 1960s protest. The
war in Vietnam made the metaphor of a sick, destructive society hor-
ribly real. There was a widely shared sentiment that if "normal,
healthy American boys reared in normal, healthy American families
were prepared to go on bombing missions dropping napalm on North
Vietnamese villages,"[14] then something was deeply wrong with both
society and the family. It was this vision that provided the moral
justification for the willingness of many middle-class people in the
1960s, and not just the young, to liberate themselves from the con-
fines of traditional norms and conventions.

In the widely popular genre of "antipsychiatric" films that appeared in the 1960s and 1970s, madness is considered a higher form
of sanity.[15] Films like *King of Hearts* and *One Flew over the Cuckoo's Nest*
follow a formula: the hero, a mental patient, is portrayed as more
rational and moral than the "normal" society around him. The "system" is so blind to its spiritual bankruptcy that it takes an apparently
mad outsider to see reality. In the end, however, because the hero's
vision poses a profound threat to the system, he must be destroyed.

The power of this vision of society can be seen in the contrast between the great radical drama of the 1930s and its counterpart in the 1960s. When Clifford Odet's Depression-era *Waiting for Lefty* ended, the audience typically chanted, along with the "workers" on the stage, "Strike, strike, strike." The last scene in Peter Brooks's *Marat/Sade* set off a similarly impassioned audience reaction. This time, however, "the identification was not with striking workers but lunatics in an insane asylum, who sang 'We want a revolution ... NOW!' The song went on to become a kind of unofficial anthem of the Columbia strike in the spring of 1968."[16]

YOUTH AND CULTURAL CHANGE

In retrospect, the 1960s witnessed the breakdown not of American culture itself but of the peculiar tightly bound cold war consensus version of it that amounted to a secular religion. The change was so explosive in part because "the system" seemed impregnably powerful. It was also explosive because it was largely a youth revolt. Young people, particularly students, have traditionally been on the front lines of cultural and social change. Sensitive to the rumblings of economic and social structures, they have played significant roles in revolutionary movements. "If any generalization can be made," concluded one study of the student protest, it is that "student movements arise in periods of transition, when, for example, the values inculcated in children are sharply incompatible with the values they later need for effective participation in the larger society, or when values which are prevalent in universities are not supported by established political elites in the larger society."[17] In times of rapid or major social, economic, demographic, or technological change, young people moving into adulthood come face to face with the poor fit between old norms and new realities.

In the 1950s and 1960s, America and other Western countries seemed to be unlikely places for a radical student movement to erupt. Fundamental change seemed to have come to an end, ideological conflict having melted into consensus. In fact, however, these societies were in transition in a number of ways; the taken-for-granted assumptions of most of the older generation were sharply discrepant with the perceptions of most of the younger. In addition, revolutions typically break out not when times are bad but when things are getting better—when there is hope of change. The 1960s were "one of these rare decades, repeated at most once or twice a century, when capitalism seemed to promise continuous progress, and previously unheard-of social and economic possibilities were opening up."[18]

Extending Adolescence

One reason for the impact of the youth movements of the 1960s was the sheer number of young people at the time. Over the course of the decade, the baby boom generation—the largest population wave in American history—swept into the volatile eighteen-to-twenty-four-year-old age period. Between 1960 and 1970, the number of young people in that category expanded by 53 percent—an explosive increase that added up to more than eight and a half million individuals. At the same time, a greater proportion of that huge generation was in college than any generation before. Baby boomers were twice as likely as their parents and three times as likely as their grandparents to continue their education after high school.[19]

During the postwar years, as America had become an increasingly postindustrial society, educational demands for most jobs increased and jobs for those with only a high school education or less declined. This shift in the nature of work and in economic opportunity prolonged adolescence as a stage of the life course—or, rather, opened a psychosocial limbo between adolescence and adulthood.[20]

Adolescence is only partly a matter of biology; the transition of social identity from child to adult varies enormously across cultures and historical periods. Before the early twentieth century, for example, it was rarely considered a stage in human development. The concept of adolescence was a product of economic-related changes that created a need for an extended period of education.

Over the course of the nineteenth century, primary-school attendance became compulsory in America and Western Europe. In the twentieth century, mass education was extended, both in duration and availability to wider segments of the population. The new public high schools that opened around the turn of the century became warehouses for teenagers who had no place in the labor market, as well as training grounds for those with careers ahead of them.

In the post–World War II era, for similar reasons, a kind of second adolescence was added to the first. Going to college became an expected part of life for millions of young people. For many, college was a means to reach a defined occupational goal—in education, engineering, business, medicine. For others, college and graduate

school became a way of life, a time to search for an identity. Dropping out of school for a year or two became a common pattern; it
could postpone occupational adulthood until age thirty.

A "Divide of Experience"

In 1964, the first wave of baby boomers turned eighteen and entered
college. They overflowed the campuses into the surrounding neighborhoods and created entire communities of youth during the next
several years. This concentration of a vast generation in America's
colleges and nearby youth ghettos set the stage for the protest and
counterculture movements of the 1960s. Unencumbered by the burdens of earning a living, propelled by their studies toward sophistication and critical thinking, they stood in judgment of their society's
hypocrisy and moral shortcomings. Many of the young people who
had grown up during the affluent and relatively peaceful times that
followed the war came to emphasize "post-materialist"[21] goals such as
the quality of life, individual rights, and tolerance. For older people,
shaped by the insecurities of Depression and war, security—economic
and otherwise—tended to remain paramount.

Middle-class parents had struggled hard for the stability and material abundance they enjoyed. But for their sons and daughters affluence created what the sociologist Todd Gitlin calls a "divide of
experience which could never be erased."[22] The much-heralded and
exaggerated generation gap was not so much about rejecting parental
values as about differing sensibilities.

The comfortable way of life that seemed so miraculous and hard-
won to the parents was simply taken for granted by the offspring.
"Parents could never quite convey how they were haunted by the
Depression and relieved by the arrival of affluence; the young could
never quite convey how tired they were of being reminded how bad
things had once been, and therefore how graced and grateful they
should feel to live normally in a normal America."[23]

Indeed, for the best and brightest of the rising generation, America
was far from "normal." Raised by parents who prized independence
and curiosity in their offspring, rather than obedience, they looked
at their society with critical eyes. They did not see the land of milk
and honey their parents saw, or the stable, balanced social order
described by the leading policy analysts and social scientists of the
consensus era. Instead, they saw a society in which technology and

affluence had failed to solve the problems of hunger, poverty, and racial injustice. Moreover, they saw a society whose very advances had created a host of new problems: decaying cities, environmental pollution, the threat of nuclear destruction.

The bomb and the cold war marked another generational divide. Where parents tended to see rational scientists and policy makers ensuring peace through mutual deterrence, many young people saw Dr. Strangeloves—madmen who could at any moment blow up the earth. Far more than to their parents, the bomb seemed a present danger to 1950s children: "Twice a month the sirens and bells would ring and we would go to the farthest wall from the windows, [and] cover our heads so that when the bomb exploded over Los Angeles we would survive. . . . We were the first generation to live under the threat of the annihilation of the world."[24] This perception of the madness of war prepared the way for widespread disaffection among middle-class American youth with the war in Vietnam.

THE COUNTERCULTURE AND
THE SEXUAL REVOLUTION

The youth rebellion of the 1960s took many forms. The major division was between those dedicated to political change and social justice—upholding civil rights, ending the war, reforming the universities—and the cultural radicalism of the "hippie" counterculture, although there was considerable overlap among the different youth movements. Further, the style of political protest in the 1960s was different from the more ascetic Old Left, with its distrust of emotion and individuality. In its combination of political and cultural radicalism, in its taste for sex, drugs, and rock and roll, the New Left had much in common with the counterculture.

Today, to many Americans, the counterculture seems to stand for nothing more than mindless hedonism and mad, destructive excess. In the age of AIDS and a drug crisis, cultural radicalism has had a bad press. But the counterculture was part of a broader shift in sensibility to an alternative set of values that was as old as middle-class culture itself. The counterculture grew out of a bohemian, romantic strain of bourgeois culture that had originated in nineteenth-century Paris and lived on in such twentieth-century enclaves as New York's Greenwich Village and San Francisco's North Beach. For generations of middle-class youth, a bohemian-student identity was a way station en route to maturity.[25]

Bohemianism was always opposed to the traditional values of bourgeois culture, and cultivated its own set of virtues: the ideas of salvation through childlike innocence,[26] of the body as a temple and
sexuality as sacrament, of living in the moment, of transcending
mundane reality through meditation or drugs.[27] It was the sensibility
expressed by William Blake and Walt Whitman.

Although the neobohemian hippie counterculture was at the leading edge of the sexual revolution, as with the other transformations,
the dramatic shifts in sexual norms that took place in the 1960s were
in good part the culmination of changes already in process. In fact,
it was less of a break with past behavior than most people realize.
Sexually liberal attitudes had been increasing since the last decades
of the nineteenth century. The decade between 1965 and 1975 was
the second wave of a long-term trend that had crested in the 1920s.

There are a number of striking parallels between the first and second waves of the sexual revolution. Both periods were marked by
startling new styles of hair, clothing, music, dance, and the widespread use of illegal drugs—in the 1920s Prohibition era, alcohol; in
the 1960s, marijuana. In both periods, the coming of age of a new
generation marked a cultural divide; middle-class youth were at the
vanguard of cultural changes that eventually spread to other young
people and to the rest of society. Anxiety over its youth, long an
American habit, shifted from the problems of those outside the mainstream of society—juvenile delinquents, the exploited and neglected,
the children of the poor—to insider youth, the offspring of the middle class. "The issue was no longer assimilation to the mainstream,"
observes the historian Paula Fass of the youth crisis of the 1920s, "but
changes within that very mainstream which now affected every facet
of American life and the young in particular."[28]

In both periods, prosperity and the disillusioning effects of war
helped set the stage for a revolution in manners and morals. Both
periods ended when prosperity had declined, the old morality had
crumbled, and people grew tired of the excesses of the new. Despite
the sober mood after the onset of the Depression, the new sexual
patterns of the Jazz Age were absorbed and extended by middle-class
American culture.

The New Sexual Codes

While the ideology of family life, especially gender roles, grew more
traditional during the 1930s, dating, which had seemed a shocking

departure from traditional courtship, became an entrenched custom among young people.[29] When Robert and Helen Lynd returned to Middletown in 1935, they found that the liberalized manners and morals of college students a decade earlier were taken for granted among high school students. Newspaper advice columns were still telling girls not to kiss on the first date, but few young people paid attention. Sex, as *Fortune* magazine observed in 1937, was no longer news.[30]

But change was continuing, even though premarital intercourse, the standard by which sociologists measure sexual change, leveled off. Succeeding generations maintained the line that jazz-age youth had drawn between petting and intercourse. But there was a great deal of activity on the "safe" side of the line. One 1937 study found "more widespread acceptance, particularly by females, of the 'naturalness' of sex intimacies, with and without coitus; less extreme petting on first or early acquaintance, and more 'steady dating' with fewer in-hibitions as to sex intimacy following long courtship."[31]

Between the 1920s and the late 1960s, there evolved a secretive "petting culture"—an intense form of erotic play that could go on for hours, based on "an intricate hierarchy of codified pleasures, usually enforced by the girl, and doled out in portions that advanced with the status of the relationship."[32] A key part of the petting culture was the appearance of chastity on the part of the girl, however the reality might compromise it. "Of all the secrets of coming of age in the fifties," wrote Benita Eisler, "sex was the darkest and dirtiest. As sexual beings, people became underground men and women."[33]

"Technical virginity" was a compromise, a way of going as close to the line of actual intercourse as possible, without crossing it. To later generations of young people, that line would seem absurdly thin, but it had great symbolic value from the 1920s to the end of the 1960s.[34] One way of holding the line was early marriage. Sexual in-tercourse among young people was actually increasing, but the age of marriage came down to legitimate it.

The Old Double Standard

The sexual codes of the 1950s, like so many other aspects of that era, were complicated, contradictory, and frequently at odds with behav-ioral reality. The code defined sex—especially for females—as dirty and dangerous before marriage, beautiful and healthy afterward. Virginity was a major asset in the marriage market; a woman who had had sex before marriage was considered "damaged goods." Technical virginity before marriage, and faked orgasms afterward, were products of the ambiguous, ambivalent sexual culture of the era.

Unmarried women in the 1950s had to walk a tightrope between "frigidity" and "promiscuity." A girl who went "all the way" or just "too far" might lose her status as "nice girl." The film critic Molly Haskell recalls that in both the movies and real life of the 1950s, "the whore-virgin dichotomy took hold with a vengeance." Recalling her own adolescent experiences, she writes that the sexual taboos of the time, "encoded in the paralyzing edict that no man would marry a woman who was not a virgin (with the unexpressed corollary that untasted sex was a woman's prime attraction for a man) held fearful sway in the southern community where I grew up."[35]

By the late 1950s and early 1960s, researchers began to detect signs of a more egalitarian sexual standard emerging among older teenagers, especially college students. The change was not so much in behavior as in attitudes. The double standard was giving way to what the sociologist Ira Reiss called "permissiveness with affection"[36]— intercourse before marriage was acceptable for both women and men if they loved each other. By 1966, Reiss was predicting another upturn in sexual liberalization: "the stage is set for another upward cycle of increasing sexual behavior and acceptance."[37]

In the late 1960s rates of premarital intercourse seemed to rise dramatically again, although, as we have seen, this is more correctly viewed as the continuation of a trend that began at the turn of the century.[38] In 1938, the researcher Lewis Terman predicted that if current trends continued, after 1940 no girl would enter marriage a virgin. But the rates leveled off in the 1940s and 1950s.[39]

The change in the late 1960s was mostly made up of young women catching up to young men; male rates did not go up by much. This was not so much a revolution in behavior as in norms; young people were not abandoning the expectation of marriage, but they were no longer "scheduling marriage on their life agenda simply to gratify their sexual needs or in order to legalize their sexual relationships."[40] In effect, the petting culture of the 1950s had evolved past the barrier of technical virginity. Young women abandoned their desperate struggle to remain categorized as virgins. The media uproar over Linda Leclair and her battle to live with her boyfriend was the sound of this symbolic barrier breaking.

The Pill and the Normalization of Sex

Youthful rebels were not the only ones challenging traditional sexual norms. Americans in general were increasingly willing to separate sex from reproduction, to value sexuality itself as a vital part of marriage and to accept it as part of adult life, married or not. In 1962— long before Linda Leclair's battle, the rise of the counterculture, or the rebirth of a feminist movement—Helen Gurley Brown's *Sex and the Single Girl* became a best-seller. Brown argued that "nice" girls could have affairs—in fact, *were* having affairs—without ruining their reputations or their emotional health.

In her breezy "Cosmo" style, Brown preached a message of female sexual liberation and financial independence that was way ahead of its time. Yet Brown's book did reflect the growing "singles culture" that was springing up in American cities—the bars, resorts, and neighborhoods where singles of the surging baby-boom generation gathered. By and large, these were mainstream, college-educated, white, middle-class Americans, uninvolved in political movements or the counterculture. Yet without rejecting plans for eventual marriage, they were making casual sex a normal part of life for single men and women.[41]

One indicator of changing American attitudes was a growing acceptance of birth control. In the early decades of the century, it had been considered a dangerously radical and obscene idea, as well as a threat to the moral order. Federal law prohibited the importation and interstate shipment of contraceptive information or devices, and individual states had their own anti–birth control laws.[42]

As late as 1965, in Connecticut, it was still illegal for a druggist to sell contraceptives or for a doctor to prescribe them. In that same year, in the Griswold case, the United States Supreme Court declared the Connecticut statute unconstitutional on grounds that it violated the right to privacy. A few years later, the court extended the right to unmarried couples.

Over the years birth control had been transformed from a "private vice" to a "public virtue" and mainstay of the social order.[43] For the middle class, planning and spacing children had always been fundamental to a well-organized life. Now birth control also became an essential weapon against poverty in America and the dangers of overpopulation around the world.

When oral contraceptives came on the market in the early 1960s, they were widely publicized and hailed as a great advance in contraceptive technology. The pill—a watershed in the sexual revolution of the 1960s—was not only more effective than other methods but, for the first time, permitted the separation of birth control from the sex act itself. Some in the media speculated that the revolutionary change in contraceptive technology might also revolutionize sexual morals, but there was relatively little alarm about these implications.

By privately and routinely taking a pill, as they might take a vita-min, women were suddenly liberated to experience their sexuality unaccompanied by the fear of pregnancy. In the years before the hazards of oral contraceptives became known, the pill seemed an-other wonder drug, like penicillin and the other antibiotics. These drugs too, apart from their general uses, had influenced sexuality by making it possible to cure venereal disease.

For a brief time, sexuality was miraculously freed from the twin terrors of disease and pregnancy that had haunted it throughout the ages. It was also freed from shame. The wave of publicity that greeted the pill helped to confirm the behavioral changes that were already pervasive. "The existence and widespread marketing of a technology for presumably effortless contraception was evidence that millions of women . . . single as well as married, were 'doing it'—and, apparently with the blessings of the medical profession, getting away with it, too."[44]

Although the virginity norm had been crumbling since the early 1960s, the end did not come until the early 1970s. Sex lost not only its biological connection to reproduction but also its normative con-nection to marriage. Now it came to be defined as an expected com-ponent of dating and love relationships.[45] The average age at marriage rose to what it had been before the early-marrying 1950s. Further, there was increasing support for a still more lenient sexual standard, "permissiveness without affection."

The war in Vietnam, coming on the heels of the civil rights and protest movements, added ideological force to the sexual revolution already in progress in American culture. Wars often "loosen" mor-als—World Wars I and II had also had that effect. Vietnam, the most unpopular war in American history, delegitimated not just the gov-ernment but the American way of life itself, including its notions of sexual propriety.

ALTERNATIVE LIFE-STYLES

Despite the upheavals and changes that had already taken place when Linda Leclair's decision to live with her boyfriend became known to the public in 1968, it was shocking for several reasons. She was not only openly proclaiming her nonvirginity but, in moving in with her boyfriend, engaging in a behavior long associated with the lower classes. Also, "cohabitation," to use the sociological term, seemed to be one of the alternative life-styles that blossomed at the time and included communes, open marriage, group marriage, and swinging. To many observers, it seemed as if these shocking new living arrange-ments were the wave of the future.

Cohabitation

Cohabitation in particular seemed likely to replace marriage. For many older Americans, it meant only one thing: men were now get-ting "for free" what they used to have to "pay for" by getting married. Now why would they ever tie the knot? In the end, however, cohabi-tation turned out to be not a permanent substitute for marriage but, for the majority of those who tried it, a step along the way toward an eventual wedding. Further, the practice of living together has not diminished the symbolic meaning of marriage. (Nor does it reduce the likelihood of divorce.)

Living with a lover—or living alone—was for most young adults a substitute for the early marriages of the 1950s. Marrying in one's teens or early twenties became increasingly ill-suited to the length-ening educational plans of both sexes and the increasing need for two incomes in the family. By the early 1980s, cohabitation had be-come widely acceptable to young Americans, and had even won the approval of many of their parents. Reassured that their children would eventually "slide from dating into shacking up into marriage," middle-class parents came to accept the practice, and even to prefer it to early marriage.[46] (Cohabiting couples are almost as likely as those who have not lived together to have large weddings, complete with bridal gowns, champagne, rice, and bouquet tossing.)

At least one perceptive observer had seen the change coming. In 1964, when divorce and remarriage rates had already started to rise, the sociologist Bernard Farber suggested that these trends were changing the nature of *first* marriages. Getting married was no longer the once-in-a-lifetime fateful decision it had been. Marital mistakes could be rectified by divorce. Further, Farber observed, the rise in remarriage was undermining the market value of virginity.[47]

Finally, he pointed out that a blurring of the lines between court-ship and marriage had been going on for some time. Before the 1950s, marriage had been the end point of a series of distinct stages: dating, keeping company, going steady, engagement. Each step in-volved a greater degree of commitment and physical intimacy, al-though intercourse was supposed to be saved for marriage. By the 1950s this system had given way to a series of "involvements"—relationships that were both more intimate and more fragile than courtship. Marriage was coming to be simply a more intense involve-ment. Farber underestimated the special significance that formal marriage would retain, even in a society with a high divorce rate, but his vision of how the traditional model of courtship and marriage would evolve into later patterns of couple relationships seems re-markably prescient.

Mate Swapping and Open Marriage

With the old norms and patterns no longer powerful, and no new ones available, both young and older people improvised and exper-imented with alternative forms of family. Aside from cohabitation, these alternatives proved to have little staying power even though they appeared as serious threats to the conventional family in the 1960s.

One widely popularized but much less widely practiced alternative of the time was "swinging," or mate swapping. Estimates in the 1970s claimed that about 1 to 2 percent of married couples had tried it; they were described as otherwise conventional, conservative, middle-class people, mostly in their thirties, not part of the counterculture.[48]

Although the group sex practiced by swingers fitted the definition of an orgy, it had strict rules. Participants were limited to married couples, who were supposed to keep their extramarital relationships sexual, not personal. The aim was to enhance marriage by allowing a "safe" form of infidelity. Eventually, most swingers grew tired of the practice and gave it up. It was usually the man who wanted to quit, although typically it was he who had talked his wife into swing-ing in the first place.[49]

Another "safe" form of infidelity was open marriage, popularized

in the 1969 film *Bob and Carol and Ted and Alice*, and in a 1972 book
by the anthropologists Nena and George O'Neill entitled *Open Marriage*. The O'Neills did not explicitly advocate sexual relationships
outside marriage; they claimed they were merely arguing for complete frankness, flexible roles in marriage, and openness to outside
friendships. Nevertheless, "open marriage" was generally interpreted
to mean a marriage in which both spouses are free to have affairs
with other people. The idea was to have the best of both worlds—
marital intimacy and stability, as well as sexual variety. In practice,
open marriage turned out not to be a viable arrangement. Couples
tended to become unhappy and either give it up or break up the
marriage. There is conflicting evidence about whether men or women
tended to be most unhappy with open marriage.[50]

The Rise and Fall of the Communal Ideal

In 1971 Jay and Heather Ogilvey, an academic couple from Yale who
had lived in a commune in New Haven for two years, described the
answer a "bright, articulate Ivy League drop-out" might give to a
distraught mother who asked her son or daughter, "Why, in God's
name, are you joining this commune?": "Phillip Slater says we need
a new society stressing cooperation rather than competition, and Paul
Goodman shows the need for community as a decentralized alternative to our inefficient, centralized mass society, and just about all the
sociologists show that the nuclear family is a mess, mother."[51]
     At the time they appeared, communes seemed a serious alternative
to traditional marriage and family life. More than any other alternative family form, the commune was looked to by many people as the
hope and model of the future. Not all of those who joined communes
in the 1960s—dropouts or otherwise—were from the Ivy League.
Nor could all of them have traced the connections between communal living and the ideas of an older generation of rebellious intellectuals.
     Like the rest of the counterculture, the theory and practice of
communes radiated outward from Berkeley, Cambridge, and Ann Arbor; these were centers of cultural ferment and places harboring large
numbers of unattached young people for whom group living arrangements would not be unfamiliar. As the communal idea developed, it
attracted couples, families, and older adults. It is impossible to know
exactly how many communes there were, or how many individuals

lived on them, but the evidence suggests at least ten thousand separate communal experiments between 1965 and 1975. It seems unlikely, though, that more than a tiny fraction of the U.S. population lived in them. Still, despite the small number, communes attracted enormous attention from the media and social scientists.

Although they seemed to spring up out of nowhere, the flowering of communal living experiments during the late 1960s was nothing new; it was the revival of an old American tradition. During the social upheavals that had led to the emergence of the Victorian family, about a hundred utopian communities were founded, mostly before 1850. Among the best known were the Mormons, the Shakers, and the Oneida community. Like their 1960s counterparts, these societies were also composed of middle-class people disaffected with prevailing values, involved in the reform movements of their time (antislavery, temperance), believing in the "radical and immediate perfectibility of man."[52] As we saw in chapter 1, the Victorian nuclear family was itself viewed as a utopian community; utopian themes of retreat from urban chaos, conscious design, and perfectionism permeated writings on the family in that era.[53]

Communes varied a great deal in size, ideology, and living arrangements. Yet those who entered them generally shared a similar set of goals. They sought to combine the presumably warm and supportive group life of the extended family—on the basis of fellowship rather than kinship—with a greater degree of personal freedom than could be found in the conventional middle-class family. Further, there was a strong pastoral, "back-to-the-land" strain even in urban communes, whose members often talked about getting some land and moving to the country; people in rural communes almost never talked about moving to the city.[54]

Unfortunately, utopian visions of harmonious, loving, extended families were not realized in the communes easily or for long. In part, the difficulties could be blamed on the strains of building a new kind of family and community from scratch, at odds with the surrounding culture and its deeply ingrained norms about sexuality, work, marriage, and child rearing.

But communes also foundered on contradictions among their values: freedom versus commitment to the community; privacy versus openness; a "hang-loose" ethic of spontaneity versus the need to milk the goats, make the meals, wash the dishes.[55] These tensions emerged in the form of disputes over privacy, property ownership, and the distribution of labor.

One researcher, Ben Zablocki, noted that while most communes eventually were undone by these difficulties, many experienced a "brief golden age"—a honeymoon period—at their outset:

> Visiting a commune early in its history, one often feels that a new age has already dawned for mankind. Superhuman labors are accomplished with no apparent strain. Money is simply kept in a pot to which anyone can go and take what he needs. Mothers, fathers and childless people cooperate in taking care of children.... Portents of later conflicts are visible, but usually are not disturbing.[56]

As the golden age receded, however, Zablocki found that communal life could turn ugly. For example, anarchism could turn into a tyranny of the strong over the weak. One highly sympathetic study noted that often only males were considered full-fledged members, women ranking somewhere between objects and pets.[57] Generally, rural communes had a traditional sexual division of labor: men would tend the land, chopping wood and the like, and women would be assigned to the kitchen.

In their attempt to maximize sexual freedom and overcome jealousy, commune members faced complications similar to those experienced by swingers and devotees of open marriage. It was one thing to denounce jealousy and sexual possessiveness; it was quite another to avoid the strong emotions that sexual relationships can arouse. Further, in all these arrangements, a "sexual marketplace" developed—some people were sought after, while others suffered the pain of being ignored or rejected. Some communes tried to deal with the problem by making celibacy the rule; others demanded traditional monogamy; a few instituted rotation of sexual partners.

Strangely, communes seem to have been undone by love as well as sex. Studying 120 communes from 1965 to 1978, Zablocki found that the most unstable communes—the ones that lasted the shortest amount of time—were those with the greatest number of love bonds in them, sexual or otherwise. Zablocki suggests, among other reasons, that this was because individuals who felt left out in close-knit communes may have seceded more readily. But the sociologist Randall Collins points out that the most close-knit communes, where practically nobody was left out, were the most unstable of all. He suggests that the volatility of close emotional relationships—especially when a number of them are linked together—accounted for the instability.[58]

Communal life was pervaded by still another problem: emotional turmoil, or "freaking out." The use of drugs, the emphasis on expressing deep feelings, and the general lack of structure could unveil deeply repressed feelings and impulses. Getting intimate with so many other people could lead to frightening sensations of ego loss. In the face of emotional turmoil, communes could switch from anarchism to extreme authoritarianism. One long-lasting commune seemed to owe its survival to having abandoned its earlier principles of free love and egalitarianism; instead, its members insisted on monogamous marriage and embraced their leader as an unchallengeable authority.[59]

That communes could dissolve or become authoritarian or exploitative does not necessarily invalidate the communal ideal. But, as a solution to strains in conventional marriage and family life, communal arrangements turned out to be deeply problematic. Indeed, one of the basic flaws in the commune may have been its resemblance to the suburban nuclear family it was ostensibly rejecting. Both sought to retreat from the problems of urban life and to find fulfillment in a warm and secure togetherness.[60]

Eventually, most participants in the life-style experiments of the 1960s drifted back to more conventional family arrangements. A recent study of former commune members found that a majority of them had married. For many, the experience had offered a moratorium, a time out before going on to make fateful commitments to work and marriage. One woman, for example, described the commune experience as a turning point in her life—it was where she first got the idea of going to law school, and the encouragement to do it. On the other hand, significant numbers of former members were unmarried and still ideologically committed to alternatives to traditional family arrangements.[61]

Although a few communes survive to this day, the movement faded away toward the end of the 1970s. It had not found a recipe for perfected family life, but its very failures were instructive. At a time when the prevailing norms of family life no longer seemed to fit the new circumstances facing young adults, the commune movement expanded the meaning of "family."

THE END OF AN ERA

"Somebody had blundered and the most expensive orgy in history was over." So said F. Scott Fitzgerald in 1931, looking back at the Roaring Twenties in the aftermath of the 1929 stock market crash. "It ended two years ago," he went on, "because the utter confidence which was its essential prop received an enormous jolt.... Now once more the belt is tight and we summon the proper expression of horror as we look back at our wasted youth."[62]

There was no stock market crash to mark the turning of the cultural tides in the mid-1970s. By 1975, the Vietnam War was over. An energy crisis and *stagflation*—an odd combination of high unemployment and high inflation—ended the era when prosperity could be taken for granted. The 1960s as a political era had ended earlier, when segments of the New Left turned violent and a backlash by the "silent majority" of middle-class Americans helped bring Richard Nixon to power.

The political and cultural upheavals came at the crest of America's longest economic boom. They cannot be understood apart from that fact. Both sides in the struggles of the time, the Establishment and the protesters, shared in the postwar belief in a boundless future. The age of scarcity was past; prosperity would continue and make all things possible. For reformers, it meant that poverty and other social problems could be ended. Political analysts foresaw a time when the central issues of American public life would no longer be economic matters such as wages, farm prices, or social security. With no foreseeable need to "refuel the economic machine," observed Arthur Schlesinger, Jr., in 1960, the new issues would be "fighting for individual dignity, identity, and fulfillment."[63]

The cornucopia had kept aloft the "post-materialist" spirit of the counterculture and the youth movement and the experimental spirit of the middle class. "Tune in, turn on, drop out": give up the job, the practice, the rat race; go back to the land; hitchhike across the country. You can always drop back in later. There will always be a place in college, another job. It didn't matter to your future if you stepped off the escalator for a while.

The restrictive, tightly bound consensus culture of the two decades following World War II was at odds with the expanding possibilities of middle-class life. Education, leisure, and affluence had worked profound changes in the sensibilities of millions of Americans. They discovered that when economic security was no longer a central issue, new discontents arose, more psychological and spiritual. The old rules and roles stopped making sense; they seemed, in the language of the time, "uptight," "plastic," and "racist."[64] A host of cherished cultural assumptions lost their self-evident validity: my country, right or wrong; the experts know best; technology can solve it; white Anglo-Saxon males are the rightful heirs to power in America; women's place is in the home; stay married, even if you no longer have anything in common; what will the neighbors think?

In the end, when the public upheavals of the 1960s were over, it was private life that had changed the most. For most of the middle class, the last vestiges of Victorianism had shriveled and disappeared. The whole apparatus of middle-class respectability—its sexual norms, its rules of dress, its patterns of deference and demeanor—fell away. It was as if, in a game of tug of war, one team suddenly let go of the rope, leaving the opposite side in a free-fall.

By the middle of the 1970s, the new cultural mood clashed with the new economic realities. "In a matter of a few years," observed the pollster Daniel Yankelovich, "we have moved from an uptight culture set in a dynamic economy to a dynamic culture set in an uptight economy."[65] Toward the end of the decade, the rhetoric of liberation had lost its appeal. Even before herpes and AIDS brought terror back to the bedroom, the thrill of casual sex had faded, especially, but not only, for women. The sexual revolution had not solved "the most vexing problem of human sexual psychology: the paradoxical need for both companionship and variety."[66]

The let-it-all-hang-out mood gave way to a search for intimacy and stability, a longing for emotional attachment, for community, for a sense of order and meaning. Too much change too soon had brought culture shock. The struggle to hold on to a sense of personal identity and cultural meaning centered on the institution most shaken by change: home and family. "Family life, devalued for years, looked good again," observes Todd Gitlin, speaking for the veterans of the 1960s dissident movements. "We became professionals and managers, and made the acquaintance of credit cards and small domestic pleasures."[67]

A GREAT AWAKENING

Today's conventional wisdom blames "the sixties" for the ills that befell American society in the two decades that followed, from economic and military decline to the weakening of the American family. The current nostalgia for the 1950s, writes the literary critic Morris Dickstein, "speaks to our wish to have done with these problems; it tells us we can return unscathed to an idealized time before life grew complicated."[68] Yet, as we have seen, by the end of the 1950s, the country was poised on the edge of change.

The huge baby-boom generation, with its dramatically different vision of the world, was coming into adulthood. The race issue, a traditional American conflict, was heating up well before the 1960s: Southern blacks had been moving en masse to Northern cities, segregation had been damaging America's cold war search for allies by alienating Third World countries; the first stirrings of the civil rights movement were beginning to be felt. Women were chafing against the constraints of hyperdomesticity, and Americans in general, as Schlesinger had observed, were growing psychologically restless. The economic boom could not have gone on forever. Doubts about technology and the beginnings of concern for the environment were already being voiced.

The historian William G. McLoughlin argues that the period from the 1960s through the 1980s was a turbulent cultural watershed that resembles earlier upheavals called Great Awakenings. Traditionally, these episodes have been studied as periods of religious revival and transformation, and research has focused on doctrinal changes, religious leaders, and conversion experiences.[69] McLouglin, however, influenced by anthropological studies, argues that religion is just one aspect of a wider ideological transformation prompted by social structural change.

At the core of any new awakening is a "jarring disjunction" between the prevailing cultural norms and images and the daily experience of large numbers of people. Adopting the anthropologist Anthony Wallace's analysis of culture change in "primitive" societies,[70] McLoughlin argues that awakenings follow periods of significant economic, cultural, or political change. These shifts lead to a time of cultural confusion, as people find their daily behavior departing from expectation.

Cultural strain shows up first as trouble in the family. Generation gaps grow wider, as parents become uncertain in guiding their children under new circumstances. Schools and churches provide conflicting guidelines; the courts continue to punish behavior that has become common. Wallace calls this the "period of individual stress." People experience psychological and physical symptoms; family conflict increases as husbands and wives quarrel, and children rebel against parents.

In the next stage, private stresses become public issues. People attribute their discontents to malfunctioning institutions: the church, schools, the law, the government itself. Public protest takes to the streets, and religious rebels appear, speaking directly to God or Jesus, or founding new churches. Adding to this formulation by Wallace and McLoughlin, the historian Carroll Smith-Rosenberg points out that during these periods of cultural strain, repressed groups—women, minorities, and young people—see an opportunity to gain more power and redefine their roles.[71] In response to these challenges, established authority fights back. The populace is divided. A nativist revival emerges, attempting to reverse social change and to restore tradition. The period of cultural confusion and conflict lasts until some new, emotionally convincing ideology emerges.

In the Great Awakenings of earlier times, the cultural tensions were resolved when a prophet or moral leader appeared—a Martin Luther, a Jonathan Edwards, a John Wesley—who offered a widely acceptable revision of cultural tradition, aligning cultural norms and everyday life. A period of relative stability and order would set in as protest and resistance faded away. The new ideological and social arrangements persisted until forces of social change created another "jarring disjunction" between cultural norms and everyday experience.

The period to which this model of cultural transformation has been most extensively applied is the era before the Civil War. This era witnessed the second Great Awakening—a series of religious upheavals, which produced the evangelical form of Protestantism. And as we saw in chapter 1, it was during this time that the family economy began to give way under the pressures of a new world of commerce and industry. A number of scholars has examined the transformation of the family, and the emergence of the Victorian ideology of family life.[72] The era also produced a number of reform movements, including the first wave of feminism and the antislavery movement, as well as the creation of the Victorian utopian societies. In one region of the country, upper New York State, rapid social and economic change was followed by such an intense wave of religious frenzy, communal experiments, and social movements that the area became known as "the Burned-over District."

In many ways, the upheavals of the 1960s fit this model of cultural transformation. Starting in the 1950s, McLouglin argues, America entered another period of cultural disjunction. As he and others have pointed out, widespread disillusion set in with various aspects of industrial society: bureaucracy, the large corporation, science and technology, the idea of progress. The middle class discovered that affluence itself brought new discontents; those left out of the affluent society wanted their share of the pie. The American dream, at the moment of its greatest realization, seemed to be flawed.

In addition to the more dramatic sources of disillusion that came in the 1960s and 1970s—assassination, violence, Vietnam—was a more subtle disjunction between the old myths and the realities of everyday life, a disjunction that persists today. Postindustrial Americans still believe in the myths of rural and small-town virtue, of the self-made person and the self-sufficient family, yet, they live "crowded into dense metropolitan areas in a culture that has little good to say about Megalopolis, struggling to get ahead in a culture that disdains status seekers, working in enormous bureaucracies while taught contempt for Organization men."[73]

The stress and change of the previous two decades had calmed down by the 1980s, but the reverberations of those upheavals persisted. America remained—and still remains—a society in transition. Despite its seeming failures, the 1960s irrevocably altered the political landscape and transformed culture and private life. Nowhere was this more evident than in the social role of women and in the relations between men and women. In the next chapter, we turn to the rise of the new wave of feminism.

C H A P T E R 4

Half a Revolution: The Second Wave of Feminism and the Family

*For many of us, the initial feminist understanding came as a kind of explo-
sion: shattering, scattering, everything tumbling about, the old world splintering even as the new one was collecting.*   —Vivian Gornick
                                                                 Essays in Feminism

In September 1968 a group of radical women staged a demonstration
against the Miss America Pageant in Atlantic City. The event appeared on millions of television sets all over the country, and gathered much more space in newspapers than did the contest itself.[1] The
second wave of feminism had burst into American consciousness.

About two hundred women took part in the demonstration,
aided by the media and a crowd of hecklers. Outside the convention hall, they marched and sang, bearing signs with messages such
as: "Welcome to the Miss America Cattle Auction"; "I am a
woman—not a toy, a pet, or a mascot"; and "Can make-up cover
the wounds of our oppression?" The women crowned a live sheep
Miss America, "to parody the way the contestants . . . are appraised
and judged like animals at a county fair." Though the media described the protesters as "bra burners," nothing was actually
burned. But the demonstrators did dump bras, girdles, high-heeled

shoes, dishcloths, false eyelashes, and other "instruments of tor-
ture to women" into a "freedom trashcan."[2]

The climax occurred inside the Convention Hall after the new Miss
America was crowned; a white bedsheet floated down from a balcony
bearing the message "Women's Liberation" to viewers across America. Denouncing "the Libs" for desecrating one of America's most
beloved rituals, the writer Frank Deford observed: "To the women's
liberation movement, the skirmish at Convention Hall is roughly
analogous to the Boston Tea Party."[3]

He was more prophetic than he realized, or would have wished.
The Atlantic City demonstration did amount to a call for a new
American revolution. Of all the movements of the 1960s, the one with
the most lasting and profound influence on both public and private
life in America has been the second wave of feminism. Despite its
shocking arrival on the scene, and although it is far from complete,
the new feminist movement has brought about changes as dramatic
and far-reaching as any that have occurred in the twentieth century.

TAKING OFF: REBIRTH OF A
WOMEN'S MOVEMENT

The roots of the feminist revival reach back into the 1950s. Despite
that decade's glorification of domesticity and togetherness, there was
a growing gap between the public images of smiling, home-all-day
suburban housewives and the private realities of everyday family life.
Behind the rhetoric of domestic bliss seethed a vast, only partly hidden reservoir of frustration and discontent.

The Atlantic City demonstration and other events like it marked a
turning point. Although the women's movement had been stirring
for years before these eruptions, the public was largely unaware of
it. Miss America protesters came from the more radical wing of the
women's movement, younger women whose political style and rhetoric had been shaped in the protests and confrontation of the 1960s.
A second branch consisted for the most part of older, established
professionals with a more mainstream political style, who focused on
legal and policy changes as the route to equal rights for women.

Eventually the movement grew beyond these two distinct categories
into a vast collection of groups, large and small, devoted to different
purposes—political action, consciousness raising, child care, rape crisis centers—and split along a variety of dividing lines: radical versus

liberal, straight versus lesbian, those seeking gender equality versus those centered on women's differences from men.

Whatever their internal conflicts, feminists shared a common core of beliefs. Feminism in the 1960s and 1970s was, in essence, as much an emotional and intellectual understanding as a political movement. It was like a psychoanalytic insight, or the "aha" experience in prob-lem solving—the shift in perception that enables a person to see a problem differently. It was "a profoundly new way of interpreting human experience ... a vital piece of information at the center of a new point of reference from which one both reinterprets the past and predicts the future."[4] The journalist Jane O'Reilly described the "click" of what she called the "housewife's moment of truth"—the shock of recognizing that the everyday assumptions and patterns of behavior governing sex roles were unfair and arbitrary.[5]

To those who heard the click, women's oppression was seen as being as pervasive and crushing as that of other disadvantaged groups. Ranging from vast inequities in the workplace to the seemingly in-escapable constraints and expectations in private life, women's second-class status was suddenly recognized not as natural and inev-itable but as a social construct, based on power and the assumption that women are naturally inferior to men. As O'Reilly put it, "We have suddenly and shockingly perceived the basic disorder in what had been believed to be the natural order of things."[6]

The new wave of feminism challenged cultural understandings of home, family, femininity, masculinity, and sexuality in a more pro-found way than its earlier counterparts had. Few of the first wave of feminists in the nineteenth century had directly challenged the fam-ily. They were willing to accept celibacy and spinsterhood as the price of carving themselves a place in the world outside the home.[7]

In the second wave, however, even moderate feminists were calling for a transformation of marriage and family life. The NOW manifesto of 1966 declared:

> We do not accept that a woman has to choose between marriage and motherhood on the one hand, and serious participation in industry and/or the professions on the other. . . . We believe that a true part-nership between the sexes demands a different concept of marriage, an equitable sharing of the responsibilities of home and children and of the economic burdens of their support.[8]

More radical voices in the movement argued for more extreme solutions and attracted a great deal of media attention. Shulamith

Firestone called for artificial reproduction to free women from the oppression of their biology; Ti-Grace Atkinson called for communal child rearing, arguing that women could not be free "unless you get the childrearing off their backs." Others argued that marriage was a central part of the "total oppression" of women: "We are exploited as sex objects, breeders, domestic servants and cheap labor," declared the 1969 manifesto of the Redstockings, a radical feminist group in New York City. "We are considered inferior human beings whose only purpose is to enhance men's lives."[9]

News of the women's liberation movement spread with incredible speed. Within five years of the Atlantic City protest and its spectacular breakthrough into public awareness, feminism had become a grass-roots mass movement. But the ideas of the movement spread far beyond activists and those who identified themselves as "feminists." In the 1970s and 1980s, the general public would come increasingly to support the aims of the women's movement. And despite the successes of the antifeminist New Right, feminist positions have continued to represent the views of the majority of Americans.[10]

But widespread acceptance was a gradual process.* Initially, news of the movement was greeted with humor or puzzlement. Even years of student protest, civil rights marches, and antiwar demonstrations had not prepared Americans for this. The media often treated the movement as a joke, focusing on the sensational side, like the alleged Miss America "bra burning." The Feminist was often portrayed as a frustrated, unfulfilled man hater. Many people, women included, were confused, and reiterated Freud's question: "What do women want?" Many men felt themselves under attack; indeed, some feminists had declared men "the enemy," though most simply challenged the age-old custom of male privilege and power. At the very least, observed the sociologist William Goode, men experienced "a loss in centrality, a decline in the extent to which they are the center of attention."[12] At worst, they saw the feminist challenge as a threat to their very identity.

Meanwhile, women who had settled comfortably into traditional domesticity, who had staked their lives on the traditional marriage

---

*Jo Freeman points out that like other successful innovations, the spread of movement ideas followed a bell-shaped curve. At first, a few people, the Innovators, advance the new idea; a larger group of Early Adopters comes next, followed by Early and Late Majorities, and finally, Laggards—a small group of late acceptors. The critical point is where the curve shoots upward—the "take-off" point.[11]

bargain by which a woman traded her service as a wife and mother for a lifetime of support, felt that the movement had nothing to say to them. Worse, it seemed to be telling them that they had wasted their lives or, worse still, that men no longer had to keep their end of the marriage bargain.

Early converts to feminism often found themselves out of step even with close friends. In 1969 the journalist Vivian Gornick was astonished at her friends' response when she mentioned she favored the women's liberation movement. One man asked, "Jesus, what is all this crap about?" while his wife, a scientist who had given up her work to stay home and raise their children, said, "I can understand if these women want to work and are demanding equal pay. But why on earth do they want to have children, too?"[13]

Yet soon large numbers of Americans were rethinking sex roles both inside and outside the family. In 1969, when the editor of *Harper's Bazaar* traveled the country interviewing married American women, hardly anyone had heard of radical feminism; a year later, she found hardly anyone "whose thinking about herself in relation to men had not been shaken up or altered by the widening feminist clamor for women's rights."[14]

The takeoff point for the women's movement was in the early 1970s (the sociologist Jo Freeman pinpoints the date to 1970). Surveys taken at the time confirm it as a dramatic turning point in sex role beliefs as well as in the acceptance of the women's movement itself.[15] Traditional concepts of sex roles in family and marriage—for example, the notion that married women, especially mothers, should confine their activities to the home—gave way to more "modern," egalitarian attitudes. In a 1973 survey of its readers by *Redbook* magazine, two-thirds favored the movement, and less than 2 percent believed that women could fulfill their potential through marriage and motherhood alone.[16] A Gallup poll tracking women's answers to a question about sex discrimination reveals the movement's influence: in 1962 two out of three women denied having been treated unequally; in 1970 half said they had been discriminated against; in 1974 two-thirds reported unequal treatment and were in favor of efforts to improve women's status[17]

Underlying attitudes on particular issues was a sea change in perceptions of women, a new view of women as individuals able to make choices about their lives—working, marrying, child rearing—along with a new tolerance for whatever choices they might make. These changes showed up first among the college-educated and college stu-

dents themselves, but eventually crossed class, educational, and regional lines.

The shift, of course, was not unanimous. The 1970s also witnessed
the rise of antifeminism. Spurred by the Supreme Court's legalization
of abortion in *Roe v. Wade*, as well as by the early success of the Equal
Rights Amendment (and the prospect of its passing if three more
state legislatures voted for it), the backlash against the women's movement grew into a powerful political force. It was both an ironic sign
of the movement's success[18] and a measure of the deep anxieties and
cultural conflicts aroused by the ideas, as well as the reality, of family
and gender role change.

THE ROOTS OF CHANGE

Given the speed with which attitudes shifted following the sudden
emergence of the women's movement, it is not surprising that feminism has been held responsible for many of the changes, good and
ill, affecting women and family life in the 1970s and 1980s. As the
historian Ruth Rosen observes:

> Feminism has been blamed for the destruction of the family, women
> working outside the home, the high divorce rate, the neglect of chil-
> dren, the feminization of poverty, the lack of child care, women's
> failure to find marriage partners, women's infertility, men's sexual
> impotency, the superwoman syndrome, the nation's moral flabbi-
> ness, rising unemployment, and the debasement of the nation's
> moral standards.[19]

Yet the evidence shows that, in fact, the behavior changed first and
the feminist ideology came later.[20] Increasing levels of education for
women, rising employment rates of wives and mothers, the lengthening and changing shape of the life course, the liberalization of
sexual norms, the greater control over reproduction made possible
by the pill, rising divorce rates—all these shifts in work and family
life *preceded* the spread of the women's movement, and to a certain
extent, helped cause it. If feminist ideas were "social dynamite,"[21] it
was because millions of women could connect them to changes and
discontents they were already experiencing at home, in the workplace, and in American society in general.

In the following pages, I will discuss three phenomena we must understand in order to make sense of the rise of the second wave of feminism: the nature of the economic and demographic changes that altered women's lives and roles in the twentieth century; the ways in which widely held cultural images and assumptions can mask changing structural realities; and the speed with which ideological change can take place, given a vast disjunction between cultural norms and the experiences of daily life.[22]

Beyond the "Marriage Plot"

Traditionally, women's lives have followed what literary critics have called the "marriage plot," one of two basic story lines found in novels and other literary works. (The other is the "quest," or adventure story, whose hero is almost always male.) The marriage plot is a convenient way to describe the traditional domestic goals and norms that have governed women's lives.[23]

Though it has many variations, the marriage plot always centers on a heroine who searches for love, marries, and lives "happily ever after," secure at home where she nurtures her children and her husband. For centuries, this has been the paradigm for women's lives, married or not, and the standard by which they have been judged, whether they accepted it or not.

Until the end of the nineteenth century, the marriage plot was a fair approximation of the realities of most women's lives. A shorter life span, larger numbers of children, and the demands of running a home without the benefits of modern household technology or modern medicine meant that most women's lives were dominated by the tasks of motherhood. In 1900 only 6 percent of married women worked—mostly poor, black, and immigrant women, whose departure from the prevailing norms excited little controversy.[24]

Half of all women, however, never experienced the full family life cycle of reaching adulthood, marrying, and living long enough to see their children married.[25] The lengthening of the life span is arguably the single most important change in American society, having a profound impact on individuals and all aspects of family life.[26] (See chapter 6 for a fuller discussion of the longevity revolution.) Along with their new presence in the workplace, women's longer life span changed their place in the social order as well as the patterns of their lives.

In the postwar decades the average woman could expect to live half her life without having small children to care for. Even if she had returned to the Victorian standard of having three or four children, the 1950s mother would have borne them closer together than in earlier times, all the sooner to get out from under diapers, bottles, and sleepless nights. Extended life expectancy and the use of birth control had made many years of "empty-nest" living a normal part of the late life course. Further, the gap between male and female life expectancy made a decade or more of widowhood another normal phase of a woman's life.

Thus the traditional, child-focused image of the nuclear family—a mother and father surrounded by their young children—came to be a snapshot from a relatively short phase of a woman's life. In the late 1950s magazines like *Life* wondered what women would do with their time once their children had grown: "a housewife . . . lacking outside interests and training, is faced with vacant years . . . bored stiff with numbing rounds of club meetings and card playing."[27] They did not realize that transformations already taking place would make such speculations obsolete.

Economic as well as demographic change had been rewriting the marriage plot all during the 1950s. Despite the prevailing image of woman's place as only in the home, women were entering the labor force in increasing numbers. Rosie may have had to give up riveting after the war, but by 1947 women's employment had returned to its wartime peak and continued to grow.[28] By 1960, 40 percent of women were in the work force. Their ranks included large numbers of married, white middle-class women; almost half were mothers of school-age children; and a surprising one out of five had children under the age of six.[29] A U-shaped pattern appeared in women's employment across the family life course: work until marriage or the birth of the first child; quit work until the last child enters school; return to work.

Significantly, the class implications of women's employment turned around in the postwar years. Before the war, a working wife was a family's badge of lower-class status, a sign that a husband was not earning enough to support the family. The "family wage" had long been a goal of the working class; the postwar prosperity enabled many working-class men to attain the middle-class ideal of owning a home and being married to a full-time homemaker. Ironically, just as working-class and lower-middle-class families were finally attaining the old breadwinner/housewife ideal of domesticity, the educated upper middle class was revising it.

By the early 1960s the majority of women college graduates were in the work force, in contrast to slightly over a third of high school graduates. The ranks of professional women swelled by more than 40 percent during the 1950s, faster than any other occupational category except clerical work.[30] The increase in women's employment was being led, as the historian William Chafe observes, "by the same middle class wives and mothers who allegedly had found new contentment in domesticity."[31]

Why did married women swarm into the paid labor force? The answer is a complex mixture of supply and demand, structural change, and individual motivation. More and more scholars see women's departure from economic production during the Industrial Revolution—as much as their recent return to it—as a phenomenon that needs to be explained. The breadwinner/housewife system, as Kingsley Davis has found (see introduction), was a short-lived arrangement associated with the early stages of the Industrial Revolution. Beginning in the small but growing middle class, it slowly reached a peak in which few married women were employed. Davis places the heyday of the breadwinner family in the United States in the years between 1860 and 1920, after which it declined as more and more wives entered white-collar work in offices, stores, schools, and hospitals. Looking at other countries at various stages of industrial development, he finds that the rise and decline of the breadwinner family traces a similar curve.[32]

For individual married women, the motivations for returning to work are complex. Most women did not enter the labor force for either of the two diametrically opposed reasons usually assumed in discussions of women's work: dire economic necessity or "selfish" purposes, such as gaining autonomy or earning "pin money." The very terms of the debate assume that women's work outside the home is illegitimate. The "pin money" myth has traditionally been used to deride women's employment and justify keeping their earnings lower than men's.[33] Ironically, during the Depression when women's work often provided the only source of family income, this myth was propagated especially widely.

In the postwar years, married women's wages made it possible for millions of families to afford the basics of a middle-class standard of living: mortgage payments, college tuition for the children, family vacations, braces, savings for a "rainy day." As long as a woman did not entertain dreams of a career, but fit her work to the needs and demands of the family, she met with little disapproval. She could still be safely called a "housewife," living out the script of the marriage plot.

Women's need to find work was matched by a vastly expanding

demand in the postwar era for white-collar workers—secretaries, clerks, nurses, teachers, retail salespeople. This dramatic shift from manual, or blue-collar labor, to a predominantly service and white-collar work force had taken place by the mid-1950s. Unlike factory and domestic work, office work was respectable for middle-class women. And, despite the fact that the jobs most women held, then as now, were low-paying, dead-end jobs in the female sector of the economy, the expansion of the world of paid work to include most women at some point in their lives helped prepare the way for the ideological changes of the 1960s and 1970s. Although some women hated working, many others enjoyed a surge of independence and self-worth and the companionship of fellow workers. In a study carried out in two cities in the late 1950s, 90 percent of the women interviewed said they liked their jobs.[34]

More recent research also reveals the complexity of women's feelings about work. For example, in the sociologist Lillian Rubin's study of mid-life women, one subject spoke of her anger at her low pay as a mail clerk, yet also of the benefits her job brought her: "It may not be much money, but it feels wonderful to know that somebody's willing to pay me for working. . . . No matter what anybody says, there's more status involved when you're working and earning your own money." Many women in Rubin's study enjoyed the freedom from total financial dependence on their husbands: "I don't have to ask if I want to buy a new dress or something nice for one of the grandkids."[35]

Women's work had significant effects on family life as well. Sociological studies of the family in the 1950s found that women's employment subtly modified the traditional patterns of household work and decision making. Working wives had greater influence in making major economic decisions for the family, and their husbands did more household chores. Commenting on these findings in 1955, one family researcher found evidence for the "twentieth century democratizing of the home."[36] But it was a pragmatic kind of democratization, an adaption to household realities that did not openly challenge traditional gender roles.

Women's discontents within the workplace—like those of the mail clerk in Rubin's study—also helped pave the way for a feminist revival, especially the demand for "equal pay for equal work" and equality of opportunity. Aside from the obvious grievances of low pay and monotonous work, women in the workplace were exposed to what would later be defined as sex discrimination—problems such as sexual harrassment and being passed over for promotion in favor of a less experienced man. Professional women were also hampered by severe constraints. "Women scholars are not taken seriously," concluded a 1959 study of academic jobs, "and cannot look forward to a normal professional career."[37] Despite all these frustrations, the inexorable march of women into the workplace continued.

The Feminine (and Masculine) Mystique

Assumptions about male and female roles in the 1950s were so entrenched that questioning them seemed foolish. Despite the discrepancy between cultural images and a changing economic and social reality, there was little challenge to the prevailing definitions of women's place. Feminism, when recalled at all, was part of a long-gone historical era—a dimly remembered movement of cranky old maids. Indeed, an explicitly antifeminist gender ideology had an almost airtight grip on American culture, low and high—from the movies, to the women's magazines, to the college campuses, to sociological theory, to psychoanalysis. As we have seen, there was an aura of pathology and subversion about any kind of dissent in the 1950s, especially dissent from the "natural" order of gender arrangements.

A great cultural anxiety about masculinity also haunted that decade. Social critics feared that women were powerful and growing more so, and that men were weak and becoming ever more effeminate and emasculated. This "masculinity crisis" is one of the more striking paradoxes of the time. "Why," asked Arthur Schlesinger in 1958, "is the American man so unsure today about his masculine identity?"[38]

To the postwar critics of suburban matriarchies and the homogenization of the sexes, the rise of the new white-collar middle class implied a feminization of the workplace. Indeed, fewer men were running their own businesses, farming, or doing heavy manual labor. Fewer men achieved success though the old-fashioned school of hard knocks. More pushed paper—working in large organizations as salesmen, middle managers, engineers, technicians, academics.

Some sociologists at the time described these shifts as an "upgrading" of the work force; many noted that the new workplace demanded personality as well as job skills—being a "nice guy," the ability to get along well with others, became a factor in a middle-class man's occupational success.[39] Throughout the 1950s, social critics mourned the passing of the rugged "real men" of the nineteenth century: the frontiersman, the bold entrepreneur, the strong Victorian patriarch. Many of their critiques—contained in such concepts as Whyte's conforming organization man and Riesman's other-directed personality, as well as conformity and consumerism—now appear to be veiled complaints about gender issues.[40]

Sometimes the complaints were not so veiled. Phillip Wylie, who had launched an openly misogynistic attack in the 1940s on the over-bearing, domineering figure of "Mom," argued in the 1950s that women actually owned and controlled America's corporations.[41] In 1961 Paul Goodman wrote approvingly of the Beats and other alienated angry young men who argue that "a man is a fool to work to pay installments on a useless refrigerator for his wife. The structure of the society that has become dominant in our country is disastrous to the growth of excellence and manliness."[42]

Unease about gender roles was a response to both the real changes going on in postwar American life and the ideology of togetherness and companionate marriage. In the nineteenth century, a similar crisis of masculinity had followed the feminization of American culture that accompanied the rise of the cult of domesticity.[43] Even the advocates of togetherness seemed uneasy with conflict between house-hold equality and masculinity.

Although married men in the 1950s did not live up to the new ideal of household democracy, polls showed, as I noted earlier, that they were more involved in sharing household chores and child care than were earlier generations. Further, the suburban fathers of the 1950s were domestic in different ways than earlier generations of men: not only were they spending more time at home but they also found ways to carve out niches of masculinity around the house, in such activities as do-it-yourself carpentry and outdoor barbecuing.*

Even these modest steps toward the companionate ideal were enough to make one social critic declare men to be "the new servant class." In 1953, Russell Lynes complained that men had failed to "preserve at all costs" the distinction between the sexes; a woman now took it for granted that when she married, she would get "a husband who is also a part-time wife. . . . Man, once known as 'the head of the

---

*The historian Robert Griswold suggests that the domesticity of middle-class men in the 1950s may have reflected a wish to differentiate themselves from working-class men, who had recently crossed the traditional middle-class boundary of homeownership.[44]

family,' is now a partner in the family firm, part-time man, part-time mother, and part-time maid."[45]

Despite the undercurrents of discontent and the complaints of social critics, most middle-class men in the 1950s accepted the corporate/suburban way of life. In a host of studies carried out at the time, in-depth interviews as well as surveys, the overwhelming majority of men found contentment in their marriages; women tended to express much more discontent. In the Kansas Longitudinal Study, for example, while almost half the women confessed to having considered divorce, only a third of the men did so. Men complained a good deal about their work, and looked to home and family for personal fulfillment.[46]

Further, despite the cult of *Playboy* magazine and other glorifications of the single male in American culture, single males have been found to be an "exceptionally stressed" part of the population. Surveying two decades of such findings in her 1972 book *The Future of Marriage*, Jessie Bernard argued that marriage is good for men but bad for women; subsequent research does not support this extreme statement, but the general idea remains valid: men derive more satisfaction from marriage than women do.[47] For women in the 1950s, there was no place for their discontent to go.

Awakenings

Although a distinct feminist consciousness was slow to develop, the renewed possibilities of social change in the Kennedy era helped lay the groundwork for it. In 1961 Kennedy appointed a Presidential Commission on the Status of Women. This commission, and the host of state commissions that sprang up after it, set the stage and supplied many actors for the women's movement. While the final report of the commission, issued in 1963, emphasized the importance of women's traditional roles in the home, it also documented pervasive patterns of sex discrimination in education, government, and the workplace.[48]

In a surprising twist, the experience of working on these reports turned out to be more significant than the reports themselves. Many of the hundreds of men and women who gathered data for the commissions were shocked and radicalized by what they found. One senator from Mississippi described her discovery that women were second-class citizens: "I succeeded in getting Mississippi women the right to sit on juries; the opposition's arguments were appalling."[49]

Such findings, however, had less public impact than a book published in 1963, the same year as the final report of the National Commission—Betty Friedan's *The Feminine Mystique*. It did not focus on the kinds of discrimination the commissions were documenting; rather, Friedan uncovered the private discontent that "lay buried, unspoken, for many years in the minds of American women."

Like the student movement and the social critics of the 1950s, Friedan denounced the boredom of suburban life and the sterility of the consumer culture. A suburban housewife herself, Friedan gave voice to the discontent of large numbers of middle-class women. The "feminine mystique" was the traditional message, updated in Freudian terms, that happiness was to be found in the fulfillment of woman's biological nature as wives and mothers. Interviews with two hundred members of her own class at Smith College fifteen years after graduation, and with numerous other women, revealed to her the contours of the disjunction between women's lives and the mystique. Friedan called it the "problem with no name":

I feel as if I don't exist.

I love the kids and Bob and my home. There's no problem you can even put a name to. But I'm desperate. I begin to feel I have no personality. I'm a server of food and a putter-on of pants and a bedmaker, somebody who can be called on when you want something. But who am I?

I seem to sleep so much. I don't know why I should be so tired. . . . I just don't feel alive.[50]

Millions of women responded to the book, no longer feeling that they alone suffered from the problem with no name. Written out of Friedan's personal experience, the book spoke most directly to white, middle-class, college-educated women, and especially those who, like herself, had given up career plans for domesticity. Such women were more likely to experience "relative deprivation"—to feel more of a sense of deprivation than others who might be worse off in "objective" terms. Regarding themselves after sixteen years of education as the intellectual equals of their male classmates, they were more likely to feel frustrated later on in life, comparing themselves to their husbands, brothers, and male classmates. But the appeal of the book was not limited to women who fit Friedan's demographic profile. An instant best-seller, *The Feminine Mystique* would go on to sell three million copies. It would reach millions more through excerpts published, ironically, in the same women's magazines that had peddled the feminine mystique: the *Ladies' Home Journal*, *McCall's*, *Good Housekeeping*.

But Friedan had not been the first to call attention to widespread female discontent in postwar America. In 1957 the political analyst Max Lerner devoted a large section of his book *America as a Civilization: Life and Thought in the United States* to the "ordeal" of modern women, pointing out that the "unhappy wife has become a characteristic American culture type."[51] Between 1960 and the publication of Friedan's book, the plight of the trapped housewife became a media obsession. Magazines, newspaper columns, television panels, books, and conferences pondered her predicament.

Most discussions concluded that the source of the problem lay with women themselves. Some observers argued that the American woman failed to appreciate how lucky she was. As a 1960 issue of *Newsweek* put it:

> She is dissatisfied with the lot that women of other lands can only dream of. Her discontent is deep, pervasive, and impervious to the superficial remedies which are offered at every hand.... From the beginning of time, the female cycle has defined and confined women's role. As Freud is credited with saying: 'Anatomy is destiny.' Though no group of women has ever pushed these restrictions as far as the American wife, it seems that she still cannot accept them with good grace.[52]

Newsweek, along with other observers, concluded that education was the culprit; too many years in school had made women unfit for wifehood and motherhood. Such arguments echoed the century-old fears of some Victorian physicians that the mental exertions of college would lead to exhaustion and disease among women.[53] Some educators proposed that women no longer be admitted to universities; others prescribed more high school and college courses on home management and family life.

Friedan took this ongoing debate and turned it around: the fault was not in women but in a social system that assigned to them roles no longer fitted to modern life, denying women the right to develop as complete human beings. The real culprits were the women's magazines, advertisers, educators, Freudian analysts, and sociologists who had sold women a false bill of goods: the feminine mystique. By convincing women that they had no legitimate role in the outside world, these professionals had turned the home into a "comfortable concentration camp."[54]

Perhaps the most powerful source of the feminist awakening was the civil rights movement. In the nineteenth century, the first wave of feminism had been set in motion by women's participation in the antislavery movement. The modern fight for civil rights revitalized the concept of human equality as a moral ideal. The parallel between race and sex is not precise, but if it was immoral to deprive people of social and economic opportunity because of skin color, was it not also wrong to treat half the population as inferior because of their sex?

Apart from supplying a message and a model, the civil rights movement, and the other movements of the 1960s, gave women direct experience with sex discrimination. On the one hand, women were in the front lines of these movements during bloody struggles, joining picket lines, registering black voters, going to jail for their efforts. Courageous black women, such as Fannie Lou Hamer of Mississippi, were an inspiration to white women volunteers. Yet despite their significant leadership roles, movement women still felt encumbered by a "common-law caste system" that forced them "to work around or outside hierarchical structures of power which may exclude them" and that put them in a "position of assumed subordination" in personal relationships as well.[55]

In the student movement and other New Left organizations, the situation of women was often worse. Typically, women were excluded from leadership positions and handed the standard female tasks of typing, serving coffee, cleaning up, and making themselves available for sex. Not every woman experienced such treatment,* but many did, and worse. In one notorious example, a woman who addressed a meeting of movement "heavies" was hissed down with cries of "take her out and fuck her."[57]

In the late 1960s, radical women left to form their own women's liberation movement. These refugees from other movements formed the flamboyant left flank of the women's movement, adapting to new ends the methods they had used in earlier struggles. While they were ridi-

---

*Mary King disputes the argument that movement women were uniformly treated as secretaries, housekeepers, and sex objects by their male comrades. That was not her own experience in the Student Nonviolent Coordinating Committee (SNCC).[56]

culed by the media, they made more moderate groups like the National
Organization for Women seem respectable rather than far-out.

"THE NEXT GREAT MOMENT IN HISTORY IS THEIRS"

By the middle of the 1970s, the second wave of feminism had reached
its crest. For millions of women who had heard the "click" of feminist
insight, it was a time of high hopes; it seemed as if the dream of
equality in the workplace and equal partnership in the home might
be coming true. Dramatic changes in the law symbolized a transformation of women's place in the social order. In 1972 the Senate
passed the Equal Rights Amendment by a vote of 84 to 8. By the end
of 1973, the ERA had been passed by twenty-two state legislatures
and seemed on its way to early ratification. In January of the same
year, the Supreme Court, by a 7 to 2 vote, had made abortion legal,
on the grounds that the right to privacy, "whether it be found in the
Fourteenth Amendment's concept of personal liberty ... or in the
Ninth Amendment's reservation of rights to the people, is broad
enough to encompass a woman's decision whether or not to termi-
nate her pregnancy."[58]

In retrospect, the hopes of the heady days of the early to middle
1970s look naive and misguided. After its initial success, the ERA
began to lose in state legislatures across the country. Feminists became painfully aware that their movement did not speak for all
women; instead, it had begotten its own antithesis—a powerful grass-
roots movement of women opposed to the ERA and the right to
abortion, and dedicated to preserving the family and traditional female roles.

By the end of the decade, antifeminism, allied with other "pro-
family" conservative movements, helped to sweep Ronald Reagan into
the White House. The election of 1980 was widely seen as marking a
realignment in American politics, the onset of a new conservative era
that would roll back the social changes of the 1960s and 1970s. This
expectation was not fulfilled, but the election did reflect a change in
the national mood. By the end of the 1970s, the rhetoric of equality
and liberation had lost much of its appeal even to feminists. The
movement experienced its own internal backlash, as some feminists
began to have "second thoughts about the second wave."[59]

Yet, if we look back at the golden age of feminism in the mid-70s, the great expectations of gender equality do not seem so naive. Apart from the legal victories, evidence of a sex role revolution was every-where—on the newsstands, on television screens, in the movies, in the bookstores, on the street, in the small rituals of everyday life: Should men open doors for women, light their cigarettes, pick up the check for dinner or lunch?

Ms. became the first mass-circulation feminist magazine in history. Appearing in January 1972, it was intended to be a one-time-only publication. It sold out practically all 250,000 copies in eight days, and gathered 35,000 paid subscriptions, enabling the magazine to publish as a monthly. Over the course of the 1970s the mainstream media became increasingly receptive to feminist views: in 1975, *Time* magazine's Man of the Year was twelve women; in 1979 thirty-six American women's magazines ran pro-ERA articles; in 1976 Dr. Spock revised his best-selling *Baby and Child Care* to eliminate sexist biases.

The ideal of women's equality advanced across the national land-scape, seeming to dismantle, brick by brick, the still imposing struc-ture of disadvantage. Women ran for the first time in the Boston Marathon. Girls joined the Little League. Rape crisis centers and bat-tered women's shelters opened all over the country. Women entered politics, as well as medical, law, and business schools in record num-bers. As women's roles shifted, new kinds of male roles appeared in the media, including the sensitive, non-macho "new man."

Public opinion polls confirmed that the ideas of the movement had passed from heresy to acceptance in a remarkably short time. Men pushing baby carriages and wearing infants in Snugglis on their chests became common sights on city streets. Newspapers showed President Ford making his own toast for breakfast. In 1975 Ford created a national commission on the observance of International Women's Year. In 1977 the first National Women's Conference was held in Houston. It was attended by 15,000 women as well as three First La-dies—Betty Ford and Roslyn Carter, who were avowed feminists, and Lady Bird Johnson.

For women who had been touched by the movement or its insights, there was a sense of momentum, of riding the wave of the future. The title of a 1969 essay by Vivian Gornick—"The Next Great Mo-ment in History Is Theirs"—had turned out to be prophetic.[60] In 1975 Robin Morgan, who had organized the Miss America demonstration, looked back at how her own life had been changed by the women's movement: "Ten years ago, I was a woman who believed in the reality of the vaginal orgasm (and had become adept at faking spiffy ones).

I felt legitimized by a successful crown roast and was the fastest hand in the east at emptying ash trays." Then came the "radical chic" of the late 1960s: "I learned to pretend contempt for monogamy as both my husband and I careened . . . through the fake 'sexual revolution.' " Then came the women's movement:

> years of . . . joy, misery and daily surprise; my first consciousness raising group . . . the marches, meetings, demonstrations. . . . And all the while, the profound "interior" changes: the tears . . . and laugh-ter and despair and growth wrought in the struggle with my hus-band. . . . There are millions of us now. . . . we've only just begun, and there's no stopping us.[61]

THE MOMENT PASSES

But the momentum of the movement did stop. The event that sym-bolized the movement's failure for both its supporters and oppo-nents, was the failure of the Equal Rights Amendment. What went wrong? Theories about the alleged "failure of feminism" abound, especially among feminists themselves. The movement was charged with neglecting the needs of working-class, poor, ethnic, and minority women; with not speaking to women who were happy to stay home and take care of their kids. It was charged with pouring too much money and effort into the ERA struggle and other equal rights issues, emphasizing equality at the expense of women's special needs—child care, child support, maternity leave. If only the movement had not been so strident about the family, so beset by feuding factions, so far-out, so lesbian. . . .

Whatever the validity of these specific charges, it seems misguided to assume that the difficulties the movement encountered were due to the wrong language or the wrong tactics. Nor is it clear that by using a different rhetoric, the women's movement could have fore-stalled the growth of an antifeminist backlash. The historical record shows that social change itself, as well as movements that push for social change, gives rise to backlash movements aimed at reversing its effects. Change that affects the family, and women's roles in the family, is profoundly disturbing, touching on deeply rooted cultural anxieties.

It is therefore not surprising that the women's movement would provoke hostility and sharp cultural anxiety. Gender, along with race and class, is one of the fundamental organizing principles of American society. Even the seemingly modest proposal NOW put forth for a true partnership between the sexes—the "equitable sharing of the responsibilities of home and children and the economic burdens of their support"[62]—constitutes a fundamental challenge to the social order. Any change in women's place affects men, children, the economy, conceptions of human nature—and, above all, the family.

The antifeminist backlash was a response not just to feminism itself but to the same changes that had led to feminism in the first place. A similar sequence had occurred in earlier women's movements: socioeconomic and cultural change alters women's lives, especially the lives of middle-class women; a women's movement arises, led largely by middle-class women most affected by the changes; women who see their interests threatened by a shift in women's roles and by feminist arguments join with conservative clergymen and business interests to oppose the changes and the demands of the women's movement. In the late nineteenth century, women were becoming increasingly literate, attaining higher education (many women's colleges were established at this time), entering professions such as schoolteaching and social work, as well as the commercial and industrial segments of the economy. The "New Woman" appeared on the scene—the highly educated professional woman who challenged traditional gender roles and fought for suffrage and other rights for women, as well as a host of other social reforms. Still, in the nineteenth century, the socioeconomic trends favoring a women's movement were much less strong than they would be later. The New Woman was a tiny, if vocal, minority among American women.

Like their nineteenth-century counterparts, the supporters of the modern antifeminist backlash were responding to realistic threats to their own self-interests and identity. Then as now, women were divided into two antagonistic groups: "traditional" women, who remain "encapsulated" in the home and find fulfillment there, with a vested economic interest in their roles as wives and mothers; and women with "expanded" roles, which bring them into the public world outside the home.[63]

A 1984 study of pro-choice and right-to-life activists shows the contrast clearly. The pro-choice group tended to be highly educated working women with small families; the pro-life group tended to invest their self-esteem mainly in their large families, rarely working outside the home or, if they did, in low-paying jobs.[64] But some pro-life women were middle- to upper-middle-class housewives, often well

educated. Usually religiously and politically conservative, antifeminist women, whatever their economic situation, feel threatened by
feminism's challenge to the economic bargain embodied in the
breadwinner/homemaker marriage.

Traditional women have been threatened not just by feminist
rhetoric but by the social fact of the massive entrance of women,
especially middle- and upper-middle-class women, into the labor
force. In the 1970s, it became "déclassé" to be "just a housewife."[65]
The homemaker/breadwinner bargain was also being undone by the
other dramatic changes in the family that took place in the 1960s and
1970s, especially rising divorce rates.

Of all the shifts in family life, skyrocketing divorce rates caused the
most widespread alarm. Antifeminists blamed the women's movement for the general breakdown of the family. In fact, divorce rates
had been rising steadily since the middle of the nineteenth century.
The decade or so that followed World War II, however, departed
from this long-term trend: 1950s divorce rates were relatively low,
and the generation of couples who married in the postwar years was
the only one in the last hundred years that would undergo fewer
divorces than the historical trend would predict. By the early 1960s,
however, divorce rates began to resume their upward course. This
increase in divorce came well before public attitudes toward divorce
became liberalized.[66] It also came well before the rise of "women's
liberation." In fact, the growing instability of marriage may have
helped set the stage for the reemergence of feminism.

Because of the divorce revolution and other changes in the family,
feminism came to confront a dramatically different social landscape
than the one that had inspired it in the first place. The problem with
no name was transformed into a set of problems with various names:
single motherhood, the displaced homemaker syndrome, the double
day of work, the loneliness of the single life.

While women suffered from new conflicts arising from family
change, they faced persisting disadvantages that legal changes favoring women's rights had not been able to address. The feminist movement shared the tragic fate of other "successful" movements for
dramatic social change; after the moment of elation and utopian
hopes passes, reality catches up. The same sequence occurred when
women won the right to vote in 1920. To many women at the time,
the victory signaled that the long battle for equality had been won.
Now that women had the vote, they would have the power to sweep
away the remaining barriers to full equality.[67]

Then as now, the formal equalities granted by the law did not change the difficult realities most women faced in everyday life. Feminists after the mid-1970s also had to contend with the fact that the barriers to equality in the workplace and the home were much more formidable than they first appeared. The number of women in the workplace continued to rise during the 1970s, but so did the discrepancy between men's and women's incomes.[68] Most women remained confined to low-wage, gender-segregated occupations. Despite some headway in the 1980s, women's overall economic well-being has not improved since the 1960s.[69]

Women did not fare much better in the home. Despite all the talk of equal partnership, men ultimately proved reluctant to take up their share of the household work. No matter how sympathetic to feminist ideals their husbands might be, most working women continued to do the bulk of family chores. Even in the glory days of the early 1970s, few feminists believed it would be easy to alter the sexual division of labor within the family. "I cannot imagine anything more difficult than incurring the kind of domestic trauma I describe," admitted Jane O'Reilly in "The Housewife's Moment of Truth." A "liberated woman," she observed, is in danger of losing not only the role she has been taught all her life but her man as well: "The more we try, and argue, and change, the more we will realize that the male ego will be the last thing in the world to change. . . . Men do not want equality in the home. A strong woman is a threat, an inconvenience, and she can be replaced."[70]

Finally, the shift in the women's movement from elation to despair coincided with a shift from one historical era to another. Feminism was born in a time of economic expansion and restrictive family and sex role norms; it was the last act in the postwar drama of affluence and optimism. Both reformers and radicals had assumed that change could come easily, as, in fact, it appeared to with the ERA and *Roe v. Wade*. It did not seem farfetched to think the dream of equality might come true.

But the golden years of the feminist movement overlapped with the beginning of economic decline. "The year 1973," declared one economist, "should probably be taken as a watershed, sharply dividing the second half of the 20th century."[71] Not just in America but also in England and other Western countries, the long postwar boom came to an end. Just as the crash of 1929 and the Depression had sobered the Roaring Twenties, so did the various crises of the 1970s help put an end to the freewheeling era of "liberating" social change.

CONCLUSION

The feminist movement has been through a complex and paradoxical time since the 1970s. The Reagan revolution came to power on a wave of antifeminist backlash, yet was unable to reverse the social and cultural transformations that had already taken place: women's new roles in the workplace; freer sexuality; demographic shifts in marriage, divorce, and childbearing. Further, the antifeminist move-ment itself empowered conservative women in ways that undid the gender stereotypes of the prefeminist era that claimed women were irrational, unserious, not quite fully adult. The fact that it was Reagan who appointed the first woman to the Supreme Court testifies to the ways feminism had reshaped conceptions of gender in America.

By the end of the Reagan era, issues such as equal pay, child care, abortion, rape, and domestic violence were no longer "feminist" is-sues; they had become "women's" issues. Yet feminism emerged in surprisingly good shape after the Reagan years. Opinion polls carried out in the late 1980s showed that a majority of women identified themselves as feminists and believed a feminist movement was still necessary to improve women's situation in society.[72] In the wake of a Supreme Court decision threatening abortion rights in the summer of 1989, a powerful pro-choice movement had been mobilized.

To those who remembered the prefeminist era, it was clear that there had been a sea change in the unconscious sexism that once pervaded everyday life. For example, put-downs masked as flattery—"You think like a man"; "Don't bother your pretty little head about it"—and the assumption that victims of rape or wife battering had "asked for it" were no longer tolerated. As the writer Ellen Willis observes, there is a "profound difference between a society in which sexism is the natural order, whether one likes it or not, and one in which sexism is a problem, the subject of debate, *something that can be changed*."[73]

But if the old order had crumbled, the nonsexist future seemed a long way off. It had been only half a revolution: women had changed, the family had changed—but other institutions, and men, had not fully accepted or adapted to the changes. Further, the shape of the ideal future seemed unclear. Debates among feminist women were as fierce as those they had with their opponents. Should feminists pur-sue gender equality or celebrate female difference? Is heterosexuality a pleasure or a source of oppression? The dilemmas raised by the new reproductive technologies—dramatized in the legal battle over the custody of "Baby M"—opened up new fault lines among feminist women.

Whatever the difficulties and frustrations of an unfinished revolution, feminism has irreversibly transformed the social and cultural landscape. Yet the image of a genderless, androgynous world that some early feminists had hoped for, and their opponents had feared, never came to pass. On the other hand, in the Persian Gulf War, Americans did see a scene few could have imagined only a decade or two ago: women saying goodbye to husbands and children and going off to battle.

Paradoxically, as feminism freed women to say no to 1950s assumptions about women's place, it also freed them to embrace what had been devalued, to choose what had been obligatory—to say yes to motherhood, to domesticity, even to femininity. One card-carrying feminist, staying home with a newly adopted baby after "years of 'achievement' in the working world," recently observed: "There is a seductive grace to focusing all your efforts on making a few people happy, creating order and beauty on a small scale, bending to natural rhythms rather than time clocks or deadlines."[74] For some, the reaction against the glorification of motherhood during the years of the feminine mystique had come almost full circle. In 1987, an article in a feminist journal noted an "obsession with maternity and children that seems to pervade aging feminist circles, a romanticization of motherhood that occasionally rivals that of the fifties."[75]

For younger women, the so-called postfeminist generation, the gains of the movement—expanded employment opportunties, the decline of the sexual double standard,* a more symmetrical version of family—have been taken for granted. Today's young women are fervent believers in a new version of the American dream; they want both family happiness and success at work.[77] The difficulty they will have in fulfilling the dream on their own is eventually likely to set the stage for a restructuring of American institutions to meet to new realities of women's—and men's—lives.

*Lillian Rubin offers evidence, however, that the double standard still persists.[76]

C H A P T E R 5

The 1970s and the Culture of Nostalgia

Many millions of people, themselves caught up in the toils of the urban and suburban economy, attribute their alienation to the destruction of an imagined past. As they wander from Kmart to Pizza Hut, they look back to the good old days on Walton's Mountain, where God was in heaven and Mom was in the kitchen, when families were happy, when all towns were small and all folks were good. Carter briefly captured their interest by evoking their love for this nonexistent past, but Reagan stole their hearts by pledging to restore it. —Walter Russell Mead

Mortal Splendor: The American Empire in Transition

American institutions have had too many uncritical lovers, and too many unloving critics. —Michael Kammen

People of Paradox

In May 1971 a television camera crew entered the Santa Barbara, California, home of Pat and Bill Loud and their five children and began seven months of filming everyday life in their household. Two years later, three hundred hours of footage on the Louds had been edited down to a twelve-episode documentary entitled "An American Family," which appeared on public television stations all over the country. The Louds had their "fifteen minutes" of fame, becoming for a time the most-talked-about family in America.

Looking for "an attractive family with teen-age children," the producer Craig Gilbert had found the Louds through the editor of the women's page of their local newspaper. Bill Loud, a businessman, belonged to the "lucky generation" who grew up during the Great Depression, fought in World War II, and returned home to make good in the postwar boom years. Pat Loud, like most of her generation of college-educated women, was a full-time homemaker. The family lived in a spacious ranch house complete with sliding glass doors, patios, and swimming pool.

Although the handsome Louds looked like the cast of a family sitcom, their story, as *Time* pointed out, was "no Ozzie and Harriet confection." Shana Alexander, writing in *Newsweek*, called the series a "genuine American tragedy." Margaret Mead, writing in *TV Guide*, saw the series as a "new art form" in which the Louds had agreed "to lay their as yet unlived lives on the line, to share joys and sorrows they had not yet experienced."[1]

The Louds shared with millions in the television audience the dramatic breakup of their twenty-year marriage and the deep involvement of their eldest son in the East Village drug scene, as well as his flamboyantly gay style.* Viewers also witnessed the unwillingness of the Louds' youngest son to work hard at anything, including his rock band; the sexual awakening of their fifteen-year-old daughter; and the general aimlessness that afflicted all five children.

The Louds joined a wave of fictional families that appeared on television in the early 1970s, in such programs as "The Waltons," "Little House on the Prairie," and the most popular of the decade, "All in the Family." In contrast to the typical TV series, however, the Loud story was in many ways a real-life, updated version of an older genre stretching from Chekhov and Ibsen to Sam Shepard. Above all, it resembled the classic American plays of the 1940s and 1950s by O'Neill, Miller, and Albee, especially *Death of a Salesman* and *Long Day's Journey into Night*—plays showing "a home dissolve in full view of the audience."[2]

The appearance of the Loud saga as the centerpiece of the PBS fall season was one sign of a growing national preoccupation with the family on the part of popular culture, policy makers, researchers, and

*In 1973 homosexuality was still listed as a mental disorder by the American Psychiatric Association, and sodomy was a crime in most states.

social critics. "The family" also became an increasingly charged political symbol serving an array of contending causes. In this chapter
I will explore the forms this preoccupation took in the 1970s, the
shifting terms of the debate about the family, as well as the shifts in
family life itself that provoked concern and anxiety.

By the middle of the 1970s, American family life had been shaken
by a series of social changes as broad and traumatic as any that had
occurred in the past. If there were a Richter scale for cultural and
social earthquakes, this would have been the third Big One in American history, bigger than the one that shook the 1920s, and comparable in scope to the dislocations of the 1820s and 1830s. Standing
about in the ruins of structures that had, little more than a decade
before, seemed stable and changeless—lifelong marriage, sexual morality, parental authority, the "traditional" family—Americans groped
for an explanation of what had shattered them all. A "cultural struggle," much like those that took place in the earlier upheavals, developed as journalists, academics, and religious leaders argued about
the meaning of change and what should be done about it.[3]

"In Jacksonian America," observes Carroll Smith-Rosenberg, "many
celebrated the individualism and freedom from structure they
found. . . . Others feared that altered relations within the family paralleled the decline of a hierarchical world order."[4] Unsettled by the
disruption of taken-for-granted norms and family arrangements,
many early-nineteenth-century Americans responded to change with
nostalgia and moral panic. Yearning for an idyllic eighteenth-century
past, they made sexuality a metaphor for social disorder.

In the late 1970s and 1980s Americans confronted dramatic
upheavals in family life in similar ways. In a time of relative social
calm during the Ford and early Carter years, some attempts were
made to make pragmatic adjustments to the new patterns of family
life. But as economic and foreign policy troubles mounted, there was
a widespread fear that institutions, the government, the family, even
individual personalities, were breaking down. *Narcissism* became the
"galvanizing word" that expressed this sense of chaos and fragmentation;[5] a favorite quotation of the times was from Yeats: "Things fall
apart; the center cannot hold." Faced with rapid shifts in almost every
aspect of life, Americans lost their customary belief in a better to-
morrow; they embraced "tradition" and turned to an idealized past
for solace. The narcissistic fall from grace became the dominant
framework for interpreting social change.

There is, however, another story to be told about the social, moral, and psychological changes of the 1970s. It is a more complicated story, one that looks at continuity as well as change, gains as well as losses, and sees claims about "narcissism" as part of the story, rather than the tale itself.

FAMILY CRISIS, AMERICAN STYLE

The late twentieth century has brought to all industrial countries similar transformations in family and personal life. Only in the United States, however, have these changes been so deeply traumatic and ideologically charged. One reason is that other countries did not experience the contradictions of "the fifties" in quite the way America did. Europe did not experience as large a baby boom, nor did young Europeans in the postwar era marry at such young ages or in such high numbers as their American counterparts. Europe did not undergo a full-blown culture of domesticity. Hence the revolt against the 1950s version of the family was not as explosive, and the conservative backlash against that revolt not as powerful, as in America.

Further, practically every other industrial country has, over the postwar years, developed a system of family supports that has served to cushion the effects of changes in family structure. Conservative countries like France and the former West Germany as well as "welfare states" like Sweden have made social provisions for child care, parental leave, health benefits, and the like, which Europeans consider essential adaptations to conditions of modern life. In America, the traditional celebration of family self-sufficiency and rugged individualism, along with a traditional antipathy to government interference, has impeded some needed adjustments to change.

In the 1990s policies in support of the family are high on the national agenda. But so were they a decade and a half ago. In the middle to late 1970s, the nation seemed to be emerging from the turmoil of countercultural challenge and rapid demographic change. The passing of the 1950s pattern of family life had left in its wake a great deal of stress, anxiety, and dislocation, but efforts were being made to explore ways of overcoming at least some of the difficulties associated with change. Infused with hope and energy, an array of study groups, foundation projects, and government task forces began to examine the state of family life and to propose pragmatic adjustments to the new realities.

By the end of the 1970s, however, public discourse about the family came to be dominated by nostalgia and laments about narcissism and moral decay. A profound sense of cultural despair had set in as the country's economic and foreign problems worsened. Notions about the decline of the American family became entangled with notions about the decline of the American character, which in turn became entangled with notions of the decline of the economy and of the American empire.

Nostalgic social critics on the left and the right lamented family change, and a conservative president came to power vowing to roll it back and restore the "traditional" family. A decade-long detour ensued. While Americans daydreamed about Norman Rockwell families, the conditions facing their own families worsened.

In sum, the 1970s ushered in a period of critical change in American life, redefining cultural assumptions and transforming the terms of political debate. We need to understand both halves of the 1970s and how we made the shift from one to the other. That era's embrace of nostalgia and moralizing lamentation still shapes our public and private responses to family change.

REDISCOVERING THE FAMILY

By the early 1970s, traditional assumptions about family life had been undermined by both ideological challenge and behavioral change. The undoing of 1950s manners and morals begun by rebellious youth was spreading to mainstream America; the women's movement was reshaping public opinion and unsettling relations between men and women inside and outside the family. Meanwhile, the newly emerging gay liberation movement was challenging the norm of heterosexuality.

During this same period, Americans suddenly found themselves in the midst of dramatic demographic change. The unusual baby-boom era family patterns turned around with amazing speed: marriage rates dropped sharply, fertility rates fell and, by the mid-1970s, the annual number of divorces exceeded one million for the first time. Meanwhile, the labor force participation of married women reached a "tipping point"—half of married women were in the workplace, and the number continued to rise.[6]

These sudden changes, coinciding with well-publicized criticisms of the family by some feminists and radical psychiatrists, provoked widespread confusion and alarm. Was the family on its way out? If it

survived, could it still carry out its age-old functions? Some commentators feared that the middle class was growing more like the lower
class: high divorce rates, along with increases in the incidence of
cohabitation, single-parent families, and working mothers, convinced
many Americans that "loving, mutually supportive, traditional, long-
lasting family relationships are no more certain outside the welfare
population than within it."[7]

Much of the anxiety and uncertainty about the family focused on
children. Within the family, many parents of young offspring struggled with new complications of child rearing brought about by divorce, single parenthood, and two-job parenting in a society
unprepared for these changes. Parents of teenagers, like the Louds,
were confronted with "sex, drugs, and rock and roll"—a new youth
culture radically different from their own. To the public at large, the
changes seemed to support arguments that Americans were abandoning family ties in general and ties to children in particular.

Adding to the sense that family life was coming apart was a new
climax of openness, and not just about sex. The dark side of family
life suddenly came to light. Formerly taboo topics—from homosexuality to abortion to incest—could now be openly discussed. Family
violence was "discovered": child abuse and wife battering became
important topics for research as well as significant public issues.

In contrast to older beliefs, the new research did not view family
violence as either rare or the product of deranged personalities. If,
as Clauswitz stated, war was diplomacy carried on by other means,
domestic violence was now seen as family relations carried to an
extreme. Researchers pointed to crime statistics showing that Americans were more likely to be beaten up, sexually assaulted, or killed
by other family members than by strangers. One research team observed that "It would be hard to find a group or institution in which
violence is more of an everyday occurrence that it is in the family."[8]

The claim was not that family violence was increasing. Nor was
there evidence that it had. To the general public and much of the
media, however, the discovery of family violence was taken to mean
that abusive behavior in the home was not only widespread but reaching epidemic proportions. The sudden awareness of the problem,
along with the airing of the rest of the dirty linen of family life, added
to the sense of alarm about the state of the American family.

Yet not all of the attention to family life in the early to middle
1970s was fueled by fears of family disintegration. Sounding alarms
about a crisis in the family was often a strategy aimed at promoting

new and old social programs. Pleas for helping families often mingled arguments for new policies with therapeutic and moral complaints about the declining family. Yet many of the problems affecting families were far from new. Poverty, unemployment, poor housing, child neglect, illegitimacy, runaway youth, and juvenile delinquency, for example, had been on the public policy agenda for decades. "What is new," observed the policy analyst Gilbert Steiner, "is the discovery that all these depressing problems can be gathered under the heading 'decline of the family.' "[9]

The family was simultaneously rediscovered in the late 1970s by political activists, policy makers, and researchers in a number of fields. Educational sociologists found that family factors seemed to outweigh school or other influences in predicting children's academic success. Activists of the right and the left saw families as victims of intrusive experts and insensitive bureaucracies. Historians also "discovered" the family in the 1970s, producing a deluge of new studies that undermined beliefs about the family in history, especially the notion that there had been a golden age of family harmony and stability. New insights into family life also emerged from studies of live family interaction. Like the Louds, numerous families, both troubled and content, were recorded on film or observed through one-way mirrors by clinicians and researchers.

Observing families "live" revealed a strange yet familiar world: strange because it did not resemble the family as portrayed in textbooks, or on TV sitcoms; familiar because these families were unmistakably real. One study, comparing normal families, those of schizophrenics, and groups of unrelated people, discovered that the two kinds of families were not as different as expected. In both types of families, the ratio of pleasant to unpleasant interaction was much lower than in unrelated groups.[10] In short, normal families, as well as being loving and caring, can also be "difficult contexts for interaction." "The family is the place where," as one therapist put it, "you're dealing with life and death voltages."[11]

For a brief time, in the middle of the decade, as we have seen, it looked as if the rediscovery of the family might lead to new policies to address some of the old problems afflicting families—those based on poverty and inequality—and the newer ones created by the shifts in family structure. The climax of these efforts was Jimmy Carter's campaign promise to convene a White House Conference on the Family.

The fate of the White House conference revealed in capsule form the fate of the family as a national issue across the decade. The idea of a conference devoted to exploring the problems of families had a wide appeal. Yet its planning stage quickly became a battleground over such issues as abortion, sex education, the equal rights amendment, and gay rights. Major conflicts erupted over what constituted a family, and whether it would be appropriate to appoint a divorced mother as executive director of the conference.

Underlying these conflicts were two different visions of the family and the problems it faced. The conference planners and the family professionals tended to have a pluralistic and pragmatic outlook, accepting families as they were.[12] Acknowledging the diversity of family types in America, the planners changed the name of the conference to the White House Conference on *Families*. They assumed that the changes in family life would remain, and thought family policy should reflect these new realities. The definition of *family* they adopted, for instance, was broad enough to encompass gay partners. They also emphasized the economy as the source of pressure on families.

Opposing this liberal pragmatic view were representatives of a surging conservative backlash against feminism and the social changes of the early 1970s. The shock troops of the emerging New Right were evangelical Christians insisting on only one true family, the traditional one in which marriage is permanent, sex is confined to the conjugal bed, woman's place is in the home, and the father is both breadwinner and boss. For the religious wing of the New Right, the recent departures from this family pattern were symptomatic of moral decay; America was in danger of going the way of Sodom and Gomorrah. In the end, instead of bringing people together, the conference revealed the deep divisions in beliefs and values concerning the family. The conservative columnist Paul Weyrich, observing the controversies, predicted that the family would be to the 1980s what the Vietnam War had been to the 1960s.

FROM *THE GREENING OF AMERICA* TO *THE CULTURE OF NARCISSISM*

The upheavals in family life in the early 1970s would have been hard to assimilate in the best of times. But, as *Time* magazine noted in the summer of 1979: "Nobody is apt to look back on the '70's as the good old days."[13] By the middle of the decade the expansive, experimental mood that had bubbled through much of the middle class had faded.

There was no historical precedent for the pessimism that settled over American life at the end of the 1970s. Even during the Civil War and the Great Depression, observed the historian Oscar Handlin, there had been hope that out of suffering a better society would someday emerge.[14] In the late 1970s, such hope seemed nowhere to be found.

Two best-selling books bracket the decade, illustrating the dramatic shift in the nation's cultural mood and its reaction to transformations in family and personal life: Charles Reich's *The Greening of America* (1970) and Christopher Lasch's *The Culture of Narcissism* (1979). Each written by a radical critic of American society, they supplied catch-words that crystallized the concerns and controversies of the times. One, looking hopefully to the future, celebrated personal liberation and the peaceful overthrow of the prevailing social order. The other lamented the loss of the patriarchal, self-denying past and denounced the recent changes as evidence of moral decay and impending cultural collapse. The visions of Reich and Lasch may be seen as polar opposites in a cultural struggle to make sense of the sweeping changes in American life.

Though they offered opposing views, both books were best-sellers because they provided a language for talking about and making sense of social change. Each articulated the "structure of feelings" of a particular time—an emerging sensibility or pattern of experience—and reflected its respective side of the sociocultural watershed that divided the 1970s.

First serialized in the *New Yorker*, *The Greening of America* marked the passage of ideas from the 1960s youth counterculture into the mainstream of adult middle-class America—or, at least, to the more worldly segment of the middle class. Reich's credentials—at the time he was a Yale Law School professor—and publication in the *New Yorker* helped gain serious attention and a wide audience for his book.

Reich saw the student and youth counterculture as the leading edge of a coming revolution in consciousness, which he called Consciousness III. Consciousness I, in his view, had been the rugged individualism of the nineteenth century; Consciousness II was the mindset of the "organization men" of the liberal establishment, the corporate bureaucracy, and the military-industrial complex—the principal adversaries of students and protesters in the 1960s.

Consciousness III, or "Con III," was the spirit of the new generation. It embraced the promise of American life and rejected the "plastic" world of corporate and suburban America, along with the bland "rationality" that was ravishing nature, and which had unleashed the war in Vietnam. Con III, though it had started in one segment of youth, was spreading with "amazing rapidity." It was openness to new experience, a neverending state of becoming. Although it began with the self as the "only true reality," it did not condone selfishness: "It promises a higher reason, a more human community . . . a renewed relationship of man to himself, to other men, to nature, and to the land."[15] Reich was not explicitly a feminist, but his liberationist theme was in keeping with the spirit of the early women's liberation movement.

Reich's book was controversial from the beginning. Its rhapsodic style and its celebration of such counterculture trademarks as long hair, bell-bottom trousers, granny glasses, and pot smoking were ripe for satire. "What is interesting about this moony Rousseauian theorizing," one writer recently commented, ". . . is that it was taken seriously by so many sensible grown-ups. *The Greening of America* was a best-seller, spoken of in reverent tones, hailed as the harbinger of a new era—when it was nothing more than a fluently written piece of adolescent theorizing."[16]

Nevertheless, Reich's book reflected the mood of the early 1970s. The counterculture had raised questions about middle-class manners, morals, and values—definitions of personal authenticity, intimacy, success, respectability, meaning, material possessions, community, a concern for the environment and the quality of life—that many Americans felt obligated to answer.

In addition to the turmoil surrounding sex, marriage, and family life, America was also in the process of becoming a more open, tolerant, and democratic society. A "democratization of personhood,"[17] a new demand for equality in which minorities of every category— blacks, Hispanics, Asians, white ethnics, homosexuals, old people, the handicapped—as well as women claimed full political and cultural rights.[18]

While a relatively small proportion of the population was engaged in the more flamboyant kinds of alternative families popularized by the media, such as communes and swinging, millions of couples sought to reduce the strains in traditional roles in the family by making them more equal, more psychologically intimate, and more sexually fulfilling. Indeed, the best-seller lists in the early 1970s were full of books on sex: David Reuben's *Everything You Wanted to Know About Sex But Were Afraid to Ask, The Sensuous Woman* by "J," and Masters and Johnson's *Human Sexual Inadequacy*. The traditional, staid marriage manual gave way to sexual advice books that described sex in terms that had once been considered pornographic, and endorsed sexual practices once confined to brothels. Even the antifeminist "how-to-hold-your-man" author Marabel Morgan advised Christian housewives on how to liven up their sex lives by dressing like strippers, mini-skirted cowgirls, or spies with nothing on under their trenchcoats.[19]

A 1974 study of sexual behavior reported that the sexual liberation movement seemed to be having the strongest effect within marriage itself; Morton Hunt found a great increase in the frequency and variety of sexual relations within marriage.[20] Lillian Rubin's 1976 study of blue-collar families similarly found that new expectations for emotional and sexual intimacy were making their way into families that remained bastions of traditional family roles and values.[21]

The Turn to Nostalgia

By the mid-1970s, cultural effervescence and self-fulfillment began to collide with economic and international crisis. The longest boom in American history had fueled both the rise of the suburbs and the rise of the counterculture. It had encouraged the belief that inspired the War on Poverty—that poverty and class divisions could be ended painlessly by an ever-expanding economic pie.

Between the late 1940s and 1973, the average weekly earnings of forty-year-old men rose every year by 2.5 to 3 percent. After 1973 wages stagnated, and average family income declined.[22] Suddenly, Americans found themselves in a world they thought they had left behind in the 1930s, a world of economic contraction and scarcity. But the economy was also being devastated by stagflation, a new and puzzling malady whose combination of declining wages and high unemployment led to unprecedented levels of inflation. Inflation sent masses of women into the workplace.

The energy crisis was also a major source of economic difficulty, as well as symbolizing a humiliating loss of American dominance in world affairs. With the Arab oil embargo of 1973, followed by the rise of the Organization of Petroleum-Exporting Countries (OPEC), came the end of the cheap oil and gas that had sustained the American way of life and leisure in the postwar era. People in the coldest parts of the country saw their fuel bills reach astronomical levels; there was talk of people "freezing in the dark."

A 1976 study found that most American families were feeling the

effects of the economic squeeze. Not surprisingly, however, the sociologist David Caplovitz found that lower-income groups were suffering the most, reporting that their children had been denied things
they wanted or needed. Caplovitz concluded that inflation was widening the cleavage in America between the haves and the have-nots.
While upper-income families were not struggling to provide necessities of life like milk and shoes, they were not immune from the economic squeeze. Twenty-seven percent of those with incomes over
$20,000 also reported having to deny their children certain things.
Few people remained unaffected, even if the only change in their
lives was cutting back on steak, taxis, vacations, and theater tickets.[23]

Like other researchers, Caplovitz also found that economic hard-
ship often leads to emotional strains in families, especially marital
problems. Lower-income groups were most afflicted by worry, depression, and anger, but upper-income couples reported more arguments as a result of having to cut back on expenses. Rather than
deprivation, a new precariousness marked middle-class life; most people were still making a good living, but came to be plagued by what
Barbara Ehrenreich calls a "fear of falling"—a wariness of misfor-
tunes that might lead to a downward slide.[24]

For the first time in history, a generation of Americans faced the
prospect of doing worse than their parents had. The staples of the
good life, a home and steady, well-paying job, seemed to slip beyond
reach even for many baby-boomers who grew up in the middle class.
The 1950s of their childhood, against whose constraints they had
chafed, now took on the glow of a lost golden age. In the face of
economic uncertainty and cutbacks in public service jobs, it is little
wonder that there was a renewed interest in business careers among
college students in the 1970s.[25]

New words entered the American vocabulary: *limits, lowered expectations, lifeboat ethics, zero-sum economics.* In a society that had grown
used to affluence but now faced its worst economic crisis since the
Great Depression, the possibility of political turmoil, the growth of
intolerance, and a search for scapegoats became serious. Public opinion polls registered an unprecedented degree of distrust of American
institutions and uncertainty about the future.

For much of modern history, a politics of nostalgia has been a
recurrent response to periods of social upheaval, economic hard
times, and military defeat. By the end of the 1970s, Americans had
experienced all three. The nostalgic response to crisis typically
emerges in the form of right-wing backlash movements seeking to

restore nationalist traditions.[26] Such movements tend to view recent social change as morally corrupt, and look back to some lost age of virtue and order. In Europe the politics of nostalgic restoration has taken deadly forms. But that did not happen in America. Nor was there a full-scale revival of the nativist, anti-alien, anti-Communist movements that had risen to prominence and power in earlier eras of American history.[27]

America in the 1970s had become a more open, pluralistic, and tolerant society, accustomed to the presence of racial, religious, sexual, and political minorities. Prejudice had obviously not disappeared, but overt expressions of contempt for the usual political scapegoats had become unacceptable to the mainstream. "For the first time in its modern history," observed the sociologist Paul Blumberg, "American society seemed to be running out of witches to burn."[28]

The urge to restore a lost golden past took the relatively muted form—a "new politics of old values"[29]—of a nostalgic rhetoric of family, flag, neighborhood, and work. Despite his military buildup, Ronald Reagan was not the traditional "man on horseback," observed the political analyst Kevin Phillips, but "a Norman Rockwell figure from the front cover of the Saturday Evening Post."[30]

The culture of nostalgia that developed in response to the troubles of the 1970s muddied the classic distinction between right and left. Although the political right has traditionally looked to the past when confronting the problems of modern life, liberals and radicals have traditionally looked to a more democratic, egalitarian future. Yet liberal notions such as rights, autonomy, pluralism, reform, and progress disappeared from intellectual discourse as the rhetoric of loss and decline became the predominant language for discussing social change.

Thus the rise of the self-proclaimed "pro-family" New Right that helped propel Reagan into the White House was the extreme edge of a wider cultural shift that spanned the political spectrum. The early warning signals of the coming wave of nostalgia were evident in the popular culture of the early 1970s.[31] Television comedies such as "Happy Days" and films such as Grease and American Graffiti evoked a prettified, innocent 1950s. "The Waltons," set in the 1930s, one of the most popular TV series of the 1970s, portrayed a family with boundless love and understanding. "Roots," the eight-part saga of several generations of a black family, gathered the largest television audience in history.

Even the *Godfather* films, with all their gangster violence, portrayed the family as a "fantasy of tribal belongingness"—a world of fiercely loyal kinship bonds and clearly drawn gender boundaries.[32] The films were crowded with images of family life—weddings, christenings, funerals, family meals, and small, tender moments. Despite the fact that in the first film, Michael Corleone murders his brother-in-law, alienates his sister, and betrays the trust of his wife, its family imagery stirred up such powerful yearnings that one writer, commenting on the Loud family series, confessed, "Maybe it's better to be a Corleone than a Loud, better to be tribal and ethnocentric than urbane and adrift."[33]

While Reagan perfected the new politics of nostalgia, Carter was actually its first practitioner. Carter's ill-fated "malaise" speech (he did not actually use that word in it) of July 1979 was a beginning exercise in the new rhetoric. Billed as an address to the nation on the energy crisis, Carter spoke in apocalyptic terms about the moral and psychological failings of the American people. Only three years earlier, he had campaigned across the country telling Americans they deserved a government as good and moral and "as filled with love as the American people." But 1979 was a disastrous year for the country and for Carter's public approval ratings. In June, with gasoline lines already running five-hundred-cars-long in some places and some station attendants brandishing guns to keep order, OPEC announced a 50 percent hike in oil prices.

Now the president blamed the country's troubles not on economic and foreign policy reverses but on a "crisis in the very heart and soul and spirit of our national will." He lamented that a "preoccupation with self" and a "mistaken idea of freedom" had led Americans to lose their moral bearings: "In a nation that was proud of hard work, strong families, close knit communities and our faith in God, too many of us now tend to worship self-indulgence and consumption."[34]

Americans have a long history of linking their most vexing problems to defects in individual moral character.[35] While Carter's speech mirrored the grim public mood, its pessimism was a recipe for political failure. In contrast, Reagan campaigned the following year with a positive vision of nostalgia, a hope of restoration: the country's economic problems could be solved, our power and prestige renewed, and the traditional family restored.

The "malaise" speech may not have won Carter many votes, but the ideas it reflected dominated intellectual discussions of American culture in the 1970s. Carter had consulted an array of politicians, religious leaders, academics, and writers, among them a number of influential social critics who had recently offered deeply despairing visions of American character and culture.[36] In particular, Carter's lamentations about the "emptiness of lives" and the "worship of self-indulgence" echoed Lasch. Carter had read *The Culture of Narcissism* and recommended it to his staff. Carter found in it a message that seemed tailor-made for his political purposes: the growing pessimism about the nation's future reflected not the current economic crisis or his own failings but a deeply rooted moral and psychological ailment.

Lasch spoke to the widespread nervousness of the late 1970s, just as Reich had spoken to the effervescent mood of the early part of the decade. As the economy turned sour, notions about liberation and self-fulfillment seemed misplaced. It was a moment that closely resembled the period following October 1929, when people began to regret the "wasted decade" and took the crash as evidence of moral collapse. Discussions of the economic crisis in the early 1930s were suffused with moral condemnation of the jazz age.

Most of the social critics of the late 1970s ignored economic issues altogether. Instead, a chorus of critical voices complained that individualism, hedonism, feminism, and a new therapeutic ethic were eating away at the social fabric. Critics on the left blamed late capitalism for its culture, not its economics; critics on the right blamed the welfare state for having spawned a permissive society and an excessive sense of entitlement. There was general agreement that the new obsession with self was eroding moral standards, undermining the family, and sapping American strength at home and abroad.

The unsuccessful social experiments also fueled the malaise of the late 1970s. Alternative life-styles, from communes to open marriage, had turned out to be at least as problematic as the conventional arrangements they were meant to replace. Five years after *Open Marriage*, Nena O'Neill published *The Marriage Premise*, in which she recanted some of the implications of her earlier work: "In our haste to correct the obvious inadequacies of the old order in marriage, to revise our roles, and to eradicate the traditions we saw as confining, the baby has been thrown out with bathwater."[37] Moreover, the old order the rebels and experimenters had reacted against had itself crumbled. The rapid changes led to a widespread sense of dislocation and confusion, followed by a "normative reaction to normlessness"[38]—a revival of traditional values.

Narcissism and the Family

Despite the difficulties of pinning down its meaning, *narcissism* became in the late 1970s an instant catchword.[39] It seemed to provide
a framework for understanding most of what was troubling people—
higher divorce rates, women's influx into the workplace, the new
sexual freedom, and the younger generation's turning away from tradition and toward popular fads. At the same time, in circular fashion,
these things seemed to provide clear evidence of narcissism and family breakdown.

The publication of Lasch's book in 1979 was the climax of the
invention of the "narcissistic seventies," which subsumed the idea of
family breakdown. The birth of the narcissistic cliché took place, the
historian Peter Carroll observes, over a period of five weeks in the
summer of 1976, beginning with the appearance in *New York* magazine of Tom Wolfe's article "The Me Decade and the Second Great
Awakening." Wolfe lampooned the foibles of encounter groups and
other self-improvement fads of the time. ("Esalen's specialty was lube
jobs for the personality.")[40]

Two weeks after the article was published, *Newsweek* ran a cover
story echoing its themes. Entitled "Getting Your Head Together," it
described some of the latest offerings of the human potential movement—Rolfing, biofeedback, Feldenkreis, Arica—and defined the
trend as "a culturally pervasive movement that may well turn out to
be this century's version of colonial America's Great Spiritual Awakening."[41] Three weeks after that, Lasch's "The Narcissist Society" appeared in the *New York Review of Books*, prefiguring the arguments
that would be elaborated three years later in his book.[42]

The fads and foibles Wolfe, Lasch, and others were castigating certainly formed part of the American social landscape in the 1970s,
especially in the college towns and cosmopolitan areas that are the
natural habitat of academics, writers, and journalists. But they were
only one corner of it. To claim that these trends characterized the
American people or the American character, or even the middle class,
is a wild distortion. The narcissism critics' myopic focus ignored vast
areas of American life, especially the widespread economic hardships
that researchers like Caplovitz were documenting. As Carroll observed, "the cult of narcissism" contained "a cold disdain for the
problems of ordinary people."[43]

At a time when inflation and unemployment were increasing class
divergence and inequality and cutting into middle-class living stan-

dards, Wolfe perpetuated the myth of the affluent worker: "In America, truckdrivers, mechanics, factory workers, policemen and garbagemen make so much money ... that the word *proletarian* can no longer be used in this country with a straight face."[44] What set Wolfe's satirical juices flowing about encounter groups and the like was that people newly arrived in the middle or upper middle class suddenly seemed to be doing what their social betters, the old upper classes, had been doing all along. Wolfe pointed out, for example, that finishing schools and elite colleges in England and France were also places where the personality was "shaped and buffed like a piece of high class psychological cabinetry." Similarly, the mysterious goings-on in Yale's fabled secret societies, such as Skull and Bones, were "lemon sessions"—encounter groups much like Esalen's in which the members bared their souls and attacked one another's failings, emerging with stronger and better personalities.

The "Me Decade" half of Wolfe's title became an instant cliché. In two little words, he had satisfied the popular taste for pairing a catch phrase with a decade, skewered the latest fads in pop psychology, and articulated an emerging theme then being wheeled out by a variety of social critics.[45]

As economic indicators declined, some older intellectual enterprises flourished: the dissection of American character and culture, the pessimistic laments about modern society that intellectuals have been carrying on since the Enlightenment. Before 1960 a large body of social criticism, reaching back into the nineteenth century, complained about the pathological qualities of modern society—mass culture, mass media, mass consumption, and the alienation, isolation, and meaninglessness of urban and suburban life. The outcome of all these dehumanizing processes was a pathological new social character or personality type. Studies of the American character, like Reisman's *The Lonely Crowd* and Whyte's *The Organization Man*, were variants of the genre.

There was a lull in this literature between the mid-1960s and the mid-1970s. Instead of assuming a single monolithic American character type, there was an emphasis on specific groups in American society: the poor, blacks, women, Indians, as well as "middle Americans." Reich's book was one of the few attempts to generalize about the American character before the middle of the 1970s.

Lasch's writing, following a Frankfurt school recipe for mixing Marx and Freud, gave intellectual ballast to popular critiques like Wolfe's. Lasch linked general moral notions like narcissism, hedonism, and selfishness to a seemingly precise psychiatric diagnosis in order to argue that there had been a pathological shift in the deep structure of the modern personality.

According to Lasch, the narcissistic personality of our time is the product of a decadent social order, late capitalism, and a family that had been undermined by that system—its public and private bureaucracies, mass media, peer groups, and especially alleged experts in child rearing. Absent fathers, shallow, unloving, but suffocating mothers, and a decline of parental authority have resulted in weak, dependent personalities who were nevertheless well adapted to life in a "corrupt, permissive, hedonistic culture." Unable to form deep or lasting relationships, dedicated to "doing others in" in the guise of cooperation, the narcissistic self must nevertheless depend on the vicarious warmth of others. Fearful of dependence, it can never escape from its own inner emptiness.[46]

This personality was the dominant character type of late capitalist society, Lasch argued, just as hysteria had been the dominant disorder of Victorian times. Manifestations of narcissism could be found everywhere—in advertising, sports, the cult of consumption, the popular obsession with the rich and famous, as well as new therapy and fitness movements. In many ways, observed one historian, *The Culture of Narcissism* reads "like the sermons of Samuel Parrish, the Salem minister who warned his listeners that the devil's hand was visible in their daily lives."[47]

Lasch was not the first to use *narcissism* to describe the selfcenteredness and lack of concern for others that presumably characterizes the typical person in contemporary American (or Western) culture. But in choosing it to describe cultural change, he and others had fastened onto a word with a long history as a problematic, muddled concept in psychiatry and psychoanalysis. First defined as a sexual perversion, it soon acquired a variety of meanings.[48] Charles Rycroft, a British analyst, summed up the major difficulties with the concept: its "inescapable disparaging overtones," combined with its use "as a technical term to describe all forms of investment of energy (libido) in the self."[49] Psychoanalysts since Freud have often spoken of "healthy narcissism" or simply "narcissism" to refer to normal selfesteem.* If anything can be stated clearly about the meaning of the

---

*In the clinical literature, the term can refer, among other things, to healthy self-esteem, self-hatred, lack of empathy for others, lack of interest in others, interest in manipulating and exercising power over others, grandiosity, and exhibitionism. It has a different theoretical status in different versions of psychoanalytic theory.[50]

term, it is that it always focuses on the self and that usually, but not always, it is an expression of moral disapproval on the part of the person who uses it.

If Lasch's use of narcissism as the key to understanding American culture in the 1970s is weakened by the confusion surrounding the term, the other assumptions on which his argument rests are equally flawed. First, Lasch relies heavily on claims by some psychoanalysts that they have been seeing more narcissistic disorders in their patients in recent years. Second, he assumes such a shift in symptoms must reflect a transformation of personality in the population at large. Finally, he assumes that many aspects of American culture and society can be seen as reflections of deep personality structures deformed since infancy.

As a number of Lasch's critics have pointed out, it is questionable whether most analysts are in fact seeing more narcissism among their patients, and if they are, whether it is the patients or their own theoretical lenses that have changed. Further, even if that small segment of the population that seeks analytic treatment has shifted its symptoms, this would not necessarily imply that pathological narcissism is rampant across the entire country. Finally, to reduce cultural and social reality to symptoms of personality disorder is to engage in a highly dubious form of social analysis.

To dispute Lasch's claims about narcissism, however, is not to deny that important changes in behavior and attitudes have taken place. But as one critic concluded, "As a controversial category of clinical pathology as well as a general symbol of selfishness and alienation, the concept of narcissism merely clouds our understanding of these complex social and cultural issues, and neither measures nor explains them in an effective way."[51]

The Culture of Narcissism is the polar opposite of *The Greening of America.* Lasch's book was like Wolfian satire minus the humor. Where Reich saw counterculture fads like long hair, bell-bottomed jeans, and a fondness for unhomogenized peanut butter as symbols of purity and redemption, Lasch saw in the fads of the 1970s—jogging, health foods, encounter groups, belly dancing—signs of narcissistic despair in people who have "no hope of improving their lives in any of the ways that matter."[52] Instead of Reich's utopian vision of a greened, more gentle America, Lasch offered an apocalyptic vision of a corrupt, decaying culture. Where Reich's liberated selves will redeem their society, Lasch's narcissistic selves will destroy it.

Despite its nightmarish portrayal of American life, Lasch's book received serious scholarly attention as well as being a best-seller. Its pessimistic mixture of moral denunciation and psychological analysis resonated with a widespread uneasiness about the social changes that had swept over the nation in the late 1960s and early 1970s and the economic crises that followed them. As Reich had done earlier, Lasch provided a language for talking about a range of new concerns. Further, he permitted the reader to indulge in the same tendency he denounced as pathological—the new cultural preoccupation with the self, inner experience, and psychological modes of analysis. *The Culture of Narcissism*, argues one social scientist, offers "a delicious exercise in social criticism, an exercise that confirms the moral superiority of author and reader while providing an occasion to practice the very vice they condemn."[53]

HERE TO STAY

In 1976, just as the decline-of-the-family argument was shifting toward the narcissistic critique, Mary Jo Bane's *Here to Stay* offered the first major statement of the optimistic view of family change. Over the next decade and a half, others would follow. Bane, a sociologist, cited an array of demographic and survey data showing the family to be alive and well, and family values strong. Family disruption due to divorce was no greater than it had been in earlier times due to death. A larger proportion of children than in the past was living with at least one parent. There was no evidence that the influx of mothers into the workplace was harming children. Contemporary families have no fewer relatives, neighbors, or friends to call on than they had in the past. Even the sharp rise in divorce did not mean that marriage was dying, or that people were treating marriage like cars or clothing—to be used for a short time and replaced by later models. "[T]aken as a whole," she argued, "the data on marriage and divorce suggest that the kind of marriage Americans have always known is still a pervasive and enduring institution."[54]

The "here to stay" argument embodied certain basic truths that had been ignored in all the talk about the death or disintegration of the family. Since Bane's book, it has become clear that the rapid and unexpected changes of the 1960s and early 1970s did not mean that Americans were abandoning marriage and family life. But the optimists tended to gloss over the painful dislocations resulting from those changes.

Nor did Bane and others delve into the complex array of psycho-logical and cultural shifts that were creating a new normative frame-work for family life. Basic values had not changed, but family roles were being revised, and the emotional meaning of family life had been subtly transformed. Several studies carried out at the time make it possible to take a closer look at the changes in values and attitudes that took place during what Tom Wolfe confidently predicted would be forever known as the Me Decade. These studies show, first, that there have indeed been significant changes in values and attitudes, changes that may well justify speaking of a psychological revolution. But, second, the extent of the change has been vastly overstated by the critics. Third, the changes are neither selfish and asocial, as the critics allege, nor necessarily at odds with family obligations and com-munity bonds. Indeed, some of the changes have enriched family life.

The best evidence on changing values and attitudes in the 1970s is found in a 1981 book entitled *The Inner American*, a report of a study carried out by the University of Michigan's Institute of Social Re-search.[55] In 1957 researchers intensively interviewed a random sam-ple of over two thousand people about themselves, their families, their work, their values, their joys and sorrows. In 1976 a second survey asked the same questions, along with a few new ones, of a matched sample about the same size as the first.

The study found a "dizzying complexity" of change not easily sum-marized in phrases favored by social commentators. Social changes occurred in multiple, sometimes contradictory, directions, and un-evenly among different groups of Americans. While much of the analysis focused on differences between 1957 and 1976, many indi-cators showed surprisingly little change during this span—and many measures of psychological well-being showed no change at all. Most people were by and large shown to be lacking anxiety, satisfied with their jobs and their families, and involved with friends and kin.

Nevertheless, the authors insist that a "psychological revolution" had occurred over the twenty years between the two surveys. The "revolution," if that is the right term, was not so much about self-fulfillment or "looking out for number one" as about the "phenom-enology of perception"—a shift, in the way of looking at oneself and others, toward a more "psychological orientation to experience."[56] Increasingly, Americans had come to be more introspective. They spoke in psychological terms about the people and things that were important to them.

Whereas in the 1950s people were likely to see their identities as contained in their social roles—a man's in his work, a woman's in her roles as wife and mother, attributing their satisfactions and problems to external or material conditions such as money, health, or the outward signs of success—in the 1970s people were likely to define themselves in terms of their personal qualities and the quality of their individual experience. They were more aware of themselves as "individual beings" with "individuated ways of responding to the world."

The new tendency to appraise the self in terms other than one's social roles extended to other people also. One of the most striking changes was an increasing tolerance of other people's family styles, especially those who chose not to marry. In 1957, 53 percent of the respondents thought that a person who remained single was either sick or morally flawed—too selfish or neurotic to marry. Even those who themselves were single or divorced had a negative view of someone who chose not to marry. In 1976, only 34 percent of respondents held this negative view.

Despite the heightened individuality of the 1976 respondents, and the fact that being married was no longer such a powerful norm, America in 1976 remained a "family-centered society." Both men and women were "extraordinarily certain" that marriage and family were of prime importance in their lives. For men especially, marriage had become even more central than in the past; it was the only relationship in which they could enjoy emotional intimacy.

Paradoxically, the survey showed that while people described themselves as happier in their marriages than in 1957, they also reported more stress and problems. Indeed, the greater importance of family relationships for satisfaction and meaning in life may have exacerbated ordinary tensions. The Michigan researchers observed of marriage that: "When so much rides on a single role and a single relationship, anxiety is likely to run high and act in some way as an obstacle to realizing the easy intimacy people seek in marriage." Similarly, significant numbers of people felt inadequate as parents because they had wanted warm and open relationships with their children, but the reality did not meet their expectations.[57]

Perhaps the major finding of the study was that people had become increasingly sensitive to the quality of interpersonal relations, not only in the family but at work. In 1976 people wanted friendly, warm relationships at work and increased intimacy and emotional support in marriage. This search for intimacy explains why marriage has become more important for men as the only relationship where these needs could be met.

In general, then, few of the findings described in *The Inner American* fit the picture of America in the 1970s as a land of collapsing family life, of a people alienated from work, incapable of empathy, narcissistically abandoning family commitments in search of instant intimacy and emotional titillation. Other empirical studies at the time yielded similar conclusions.

In a book reporting on the shifts of the 1970s, *New Rules: Searching for Fulfillment in a World Turned Upside Down,* the pollster Daniel Yankelovich combines survey data with portraits of individuals and couples. Aimed more at the general reader than the Michigan study, the book sometimes sounds like another jeremiad against narcissism. In fact, Yankelovich finds a good deal to admire in the new approach to life. He opposes the idea that deep personality pathology accounts for the trends he describes and rejects Lasch's "angry and gloom-ridden images of American life," labeling Lasch's conception of the narcissistic personality "arbitrary and incoherent."

Yankelovich's own claim in *New Rules* that a traditional "ethic of self-denial" had been replaced by a pervasive new "ethic of self-fulfillment" is at odds with the report that only 17 percent of his sample followed a "strong form" of the self-fulfillment ethos. Demographically, most of the "strong formers" were relatively young, well educated, upper middle class, politically liberal—in other words, veterans of the counterculture coming to terms with adult life. Meanwhile, 20 percent of adult Americans remained completely unaffected by the "great shift in culture."

Yankelovich also acknowledges that among the large majority of his sample, traditional values persisted. They strongly believed, for example, that drug use and extramarital affairs are morally wrong, and that women should put their children and husband ahead of their careers. Fifty-one percent reported believing that "strict, old-fashioned discipline" is the best way to raise children. Nevertheless, most of the people we meet in Yankelovich's vignettes are strong formers carrying out "experiments in self-fulfillment"—a couple struggling with the emotional fallout of open marriage, a young man devoting himself more to bicycle racing than to work or family. In contrast to other social critics of the 1970s, Yankelovich admired aspects of this new ethos. The experiments in self-fulfillment were useful, if only in revealing the defects in their premises. Most Americans had become more tolerant of difference, more willing to live and let live—not only in matters of women's roles, premarital sex, and other such norms but with regard to racial and religious differences as well. Recent generations had moved beyond their parents' concern with money and respectability as central goals in life. Their focus on psychological satisfaction lent itself well to living in a time of scarcity and lower living standards.

All in all, the evidence Yankelovich presents serves as a counter-weight to the sometimes sweeping pronouncements he himself makes about a fundamental transformation of American culture in the di-rection of self-fulfillment. At the end of the book, Yankelovich re-ports findings showing a shift to a new ethic of commitment, efforts toward community involvement, and an upsurge in "reverential thinking," which could take the form of religion or reverence for nature. Yankelovich also acknowledges a striking continuity: in a 1970 survey, 96 percent of Americans declared their dedication to the tra-ditional "ideal of two people sharing a life and a home together"; in 1980, he reports, the figure was exactly the same.[58]

Still another insight into recent cultural changes comes from Cap-low's study of Middletown fifty years after the original study by the Lynds. As discussed in chapter 1, Caplow found the family in the 1970s to be not only alive and well but in much better shape than it had been half a century earlier. In the course of fifty years, the quality of family life had improved considerably. Much of the credit, espe-cially for working-class families, was due to improvements in the stan-dard of living: better pay, more leisure time, improved housing. Parents of the 1970s spent more time with their children than did parents of the 1920s. More flexible gender roles and the spread of knowledge about contraception and sexuality had also enriched the relationships between husbands and wives.

Taken together, these studies—all carried out at the height of the so-called Me Decade—yield little evidence for the claim that we had become a nation of narcissists, incapable of lasting relationships, seeking only instant intimacy without commitment. To the extent that a new American self did come into being in the 1960s and 1970s, it had much in common with earlier models. Finally, the changes were not due to moral breakdown or deep characterological change; rather, they were responses to broader social changes that brought improvements for everyone—a higher standard of living, longer and healthier lives, and, especially, widespread education.

To deny the collapse of family life and moral values is not to deny the reality of trauma, stress, and a sense of dislocation many Ameri-cans experienced as a direct result of these changes. By 1975 a ma-jority of adults in Middletown had experienced one or more divorces in their own families or those of their parents and siblings. No one could escape the repercussions of profound, unexpected changes in our most central institution. For many people, it was as if, like actors in the middle of a long-running play, they were suddenly told they no longer had to follow the script, but must improvise their lines and characters.

FROM THE MYTH OF SUBURBIA TO THE MYTH OF NARCISSISM

There is something Orwellian, Peter Carroll observes, about the way the notion of narcissism took over so quickly in the summer of 1976.[59] The media, the journalists, the social critics, were not just conveying information, or even articulating an argument, so much as assuming the reality of the narcissistic society and creating a language in which debate and discussion had to take place.

Despite its emphasis on the grimness of contemporary family life, however, the narcissistic critique did not lead to pragmatic efforts to remedy the actual problems families faced. Discussions of poverty in the late 1970s and 1980s, for example, as the social historian Michael Katz observed, "slipped easily, unreflectively, into a language of family, race, and culture rather than inequality, power, and exploitation."[60] Middle-class concerns with the quality of life and psychological matters—personal relationships, child rearing, self-understanding, and efforts to cope with stress and change—were dismissed by Lasch and others as narcissistic, foolish, evidence of corruption by professionals, experts, and bureaucracies.

Many of the themes in the social criticism of the late 1970s were a revival of familiar worries that had been expressed many times in American and, indeed, Western history. In fact, the myth of narcissism served the same polemical function in the late 1970s as the myth of suburbia had in the 1950s: it was a "packaged rebuke to the whole tenor of American life."[61] In both eras, critics seized on the novelties of the time to express larger concerns about social change.

Indeed, as the historian Rupert Wilkenson points out, Riesman's *Lonely Crowd* heralded the complaints of the later social critics to an extent that is seldom appreciated. By the late 1940s, before the spread of television or the rise of the "youth culture," Riesman was writing of:

> narcissism and "diffuse anxiety"; the shifting of authority from "do's and don'ts" to manipulation and enticement; the flooding of atti-

tudes by media messages; the channelling of achievement drives into
competition for the approval of others; and the splintering of society into myriad interest groups—all those tendencies of modern life
that so worried commentators in the 1970's and '80's.[62]

In the 1950s, as more Americans became middle class, social critics
worried that Americans were becoming soft, losing the ascetic moral
fiber of their nineteenth-century ancestors. Similarly, many Americans in the cold war 1950s and again in the 1970's worried about our
ability to stand up to the Russians.

In both the 1950s and the 1970s, the cultural critics' exhortations
and apocalyptic pronouncements amounted to little more than hand
wringing. Both contrasted the corrupt present with an idealized
nineteenth-century past, yet their vision of what was good about the
past and bad about the present shifted. In the 1950s, when they worried about conformity and the social ethic, the nineteenth century
stood for individualism, self-reliance, and entrepreneurial competition. In the 1970s and 1980s, when they railed against hedonism,
individualism, and the new therapeutic ethic, they portrayed the
nineteenth century as a lost era of duty, self-sacrifice, civic virtue, and
community. It would appear that the idealized yet strangely change-
able past serves as "a repository for all the values modern social
critics feel are missing from their world."[63]

But the social criticism of these times did reflect some real concerns. Massive social change had left formidable stress and dislocation in its wake; cultural concepts that Americans had only recently
used to make sense of their society and their families no longer fit
the realities they could see all around them. Like the religious promise of an afterlife, nostalgia—the savoring of a happier past, real or
imagined—has its uses as a coping device. Yet the social criticism of
the late 1970s did not point to ways of coming to grips with the
irreversible changes that had taken place in family life. Instead, it
contributed to a prolonged avoidance of the task.

C H A P T E R   6

Changes of Heart: The Social Sources of Psychological Transformation

[T]he patient of today suffers most under the problem of what he should believe in and who he should—or indeed, might—be or become; while the patient of early psychoanalysis suffered most under inhibitions which prevented him from being what and who he thought he knew he was. —Erik Erikson
Childhood and Society

Ask yourself whether you are happy and you cease to be so. —John Stuart Mill
Autobiography

A major threat to family well-being was recently identified in a book entitled *Rebuilding the Nest*: "We are becoming, more than ever, an atomized, adult-centered society in which expressive individualism— what has been called the 'untrammeled self'—has become a govern- ing cultural ideal."[1] In the last chapter, we saw that a significant shift has taken place in the way Americans think about themselves, their families, their work, and what they want out of life. An approach to life that had largely been confined to the highly educated in 1957 had become widespread by 1976.[2]

Looking at data from a number of Western societies, the political scientist Ronald Inglehart has found a change from "materialist" to "post-materialist" or "post-bourgeois" values—that is, from an emphasis on safety and security to one on quality-of-life issues, including a desire for a friendlier, less impersonal society, greater equality, a concern for the environment, and a tendency to challenge rather than accept central authority. Similarly, the sociologist Duane Alwin has found a marked shift in parental child-rearing values in industrial countries in recent decades; parents have increasingly come to value autonomy and independence in their children over obedience to authority, a shift closely linked to rising educational levels.[3]

By and large these changes of heart have had a bad press. Complaining of a new individualism that has gone too far, social critics have identified the villains as the Me generation and its new values, women who want to "have it all," the consumerist values of late capitalism, and the therapeutic ethic, with its emphasis on the self over traditional obligations to family and society.

What these judgments ignore is the massive shifts in the conditions of everyday life in postindustrial society that have nurtured the recent changes in sensibility. Demographic upheavals have altered the most basic aspects of human existence: birth, death, sexuality, and marriage; the spread of universal schooling and mass higher education have transformed childhood and the process of human development; the emergence of a service and information society has transformed the nature of work. As a result of these and other changes, Americans live in a world profoundly different from the one that confronted not only their grandparents and great grandparents but even their own parents.

Living in this new world demands a more elaborated sense of self. Perhaps the major source of this new sense of self is the transformation of the individual life course over the twentieth century. In modern Western societies, people live much longer than they did in earlier generations, they pass through more life phases, and they exercise far more choice about the direction of their lives. Thus the structure of families has been altered, family relationships have been remade, and the pattern of individual experience across the life span has been reshaped. These transformations have been double-edged: we have more choices than did previous generations about the kinds of lives we want to live, but the cost of this freedom from assigned identities and roles is a set of psychological burdens earlier generations did not have to face.

Yet the personal conflicts of today are a by-product of the kind of progress few of us would repeal if we could. Free from the threats of hunger, disease, poverty, and natural calamities, most of us enjoy

levels of education, health, and longevity undreamed of by our ancestors. Of course, some people still die young of accidents or disease,
appalling poverty is evident even in affluent societies, and threats of
terrorism, nuclear accident or war, and environmental catastrophe
hang over our heads.[4] But most of us nevertheless go about our daily
lives assuming that we will live to be old, that we will have the basic
physical necessities of life, and that we can exercise great control and
choice in our personal lives. These assumptions amount to nothing
less than a transformation in the human condition.

UNHERALDED REVOLUTIONS

Many of us, in moments of nostalgia, imagine the past as a kind of
Disneyland—a quaint setting we might step back into with our sense
of ourselves intact, yet free of the stresses of modern life. But in
yearning for the golden past we imagine we have lost, we are unaware
of what we have escaped.

In our time, for example, dying before reaching old age has become a rare event; about three-quarters of all people die after their
sixty-fifth birthday.[5] It is hard for us to appreciate what a novelty this
is in human experience. In 1850, only 2 percent of the population
lived past sixty-five.[6] "We place dying in what we take to be its logical
position," observes the social historian Ronald Blythe, "which is at
the close of a long life, whereas our ancestors accepted the futility
of placing it in any position at all. In the midst of life we are in
death, they said, and they meant it. To them it was a fact; to us it is
a metaphor."[7]

This longevity revolution is largely a twentieth-century phenomenon. Astonishingly, two-thirds of the total increase in human longevity since prehistoric times has taken place since 1900—and a good
deal of that increase has occurred in recent decades.[8] Mortality rates
in previous centuries were several times higher than today, and death
commonly struck at any age. Infancy was particularly hazardous; "it
took two babies to make one adult," as one demographer put it.[9] A
white baby girl today has a greater chance of living to be sixty than
her counterpart born in 1870 would have had of reaching her first
birthday.[10] And after infancy, death still hovered as an ever-present
possibility. It was not unusual for young and middle-aged adults to
die of tuberculosis, pneumonia, or other infectious diseases. (Keats
died at twenty-five, Schubert at thirty-one, Mozart at thirty-five.)

These simple changes in mortality have had profound, yet little-appreciated effects on family life; they have encouraged stronger emotional bonds between parents and children, lengthened the duration of marriage and parent-child relationships, made grandparenthood an expectable stage of the life course, and increased the number of grandparents whom children actually know. More and more families have four or even five generations alive at the same time. And for the first time in history, the average couple has more parents living than it has children.[11] It is also the first era when most of the parent-child relationship takes place after the child becomes an adult.

In a paper entitled "Death and the Family," the demographer Peter Uhlenberg has examined some of these repercussions by contrasting conditions in 1900 with those in 1976. In 1900, for example, half of all parents would have experienced the death of a child; by 1976 only 6 percent would. And more than half of all children who lived to the age of fifteen in 1900 would have experienced the death of a parent or sibling, compared with less than 9 percent in 1976. Another outcome of the lower death rates was a decline in the number of orphans and orphanages. Current discussions of divorce rarely take into account the almost constant family disruption children experienced in "the good old days." In 1900, 1 out of 4 children under the age of fifteen lost a parent; 1 out of 62 lost both. The corresponding figures for 1976 are, respectively, 1 out of 20 and 1 out of 1,800.[12]

Because being orphaned used to be so common, the chances of a child's not living with either parent was much greater at the turn of the century than it is now. Indeed, some of the current growth in single-parent families is offset by a decline in the number of children raised in institutions, in foster homes, or by relatives. This fact does not diminish the stresses of divorce and other serious family problems of today, but it does help correct the tendency to contrast the terrible Present with an idealized Past.

Today's children rarely experience the death of a close relative, except for elderly grandparents. And it is possible to grow into adulthood without experiencing even that loss. "We never had any deaths in my family," a friend recently told me, explaining that none of her relatives had died until she was in her twenties. In earlier times, children were made aware of the constant possibility of death, attended deathbed scenes, and were even encouraged to examine the decaying corpses of family members.[13]

One psychological result of our escape from the daily presence of death is that we are ill prepared for it when it comes. For most of us, the first time we feel a heightened concern with our own mortality is in our thirties and forties when we realize that the years we have already lived outnumber those we have left.

Another result is that the death of a child is no longer a sad but normal hazard of parenthood. Rather, it has become a devastating, life-shattering loss from which a parent may never fully recover.[14] The intense emotional bonding between parents and infants that we see as a sociobiological given did not become the norm until the eighteenth and nineteenth centuries. The privileged classes created the concept of the "emotionally priceless" child, a powerful ideal that gradually filtered down through the rest of society.[15]

The high infant mortality rates of premodern times was partly due to neglect, and often to lethal child-rearing practices such as sending infants off to a wet nurse* or, worse, infanticide. It now appears that in all societies lacking reliable contraception, the careless treatment and neglect of unwanted children acted as a major form of birth control.[16] This does not necessarily imply that parents were uncaring toward all their children; rather, they seem to have practiced "selective neglect" of sickly infants in favor of sturdy ones, or of later children in favor of earlier ones.† In 1801 a writer observed of Bavarian peasants:

> The peasant has joy when his wife brings forth the first fruit of their love, he has joy with the second and third as well, but not with the fourth.... He sees all children coming thereafter as hostile creatures, which take the bread from his mouth and the mouths of his family. Even the heart of the most gentle mother becomes cold with the birth of the fifth child, and the sixth, she unashamedly wishes death, that the child should pass to heaven.[19]

*Wet-nursing—the breastfeeding of an infant by a woman other than the mother—was widely practiced in premodern Europe and colonial America. Writing of a two-thousand-year-old "war of the breast," the developmental psychologist William Kessen notes that the most persistent theme in the history of childhood is the reluctance of mothers to suckle their babies, and the urgings of philosophers and physicians that they do so.[17] Infants were typically sent away from home for a year and a half or two years to be raised by poor country women, in squalid conditions. When they took in more babies than they had milk enough to suckle, the babies would die of malnutrition.

The reluctance to breast-feed may not have reflected maternal indifference so much as other demands in premodern, precontraceptive times—the need to take part in the family economy, the unwillingness of husbands to abstain from sex for a year and a half or two. (Her milk would dry up if a mother became pregnant.) Although in France and elsewhere the custom persisted into the twentieth century, large-scale wet-nursing symbolizes the gulf between modern and premodern sensibilities about infants and their care.

†The anthropologist Nancy Scheper-Hughes describes how impoverished mothers in northeastern Brazil select which infants to nurture.[18]

Declining fertility rates are another major result of falling death rates. Until the baby boom of the 1940s and 1950s, fertility rates had been dropping continuously since the eighteenth century. By taking away parents' fear that some of their children would not survive to adulthood, lowered early-childhood mortality rates encouraged careful planning of births and smaller families. The combination of longer lives and fewer, more closely spaced children created a still-lengthening empty-nest stage in the family. This in turn has encouraged the companionate style of marriage, since husband and wife can expect to live together for many years after their children have moved out.

Many demographers have suggested that falling mortality rates are directly linked to rising divorce rates. In 1891 W. F. Willcox of Cornell University made one of the most accurate social science predictions ever. Looking at the high and steadily rising divorce rates of the time, along with falling mortality rates, he predicted that around 1980, the two curves would cross and the number of marriages ended by divorce would equal those ended by death. In the late 1970s, it all happened as Willcox had predicted.[20] Then divorce rates continued to increase before leveling off in the 1980s, while mortality rates continued to decline. As a result, a couple marrying today is more likely to celebrate a fortieth wedding anniversary than were couples around the turn of the century.[21]

In statistical terms, then, it looks as if divorce has restored a level of instability to marriage that had existed earlier due to the high mortality rate. But as Lawrence Stone observes, "it would be rash to claim that the psychological effects of the termination of marriage by divorce, that is by an act of will, bear a close resemblance to its termination by the inexorable accident of death."[22]

THE NEW STAGES OF LIFE

In recent years it has become clear that the stages of life we usually think of as built into human development are, to a large degree, social and cultural inventions. Although people everywhere may pass through infancy, childhood, adulthood, and old age, the facts of nature are "doctored," as Ruth Benedict once put it, in different ways by different cultures.

The Favorite Age

In 1962 Phillipe Ariès made the startling claim that "in medieval society, the idea of childhood did not exist." Ariès argued not that parents then neglected their children, but that they did not think of children as having a special nature that required special treat-ment; after the age of around five to seven, children simply joined the adult world of work and play. This "small adult" conception of childhood has been observed by many anthropologists in preindus-trial societies.[23] In Europe, according to Ariès and others, childhood was discovered, or invented, in the seventeenth and nineteenth cen-turies, with the emergence of the private, domestic, companionate family and formal schooling. These institutions created distinct roles for children, enabling childhood to emerge as a distinct stage of life.

Despite challenges to Ariès's work,[24] the bulk of historical and cross-cultural evidence supports the contention that childhood as we know it today is a relatively recent cultural invention; our ideas about chil-dren, child-rearing practices, and the conditions of children's lives are dramatically different from those of earlier centuries. The same is true of adolescence. Teenagers, such a conspicuous and noisy pres-ence in modern life, and their stage of life, known for its turmoil and soul searching, are not universal features of life in other times and places.

Of course, the physical changes of puberty—sexual maturation and spurt in growth—happen to everyone everywhere. Yet, even here, there is cultural and historical variation. In the past hundred years, the age of first menstruation has declined from the mid-teens to twelve, and the age young men reach their full height has declined from twenty-five to under twenty.[25] Both changes are believed to be due to improvements in nutrition and health care, and these average ages are not expected to continue dropping.

Some societies have puberty rites, but they bring about a transition from childhood not to adolescence but to adulthood. Other societies take no note at all of the changes, and the transition from childhood to adulthood takes place simply and without social recognition.[26] Ad-olescence as we know it today appears to have evolved late in the nineteenth century; there is virtual consensus among social scientists that it is "a creature of the industrial revolution and it continues to be shaped by the forces which defined that revolution: industrializa-tion, specialization, urbanization, . . . and bureaucratization of human

organizations and institutions, and continuing technological development."[27]

In America before the second half of the nineteenth century, youth
was an ill-defined category. Puberty did not mark any new status or
life experience. For the majority of young people who lived on farms,
work life began early, at seven or eight years old or even younger. As
they grew older, their responsibility would increase, and they would
gradually move toward maturity. Adults were not ignorant of the
differences between children and adults, but distinctions of age meant
relatively little. As had been the practice in Europe, young people
could be sent away to become apprentices or servants in other households. As late as the early years of this century, working-class children
went to work at the age of ten or twelve.

A second condition leading to a distinct stage of adolescence was
the founding of mass education systems, particularly the large public
high school. Compulsory education helped define adolescence by setting a precise age for it; high schools brought large numbers of teenagers together to create their own society for a good part of their
daily lives. So the complete set of conditions for adolescence on a
mass scale did not exist until the end of the nineteenth century.

The changed family situations of late-nineteenth- and early-
twentieth-century youth also helped make this life stage more psychologically problematic. Along with the increasing array of options
to choose from, rapid social change was making one generation's
experience increasingly different from that of the next. Among the
immigrants who were flooding into the country at around the time
adolescence was emerging, the generation gap was particularly acute.
But no parents were immune to the rapid shifts in society and culture
that were transforming America in the decades around the turn of
the century.

Further, the structure and emotional atmosphere of middle-class
family life was changing also, creating a more intimate and emotionally intense family life. Contrary to the view that industrialization had
weakened parent-child relations, the evidence is that family ties between parents and adolescents intensified at this time: adolescents
lived at home until they married, and depended more completely,
and for a longer time, on their parents than in the past. Demographic
change had cut family size in half over the course of the century.
Mothers were encouraged to devote themselves to the careful nurtur-
ing of fewer children.[28]

This more intensive family life seems likely to have increased the

emotional strain of adolescence. Smaller households and a more nur-
turing style of child rearing, combined with the increased contact
between parents, especially mothers, and adolescent children, may
have created a kind of " 'Oedipal family' in middle class America."[29]

The young person's awakening sexuality, particularly the young
male's, is likely to have been more disturbing to both himself and his
parents than during the era when young men commonly lived away
from home. As I discussed earlier, there is evidence that during the
Victorian era, fears of adolescent male sexuality, and of masturbation
in particular, were remarkably intense and widespread.[30]

Family conflict in general may have been intensified by the peculiar combination of teenagers' increased dependence on parents and
increased autonomy in making their own life choices. Despite its tensions, the new emotionally intense middle-class home made it more
difficult than ever for adolescents to leave home for the heartless,
indifferent world outside.[31]

By the end of the nineteenth century, conceptions of adolescence
took on modern form, and by the first decades of the twentieth century, *adolescence* had become a household word. As articulated force-
fully by the psychologist G. Stanley Hall in his 1904 treatise,
adolescence was a biological process—not simply the onset of sexual
maturity but a turbulent, transitional stage in the evolution of the
human species: "some ancient period of storm and stress when old
moorings were broken and a higher level attained."[32]

Hall seemed to provide the answers to questions people were ask-
ing about the troublesome young. His public influence eventually
faded, but his conception of adolescence as a time of storm and stress
lived on. Adolescence continued to be seen as a period of both great
promise and great peril: "every step of the upward way is strewn with
the wreckage of body, mind and morals."[33] The youth problem—
whether the lower-class problem of delinquency, or the identity crises
and other psychological problems of middle-class youth—has continued to haunt America, and other modern societies, ever since.

Ironically, then, the institutions that had developed to organize and
control a problematic age ended by heightening adolescent self-
awareness, isolating youth from the rest of society, and creating a
youth culture, making the transition to adulthood still more problematic and risky.[34] Institutional recognition in turn made adolescents a
more distinct part of the population, and being adolescent a more
distinct and self-conscious experience. As it became part of the social
structure of modern society, adolescence also became an important

stage of the individual's biography—an indeterminate period of being neither child nor adult that created its own problems. Any society
that excludes youth from adult work, and offers them what Erikson
calls a "moratorium"—time and space to try out identities and life-
styles—and at the same time demands extended schooling as the route
to success is likely to turn adolescence into a "struggle for self."[35] It
is also likely to run the risk of increasing numbers of mixed-up, rebellious youth.[36]

But, in fact, the classic picture of adolescent storm and stress is not
universal. Studies of adolescents in America and other industrialized
societies suggest that extreme rebellion and rejection of parents,
flamboyant behavior, and psychological turmoil do not describe most
adolescents, even today.[37] Media images of the youth of the 1980s and
1990s as a deeply troubled, lost generation beset by crime, drug abuse,
and teenage pregnancy are also largely mistaken.[38]

Although sexual activity and experimenting with drugs and alcohol
have become common among middle-class young people, drug use
has actually declined in recent years. Disturbing as these practices
are for parents and other adults, they apparently do not interfere
with normal development for most adolescents. Nevertheless, for a
significant minority, sex and drugs add complications to a period of
development during which a young person's life can easily go awry—
temporarily or for good.

More typically, for most young people, the teen years are marked
by mild rebelliousness and moodiness—enough to make it a difficult
period for parents, but not one of a profound parent-child generation gap or of deep alienation from conventional values. These ordinary tensions of family living through adolescence are exacerbated
in times of rapid social change, when the world adolescents confront
is vastly different from the one in which their parents came of age.
Always at the forefront of social change, adolescents in industrial
societies inevitably bring discomfort to their elders, who "wish to see
their children's adolescence as an enactment of the retrospectively
distorted memory of their own. . . . But such intergenerational continuity can occur only in the rapidly disappearing isolation of the des-
ert or the rain forest."[39]

If adolescence is a creation of modern culture, that culture has also
been shaped by adolescence. Adolescents, with their music, fads, fashions, and conflicts, not only are conspicuous, but reflect a state of
mind that often extends beyond the years designated for them. The
adolescent mode of experience—accessible to people of any age—is
marked by "exploration, becoming, growth, and pain."[40]

Since the nineteenth century, for example, the coming-of-age novel has become a familiar literary genre. Patricia Spacks observes that while Victorian authors looked back at adolescence from the perspective of adulthood, twentieth-century novelists since James Joyce and D. H. Lawrence have become more intensely identified with their young heroes, writing not from a distance but from "deep inside the adolescence experience."[41] The novelist's use of the adolescent to symbolize the artist as romantic outsider mirrors a more general cultural tendency. As Phillipe Ariès observes, "Our society has passed from a period which was ignorant of adolescence to a period in which adolescence is the favorite age. We now want to come to it early and linger in it as long as possible."[42]

The Discovery of Adulthood

Middle age is the latest life stage to be discovered, and the notion of mid-life crisis recapitulates the storm-and-stress conception of adolescence. Over the course of the twentieth century, especially during the years after World War II, a developmental conception of childhood became institutionalized in public thought. Parents took it for granted that children passed through ages, stages, and phases: the terrible twos, the teenage rebel. In recent years the idea of development has been increasingly applied to adults, as new stages of adult life are discovered. Indeed, much of the psychological revolution of recent years—the tendency to look at life through psychological lenses—can be understood in part as the extension of the developmental approach to adulthood.

In 1976 Gail Sheehy's best-selling *Passages* popularized the concept of mid-life crisis. Sheehy argued that every individual must pass through such a watershed, a time when we reevaluate our sense of self, undergo a crisis, and emerge with a new identity. Failure to do so, she warned, can have dire consequences. The book was the most influential popular attempt to apply to adults the ages-and-stages approach to development that had long been applied to children. Ironically, this came about just as historians were raising questions about the universality of those stages.

Despite its popularity, Sheehy's book, and the research she reported in it, have come under increasing criticism. "Is the mid-life crisis, if it exists, more than a warmed-over identity crisis?" asked one review of the research literature on mid-life.[43] In fact, there is little or no evidence for the notion that adults pass through a series of sharply defined stages, or a series of crises that must be resolved before passing from one stage to the next.

Nevertheless, the notion of a mid-life crisis caught on because it reflected shifts in adult experience across the life course. Most people's decisions about marriage and work are no longer irrevocably made at one fateful turning point on the brink of adulthood. The choices made at twenty-one may no longer fit at forty or fifty—the world has changed; parents, children, and spouses have changed; working life has changed. The kind of issue that makes adolescence problematic—the array of choices and the need to fashion a coherent, continuous sense of self in the midst of all this change—recurs throughout adulthood. As a Jules Feiffer cartoon concludes, "Maturity is a phase, but adolescence is forever."

Like the identity crisis of adolescence, the concept of mid-life crisis appears to reflect the experience of the more educated and advantaged. Those with more options in life are more likely to engage in the kind of introspection and reappraisal of previous choices that make up the core of the mid-life crisis. Such people realize that they will never fulfill their earlier dreams, or that they have gotten what they wanted and find they are still not happy. But as the Berkeley longitudinal data show, even in that segment of the population, mid-life crisis is far from the norm.[44] People who have experienced fewer choices in the past, and have fewer options for charting new directions in the future, are less likely to encounter a mid-life crisis. Among middle Americans, life is dominated by making ends meet, coping with everyday events, and managing unexpected crises.

While there may be no fixed series of stages or crises adults must pass through, middle age or mid-life in our time does have some unique features that make it an unsettled time, different from other periods in the life course as well as from mid-life in earlier eras. First, as we saw earlier, middle age is the first period in which most people today confront death, illness, and physical decline. It is also an uneasy age because of the increased importance of sexuality in modern life. Sexuality has come to be seen as the core of our sense of self, and sexual fulfillment as the center of the couple relationship. In mid-life, people confront the decline of their physical attractiveness, if not of their sexuality.

There is more than a passing resemblance between the identity problems of adolescence and the issues that fall under the rubric of "mid-life crisis." In a list of themes recurring in the literature on the experience of identity crisis, particularly in adolescence, the psychologist Roy Baumeister includes: feelings of emptiness, feelings of vagueness, generalized malaise, anxiety, self-consciousness.[45] These symptoms describe not only adolescent and mid-life crises but what Erikson has labeled identity problems—or what has, of late, been considered narcissism.

Consider, for example, Heinz Kohut's description of patients suffering from what he calls narcissistic personality disorders. They come to the analyst with vague symptoms, but eventually focus on feelings about the self—emptiness, vague depression, being drained of energy, having no "zest" for work or anything else, shifts in self-esteem, heightened sensitivity to the opinions and reactions of others, feeling unfulfilled, a sense of uncertainty and purposelessness. "It seems on the face of it," observes the literary critic Steven Marcus, "as if these people are actually suffering from what was once called unhappiness."[46]

The New Aging

Because of the extraordinary revolution in longevity, the proportion of elderly people in modern industrial societies is higher than it has ever been. This little-noticed but profound transformation affects not just the old but families, an individual's life course, and society as a whole. We have no cultural precedents for the mass of the population reaching old age. Further, the meaning of *old age* has changed— indeed, it is a life stage still in process, its boundaries unclear. When he came into office at the age of sixty-four, George Bush did not seem like an old man. Yet when Franklin Roosevelt died at the same age, he did seem to be "old."

President Bush illustrates why gerontologists in recent years have had to revise the meaning of "old." He is a good example of what they have termed the "young old" or the "new elders"; the social historian Peter Laslett uses the term "the third age."[47] Whatever it is called, it represents a new stage of life created by the extension of the life course in industrialized countries. Recent decades have witnessed the first generations of people who live past sixty-five and remain healthy, vigorous, alert, and, mostly due to retirement plans, financially independent. These people are "pioneers on the frontier of age," observed the journalist Frances Fitzgerald, in her study of Sun City, a retirement community near Tampa, Florida, "people for whom society had as yet no set of expectations and no vision."[48]

The meaning of the later stages of life remains unsettled. Just after gerontologists had marked off the "young old"—people who seemed more middle-aged than old—they had to devise a third category, the "oldest old," to describe the fastest-growing group in the population, people over eighty-five. Many if not most of these people are like Tithonus, the mythical figure who asked the gods for eternal life but forgot to ask for eternal youth as well. For them, the gift of long life has come at the cost of chronic disease and disability.

The psychological impact of this unheralded longevity revolution has largely been ignored, except when misconstrued. The fear of age, according to Christopher Lasch, is one the chief symptoms of this culture's alleged narcissism. But when people expected to die in their forties or fifties, they didn't have to face the problem of aging. Alzheimer's disease, for example, now approaching epidemic proportions, is an ironic by-product of the extension of the average life span. When living to seventy or eighty is a realistic prospect, it makes sense to diet and exercise, to eat healthy foods, and to make other "narcissistic" investments in the self.

Further "the gift of mass longevity," the anthropologist David Plath argues, has been so recent, dramatic, and rapid that it has become profoundly unsettling in all postindustrial societies: "If the essential cultural nightmare of the nineteenth century was to be in poverty, perhaps ours is to be old and alone or afflicted with terminal disease."[49]

Many people thus find themselves in life stages for which cultural scripts have not yet been written; family members face one another in relationships for which tradition provides little guidance. "We are stuck with awkward-sounding terms like 'adult children' and ... 'grandson-in-law.' "[50] And when cultural rules are ambiguous, emotional relationships can become tense or at least ambivalent.

A study of five-generation families in Germany reveals the confusion and strain that result when children and parents are both in advanced old age—for example, a great-great-grandmother and her daughter, who is herself a great-grandmother. Who has the right to be old? Who should take care of whom?[51] Similarly, Plath, who has studied the problems of mass longevity in Japan, finds that even in that familistic society the traditional meaning of family roles has been put into question by the stretching out of the life span. In the United States, some observers note that people moving into retirement communities sometimes bring their parents to live with them. Said one disappointed retiree: "I want to enjoy my grandchildren; I never expected that when I was a grandparent I'd have to look after my parents."[52]

FROM LIFE BY CHANCE TO
THE NEW CERTAINTY

As lives have grown longer and particular life stages have been dis-covered or changed across the twentieth century, family relationships have been reshaped. But these are not the only ways in which indi-vidual experience across the life course has been altered in recent decades. The life course itself has become a more salient part of social reality than it was in the past. As John Demos observes, "our passage through life is much more highly codified—and self-conscious—than was normally the case for our forebears."[53]

In America, as in other modern industrial societies, the movement of a person through life has become more *individualized* and at the same time more *institutionalized*.[54] We must choose an identity out of the array of possible selves available. The life course is the framework about which we weave our subjective sense of self; and at the same time, it has also become part of the structure of modern social insti-tutions like school and work.

The modern self is an autobiographical self—one that experiences its life as a narrative, a story. Marti Kohli, a scholar of the life course, notes a shift in the idea of selfhood starting at the end of the eigh-teenth century. Earlier, autobiographies had been organized around frameworks external to the person, such as historical or seasonal events. They later came to be organized around a developmental, individualized conception of the self. In Germany, the beginnings of psychology as a field of study overlapped with autobiography; the first psychological journal in Germany consisted mostly of autobio-graphical reports.[55]

A heightened awareness of age is a central part of the modern self. Some of today's elderly, especially those not born in this country, may recall a time when people were not sure of their exact ages or dates of birth, and no one made a fuss about birthdays.[56] In the last hundred years we have been moving from a society where a person's age and stage of life were vague and blurry categories that mattered little to one with a strong sense of a "normative life course" orga-nized around age as a yardstick for evaluating our own and other people's progress through life.

Thus, we know without thinking that a child who enters first grade at the age of eight is behind schedule, that a bride of sixteen is marrying very young, that a forty-two-year-old man is too old to be a rock star but probably too young to be a president, that a forty-five-year-old man who leaves his wife and career and becomes an artist is having a "mid-life crisis."

This increasing "chronologization" of the life course[57] is a feature of modern industrial societies. It is rooted in the growth of schools, social welfare institutions, and legal regulations—for example, drivers' licenses, pension plans, and social security. In recent years, after a long trend toward more standardized age norms, the life course has become less standardized and more individuated, as more women become mothers for the first time past the age of forty, more people go to college at sixty, and ninety-year-olds run in marathons. But as Kohli points out, "the successful institutionalization of the life course is the basis for the present individualizing departure from it."[58]

Contrary to the myth of a stable past, our ancestors did not progress through life in an orderly way. For example, before 1900 only about 40 percent of the female population in the United States followed the "normal" family cycle of leaving home, marrying, raising children, surviving to age fifty with one's spouse. The rest never lived to a marriageable age, never married, died before having children or before their children were grown, or were widowed before age fifty.[59]

The major shift has been from "life by chance" to "the new certainty."[60] The major sources of unpredictability were not only high rates of illness and mortality across the life span but economic uncertainty. The unpredictability of the life course was most apparent in the way young adults left home and started their own lives.

The transition to adulthood consists of a number of steps: leaving school, starting work, leaving home, getting married. Outside the ranks of the economically secure, middle-class, young people in the nineteenth century could not follow regular timetables for these transitions because their decisions were dominated by family needs. In an age when most families lived near the margins of subsistence, parents considered their children an economic resource throughout their lives. Before the era of welfare-state safety nets, death, accident, sickness, unemployment, and other life crises often made it necessary for young people to drop out of school, put off marriage plans, and return to the parental home.[61]

Some of us may look back on these arrangements as evidence of the strong, loving families we have sadly lost. Yet as the historian

Tamara Hareven and others have noted, these obligations were often based on an "instrumental" view of family relationships, rather than on bonds of personal affection or sentiment.[62] The sacrifice of an education, or a chance at marriage, was not always borne lightly by those who had to make it. Ironically, the middle-class family, which cultivated intensely emotional bonds with children, granted those children greater independence in shaping their own lives.

In the twentieth century, lower mortality rates, improvements in public health, higher living standards, and the growth of insurance and pensions freed families from dependence on their offspring. The pattern of reliance on adult children persists to this day in many working-class, ethnic, and rural families, but for the majority of the population, the transition to adulthood—to work and marriage— came to be uncoupled from the needs of the family of origin, based more on the choices of the young person and the needs of his or her new family.

The modern life course began to take shape in the early decades of the twentieth century. The nineteenth-century pattern of various, often meandering paths to adulthood narrowed to a single path that led through an age-graded educational system. In 1910 half of all fifteen-year-old boys and a quarter of fifteen-year-old girls were in the labor force. By the 1930s, however, attending high school was defined as part of the normal life course for all young people, not just the well-to-do and those with academic aptitude.[63]

The new "linear life course" ideal that developed after the 1920s prescribed an orderly progression through life. A young man would start work after high school or college, get married, set up a house- hold, have children, and be settled for life. A woman would work only until marriage, then settle down to keep house and raise chil- dren. The Depression and World War II, however, caused massive disruptions in these expectations.

The young adults of the 1940s and 1950s, facing few obstacles, rushed through the transition to adulthood. In pursuit of "normal- ity," they followed a life course unlike that of any other generation, reducing the age of marriage to an all-time low and producing the baby boom. The sequence of transitions—ending school, starting work, getting married, having children—moved closer together in time. This script for entering adulthood, which consolidated in the 1950s, is the norm against which current generations of American young people are judged as a "postponed generation" lacking "com- mitment."

What currently looks like a "disorderly" transition to adulthood, however, resembles the life-course patterns that prevailed at the turn of the century. Of course, the reasons are different today—the seeming erratic patterns are due to individual choice rather than a lack of choice. Yet as the historical sociologist John Modell and others have argued, there is little evidence that the new patterns mean that young adults since the 1970s have been rejecting marriage and family life. Rather, they are altering the timing of marriage and parenthood, fashioning family decisions to meet their individual needs and desires and changes in the larger society.

Partly, their shift resulted from problems with the "ideal" pattern of family formation that did not become apparent until it was fully realized. The tightly linked sequence of events that were expected to be completed by the end of adolescence was ill suited, economically and psychologically, to life in a postindustrial, mass-longevity society. Not only have beginning educational requirements for most jobs increased but the pace of technological change has reduced the "half-life" of occupational qualifications, making skills and knowledge obsolete.[64]

The 1950s pattern of family formation required marriage as the price for living away from home and having sexual relations—at least for women. Early marriage, linked to early parenthood, forestalled the education of both spouses, especially the wife. And in an era when almost half of all young women married while still in their teens, women's chances for any post–high school education were slim.[65]

By the 1960s, both sexes were staying in school longer. Mass attendance at college, as mass attendance at high school had done earlier, was creating a new stage of life—a kind of extension of adolescence.[66] Single young adults could set up their own households, have sex, live together. Middle-class parents who had themselves followed the "tight" schedule of family formation no longer thought it desirable for their sons and daughters to rush into marriage and parenthood in their late teens and early twenties.

The other major change of the 1970s—the vast increase in divorce—may also be viewed as part of a revised life-course script. Divorce became part of the family system not because marriage was devalued or divorce taken lightly but rather because the new marriage system placed an extremely high value on marital happiness. Divorce is not, for most people, an escape from the bonds of marriage but a means of correcting a mistaken choice of partner—a "recycling mechanism permitting individuals a second (and sometimes a third and fourth) chance to upgrade their marital situation."[67]

While many of the life-course changes of recent years are linked to increased choice, changes in the economy since the 1970s have worked in the opposite direction to constrain choice and place obstacles in the way of young adults who try to fulfill their own and their parents' expectations. The stable, unionized jobs that enabled young blue-collar workers in the 1950s and 1960s to support a family have declined, making marginal men out of their sons. The disappearance of manual jobs from American cities has had devastating effects on the ability of young black people to form families.

In middle-class families, economic constriction has contributed to what has been called the "boomerang" generation, the "Hamlet syndrome," or the "incompletely launched young adult syndrome": young adults who deviate from their parents' expectations by failing to launch careers and become successfully independent adults, and who may even come home to crowd their parents' empty nests.[68] While parents and offspring may blame themselves and one another, treating the problem as a personal one, the changes are grounded in shifts in economy in recent decades: the parents came to adulthood in a time when there was an expanding array of secure, civil service–type managerial, professional, and technical jobs; the children came of age in a time when such jobs were rarer.

THE POLITICS OF PERSONHOOD

Aside from this complex set of demographic, structural, and cultural changes that have created a more individualized life course and a heightened sense of self, there is a political dimension, variously described as a "rights revolution"[69] or the "democratization of personhood."[70] At the center of this shift is the claiming of political and cultural rights by disadvantaged groups—from blacks and other minorities, to women, to gay people, to the handicapped, to the elderly.

The democratization of personhood goes beyond rights of citizenship, extending to all forms of authority and hierarchy. Within the family, we have witnessed a transition from what has been called the "positional" family to the "personal" or person-centered family. The terms stem from research by the British sociologist Basil Bernstein on child rearing, language, and social class.[71] The positional family emphasizes roles, status, hierarchy; it values conforming to rules and

respecting authority. The personal family emphasizes the individuality of each family member, feelings and motives, the reasons for
rules.

The positional family is not necessarily authoritarian or cold, but
it does observe clear boundaries between age groups and sex roles
and its structure of authority is clear-cut and, in a sense, impersonal.
Thus, a child in a positional family would be controlled by statements
such as: "Little boys don't cry"; "Children don't talk to their fathers
like that"; "You are not old enough to do it"; "People like us don't
act that way"; and "You will do what I tell you to do."

In the more democratic personal family, the child would be controlled by appeals to feelings, motives, and reasons. For example:
"Daddy will be pleased if you do that"; "Don't do that, because I have
a headache and the noise bothers me"; or "How would *you* feel if
your sister took *your* toy?"

An example from an episode on the television series "Thirtysomething" helps illustrate the contrast between the two patterns: Ethan,
a nine- or ten-year old boy, shuts himself in his room, refusing to
join his family and guests for Thanksgiving dinner. In a traditional,
or positional family, this might be treated as a serious breach of
discipline and manners. The child might be ordered to take his place
at the table; if he refused, he might be punished. In Elliot and Nancy's
personal family, Ethan's refusal is seen as a symptom of a psychological problem. Their concern is with the child's feelings and adjust-
ment, rather than with the behavior itself, and they carry on with
their dinner without him.

Bernstein and others have found that while the positional family
is found in both the working and the middle classes, the personal
family is a middle-class phenomenon, linked to the educational level
of the parents and their educational aspirations for the child. Bernstein found it especially prevalent among the new postwar middle
class employed by the university, the large corporation, and the government bureaucracy. But the personal, democratic style of family
can be traced back to the British aristocracy of the eighteenth
century[72] and to the upper middle class in the Victorian era.[73]

In the past several decades, there has been a gradual shift toward
the personal family. Alwin has observed a marked shift in child-
rearing attitudes away from an emphasis on obedience and toward
an emphasis on autonomy, which he also links to increasing levels of
education in the population.[74] But this is not an unmixed blessing.
Both the positional and personal family modes have costs as well as

benefits. In positional families, the roles and rules are clear; the issue is whether or not the child behaves, not what he or she feels. Talk in such families is not usually "a means for a voyage from one self to another."[75]

The paradox in personal families is that, while the autonomy and unique value of the child is celebrated, more of the child's self is subject to the parents' scrutiny and control. The sociologist Melvin Kohn has pointed out the complex and demanding messages in middle-class child rearing: "the child is to act appropriately, not because his parents tell him to, but because he wants to. Not conformity to authority, but inner control; not because you're told to, but because you take the other person into consideration."[76]

It can even be argued that the personal style of family life creates a double bind. For example, a college student in therapy reported that his parents had always insisted that he brush his teeth carefully and regularly. But they also told him that brushing his teeth regularly, on his own initiative, would be clear proof that he was grown up and independent. In effect, they were presenting him with a paradoxical communication: "If you do not obey, we shall be angry with you, but if you obey only because we are telling you, we shall also be angry, because you should be independent."[77] The dilemma posed by this demand is not mitigated by the fact that it is inherent in middle-class socialization or by the fact that most people, unlike the student with the toothbrushing problem, manage not to get caught on the horns of it.

The rise of the personal family can be seen as part of a wider shift in interpersonal relations. Abram de Swaan argues that much of what Lasch and others condemn as narcissism reflects the shift from "management by command" to "management by negotiation."[78] The new, less formal, more democratic mode of managing interpersonal relationships applies not only to parents and children but to men and women inside and outside the family, as well as in the workplace and in government.

Parents, bosses, managers, bureaucrats, prison wardens, and police chiefs—think of Captain Frank Furillo of "Hill Street Blues"—are no longer expected to rule simply by issuing commands or threats. Rather, they must operate with at least some consent from the managed or governed, at least giving the appearance of taking their wishes and desires into consideration. In turn, the managed have what Clecak calls an "enlarged" sense of their own rights and entitlements.[79]

The shift from "command" to "negotiation" was also grounded in a change in the nature of work. In the factories that symbolized the earlier stages of industrial society, most jobs required relatively low levels of skill and the factories could be managed from the top down. The postindustrial society, with its more complex organization and demands for a more highly trained and educated work force, necessitates a different kind of manager, one more skilled in human relations.

In many ways, the new morality of interpersonal relations is more stringent than the old. It is a mistake to believe that restraints on behavior and emotional expression have been abandoned, and that anything goes. Instead, certain socially disruptive emotions like anger and jealousy have come to be disapproved of, and suppressed more than they were in the past. "The restraint on violent behavior has not lessened," de Swaan observes, "the inhibition upon self-aggrandizement has probably increased, and the discipline in the handling of time, money, goods and the body has grown."[80]

Despite the widespread impression that family violence has increased, there is little clear evidence to support it. In fact, statistics on child abuse and wife battering may reflect shifting definitions of acceptable behavior within the family, increasing rights granted to women and children, and a growing intolerance for hitting and slapping for any reason.[81]

And despite the relaxation of sexual rules, there are new rules for taking into account the wishes and consent of one's sexual partner. For example, in sexual matters, men now have less permission to be mindlessly hedonistic than in the past; they can now take fewer of what used to be called "liberties" with women: "Rape, roughness, scorn and degradation, so common and acceptable for employers to inflict upon servants and factory girls, or customers upon prostitutes only a few generations ago, have become more distasteful to the general public."[82]

Changes in the law reflect the new, more stringent standards for consent in sexual matters. Consider the new concept of sexual harassment. Once simply taken for granted as a tradeoff women had to risk to be able to work, it has become not just unacceptable but unlawful. Similarly, penalties for rape have become more severe, and rates of conviction have risen. Many states have eliminated the cautionary instruction once required of judges to deliver to juries, that an accusation of rape "is easily made, and once made, difficult to defend against, even if the person accused is innocent." This instruction put the rape victim on trial, and resulted in a very low conviction rate.

Until recently, as the legal scholar Susan Estrich observes, a man could assume that he could force a woman to have sex against her will; and he wouldn't be prosecuted for rape as long as he knew her and didn't inflict severe physical injury. In effect, although the letter of the law said otherwise, "a woman's body was effectively presumed to be offered at least to any appropriate man she knows, lives near, accepts a drink from, or works for."[83] The law's casual treatment of such cases of "simple rape" is now changing.* Further, the current debates over date rape on college campuses reinforce the notion that attitudes toward what is acceptable male sexual behavior are being transformed.

The new management style and the new morality of dignity and personhood have not made life easier—certainly not for men, especially white men. But regardless of gender, race, age, and so on, we all have to navigate through life without the social dogmas that guided life in the past. Further, although the new relational styles promote greater equality and mutual respect, "negotiated consent" can mask real inequalites of power; negotiations between parents and children, husbands and wives, employers and employees, occur in a world in which one party generally has more power and options than the other.

The new styles also make increasing demands on personality and make intimate relations less predictable. In the workplace as well as at home, simply following or giving orders is no longer enough; new forms of self-control are necessary. Managers must display concern for the desires of those they manage; employees must develop the skills of assertiveness. Both must be sensitive to a wide range of interpersonal signals, and know how to respond to them. Temperamental quirks may now prove to be greater assets or liabilities than they were in the past. For example, among the subjects of the Berkeley longitudinal study, children with irritable, explosive temperaments and those who were extremely shy had less successful courses through life than those with more modulated personalities.[84] Little wonder, under these circumstances, that people scrutinize themselves, become introspective, consult with therapists, and frame their problems in psychological terms.

---

*California has eliminated the "resistance requirement" which made it necessary for a woman to show that she had physically resisted her attacker in order to sustain a rape charge; under the law a woman who was too afraid to fight hard was thus not considered to have been raped.

THE PSYCHOLOGICAL SOCIETY

There has indeed been a "psychologization" of modern culture. Between 1965 and 1981, the number and proportion of doctorates awarded in psychology in the United States increased dramatically, as did the number of psychiatrists. The number of new books on psychology tripled between 1960 and 1980, exceeding the general growth in publishing.[85] These indicators of a trend are confirmed in listening to everyday conversations, looking at bookstore shelves, and watching talk shows on television: psychological and sociological knowledge about personality, child development, and family relations pervade the everyday awareness of ordinary people. "Marriage and the family would not be what they are today," observes Anthony Giddens, "were they not thoroughly 'sociologised' and 'psychologised.' "[86]

The latest burst of interest in psychological matters is a continuation of a trend that began earlier in the century, and took off during the 1920s with the popular discovery of Freud. Writing of the extraordinary speed with which Freudian notions became the "dominant idiom" for talking about personalities and relationships, the social theorist Ernest Gellner observes: "There has been nothing like this since the spread of the potato and of maize."[87]

The contemporary search for the self and the rising demand for psychotherapy reflect not a new personality structure, or brainwashing by the psychological establishment, but a response to changes in social structures and institutions. As the primal anxieties that plagued earlier generations receded, issues of identity, intimacy, and human relationships have come to the fore. The realm of human relationships, observes Gellner, has replaced the natural world as the focus of our anxiety and sense of precariousness: "The price of this liberation from forcibly and/or ideologically ascribed identities, statuses, rituals, practices, employments and family links, is, notoriously a sense of disorientation and insecurity."[88]

While the dominant idiom for discussing it has changed, this concern with the inner life is not new. The exploration of the self is one of the most highly legitimated aspects of Western culture. No other culture, for example, has a practice comparable to the Catholics' confession, observes the historian Lynn White, in which individuals of every social class examine their consciences and whisper their sins to a priest: "And since knowing ourselves is the cornerstone of individualism, no other society has so motivated the development of self-conscious individuals at every social level."[89]

With the rise of Protestantism, the examination of conscience took new forms, among them the practice of the methodical regulation of life through a process of continual self-examination. In the sixteenth and seventeenth centuries there emerged a new sense of self, distinct from the religious examination of conscience. Lionel Trilling notes that something like a "mutation in human nature" took place in Western society during this time.[90]

People became aware of their individuality, especially their inner psychological life, in a way that differed from the kind of self-scrutiny religion had always fostered. Large, bright mirrors came to be widely available, portraits and self-portraits began to be painted, and people began to keep diaries and write autobiographies. In keeping with the new distinction between the outward self and the private, inner self, the notions of privacy and domesticity within the home grew, and marriage and family were newly honored as being central to the good life.[91]

Over the past century, the privileges and the burdens of choice spread outward and downward from the upper middle class, and from adolescence to later stages in the life course. We have gone from a society that gave most people their self-definition, to one in which most people developed a self-definition at the beginning of adulthood, to one in which, for many people, a large part of life is occupied by attempting to answer the question, "Who am I?"

Some people have no trouble answering the question, like a character in a short story by Lionel Trilling who, when asked to write an essay on "Who I Am and Why I Came to Dwight College," wrote: "I am Arthur J. Casebeer. My father is Arthur J. Casebeer and my grandfather was Arthur J. Casebeer before him. My mother is Nina Wimble Casebeer. Both of them are college graduates and my father is in insurance. I was born in St. Louis 18 years ago and we still make our residence there." Another essay is written by a tall, awkward, badly dressed boy named Tertan. It begins: "I think, therefore I am, but who am I? Tertan I am, but what is Tertan? Of this time, of that place, of some parentage, what does it matter?"[92]

Most people fall between these extremes, neither closing off the identity question nor becoming undone by it. In what John Hewitt calls a "pragmatic strategy" of self-construction, we cultivate a personal identity as separate and unique individuals, as well as a social identity as members of a family, an ethnic or religious group, and other forms of community.[93]

Nevertheless, people in complex, loosely bound societies face many choices for which there is no obvious or correct way of choosing. Unlike the Arthur J. Casebeers of this world or those who practice the "exclusive strategy of self-construction," submerging their personal identity or sense of self in a single community—Evangelical Christian, Orthodox Jewish, or radical—the pragmatic directly face the inherent complexity, ambiguity, and ambivalence of modern life and come up with no answers.

Having to deal with choice and uncertainty makes it necessary to "get in touch with" inner thoughts and feelings. With few clear guidelines, the individual must look inward to make choices, a task that is not always easy or successful: "Obstructed access to the inner world leaves one stranded in an empty and monotonous play of social masks. The inability to escape from the incommunicable sphere of inner experience locks away the individual in a prison of silence."[94]

In recent years, the range of choices has increased still more. Many aspects of family life that were once taken for granted have become matters of choice: whether to marry or simply to live together; whether and when to have children; whether, if a couple has trouble conceiving, to try infertility treatments, adoption, or any of the assisted reproductive technologies or surrogate motherhood; whether, if one is a single woman, to wait for the right man to come along, or to have a child without a husband.

The result of all this social complexity is inner complexity. Our emotional life, observes the psychologist Eugene Gendlin, has become more intricate. The "feelings" we are likely to try to get in touch with are not simple emotions or desires, but complex, murky mixtures of feelings. The clear-cut emotions went the way of the clear-cut social roles and rules that used to guide everyday life.

For example, "wholehearted righteous anger" is what we feel when we are not being treated the way we should be, not getting our "due." "You can't get angry whenever you like," observes Gendlin: "Somebody has to do something to make you feel angry."[95] Yet, with the old roles gone, it is no longer clear what our "due" is in our roles as men, women, parents, sons, daughters, brothers and sisters, in-laws, and so on—not to mention our complicated new roles created by divorce, remarriage, living together, and the like.

What's more, in recent times the cultural rules for anger have made it harder than in the past to deal with angry feelings. We are not "supposed" to get deeply angry at those close to us; we tend to see marital anger, for example, as a sign that the marriage in trouble. We are not supposed to express anger nakedly, but to "fight fair" or "talk it out," in the belief that communication will solve the problem.[96]

The incident from "Thirtysomething" cited earlier illustrates Gend-lin's notions about emotional intricacy. In earlier eras, if a child re-fused to come to the dinner table when asked, the parents were likely to feel that they were not receiving their "due"; they might even feel it was their obligation as good parents to "break the will" of the child who would disobey them. Instead, Elliot and Nancy experience a murky mixture of concern about Ethan's psychological state (he has had difficulty "adjusting" to his parents' reconciliation after their divorce), embarrassment before their guests, and probably some an-ger at Ethan to which they don't feel they are entitled.

CONCLUSION

In an article in the *New England Journal of Medicine*, the psychiatrist Arthur Barsky discusses "The Paradox of Health": although the col-lective health of Americans has improved dramatically over the past thirty years, it has not been accompanied by an increase in subjective feelings of healthiness. People report less and less satisfaction with their health, more symptoms, more illness.[97]

Why should this be so? First, Barsky argues, the more people who are saved from sudden death in childhood or early adulthood due to infectious diseases like TB, the more who will live to experience the chronic, disabling diseases of old age. Further, the greater emphasis on health today, and media publicity devoted to diseases, has led to greater self-scrutiny and increased awareness of symptoms and feel-ings of illness. Finally, medicine's great successes have led to a prob-lem of rising expectations: we assume we will remain healthy if we pursue healthy living, and that a cure exists for whatever ails us.

A similar paradox affects our psychological well-being. The lives of the majority of people in modern societies are no longer dominated by poverty, poor health, ignorance, unemployment, or sixty-four-hour work weeks. This is not to deny the obvious existence, especially in America, of serious social problems—but such problems are no lon-ger seen as inevitable; we believe that something should be done about them.

Most people manage to define an identity for themselves, find meaning in life, and maintain attachments to family and friends. Oth-ers find it difficult to find their way through a maze of choices in work, love, and friendship. Some fall through the cracks into loneli-ness, stress, alienation, despair. As Peter Berger and others have pointed out, intellectuals may be peculiarly vulnerable to the malaise of modern life—more removed from ordinary people and from their own roots, more attuned to cultural contradictions.[98] It may be that the true Narcissus of our time is the critic who projects his own experience onto the social world and fails to recognize himself in his own reflection.

C H A P T E R 7

Backing into the Future

One of the many mysteries of politics in the 1980's: How could a time in which feminist and permissive values continued to have so much power be considered a "conservative era" at all?   —E. J. Dionne, Jr.
                                                      Why Americans Hate Politics

In the summer of 1990, President Bush nominated a previously unheard-of New Hampshire judge, David Souter, to replace the retiring Supreme Court Justice William Brennan. A prime goal of Reagan-era social conservatives—overthrowing the *Roe v. Wade* decision—seemed close to being realized. Yet in the wake of the Supreme Court's decision restricting abortion rights the previous summer, a powerful pro-choice movement had sprung into action and had scored significant political victories. Bush could no longer nominate someone openly opposed to *Roe v. Wade*. Instead, the person he chose was quickly labeled a "stealth candidate"—a mystery man with no paper trail to reveal his legal philosophy or opinions.

By the late 1980s it was clear that the Reagan era's politics of nostalgia had not restored the "traditional family." Despite a backlash against the values of the 1960s and early 1970s, mainstream American attitudes toward women's roles, the family, and sexuality had been transformed. "The family," like the flag, had become a national icon,

179

yet wives and mothers had not left the workplace, divorce rates had leveled off but had not been slashed, sex had not been confined to the marriage bed, and gays had not returned to the closet.

In a multitude of ways, the changes were woven into the fabric of everyday life: on television, in women's presence in nearly every field of work, in how people talked about sexuality, in the words exchanged between men and women. "The word *sexist*," writes the political analyst E. J. Dionne, would have been incomprehensible thirty years ago. Now ... most people think that sexism exists, and most think it's wrong."[1]

The cultural civil war over the family persisted, but without the intensity of early 1980s. Family and social policy issues—child care, parental leave, homelessness, poverty—moved back onto the national agenda. But just as the country seemed once again on the verge of addressing the disorienting social changes of recent times, America's domestic problems grew worse and the means of addressing them were reduced. The huge deficits that had piled up in the 1980s stymied efforts to launch new policies.

The waning years of the twentieth century bear an uncanny resemblance to the "gilded age" of 1877–1900. Then as now, serious problems resulted from rapid social and economic change. Yet the political system, split by conflicts within and between parties, seemed unable to respond. Then as now, American families were in transition; a passionate ideological debate raged over what had happened to family life and what should be done in the future.

A hundred years ago, progressives and conservatives alike worried about changing social values. Stories of violent crime, child abuse, and sexual misconduct filled the media. Glittering wealth and middle-class comfort coexisted with shocking and widespread poverty. Meanwhile psychologists, physicians, and social critics raised alarming questions about the psychological effects of rapid, dislocating change.

Above all, they worried about the declining family. To a remarkable degree, current arguments recapitulate the terms of the earlier ones. Then as now, women had demanded and gained new freedoms, divorce rates had surged, birthrates had fallen, and the percentage of people who never married had reached an all-time high. At the center of the debate were questions about the meaning of family change and the future of the family, as well as about such issues as divorce, abortion, birth control, women's roles and rights, the relation between self and society. Complaints of "unfettered," "untrammeled," or "self-centered" individuals expressed widespread uneasiness that social bonds had frayed, that individuals were no longer willing to subordinate their own interests to those of family and community.[2] "The last fifty years," lamented one writer in 1887, "have apparently changed the marriage relation from a permanent and lifelong state to a union existing for the pleasure of the parties. The change ... is ... revolutionary."[3]

Concern about the family was part of a more general uneasiness about social change in the late Victorian era. Some observers of the time called their period the Age of Nervousness.[4] High levels of anxiety were reflected in high rates of alcohol and drug use—cocaine was the favored legal "nerve cure" drug of the 1890s.[5] Americans also turned to physical fitness, health foods, meditation, deep breathing, spiritualism, and hot tubs for peace of mind.

Social change seems inevitably to take people by surprise. Decades ago, the sociologist William Ogburn offered a striking metaphor. Human beings, he suggested, were like passengers in a bus barreling along at great speed. Yet everyone, even the driver, is facing backward; people cannot see where they are going, only where they have been.[6]

But while periods of major transformation in family life occur only rarely, the history of American family life suggests that change has been persistent. Across the twentieth century, for example, families have had to adapt to wars, depressions, inflation, periods of affluence, new technologies from the car to the movies to television to the birth control pill. Moreover, as citizens of a nation built on immigration, westward expansion, and geographic and social mobility, we have always been an "unsettled people."[7]

If change has been a constant in the history of the American family, so has the rhetoric of family crisis and breakdown. Since shortly after the Puritans landed, preachers, commentators, and social critics have been denouncing the declining family, the irresponsibility of parents, the waywardness of children—a wave of rhetoric that has continued without interruption into our own times. "I can think of no decade in the twentieth century," observes the historian Steven Schlossman, "when to experts and popular writers alike, the family did not appear on the verge of collapse (the pessimists) or of radical readjustment (the optimists). The vast majority of writers on the family have always seen its Armageddon just around the corner."[8]

We are currently experiencing the many discomforts of living through a time of transition, an era when long-standing cultural myths and assumptions, everyday habits, and institutional arrangements no longer fit the realities of our day-to-day lives. Yet those arrangements that would help cushion the effects of the multiple revolutions of our time—in women's roles, divorce, longevity, and other aspects of the life course—are not yet in place. We are in a period that fits the definition of *crisis* offered by the Italian Marxist theorist Antonio Gramsci: a time when "the old is dying and the new cannot be born."[9]

As a result of all this change, we are left without a clear-cut, shared picture in our heads of "the family." American families have always been more varied than stereotypical images would suggest, but the diversity of family arrangements today is unprecedented. Although the housewife/breadwinner family is far from dead, this mislabeled "traditional" family form is now in the minority, both as an ideal and as a practical reality.[10]

The most common household today is one with two adult wage earners. Single-parent families, along with the "blended" or "binu-clear" families of divorce and unmarried couples are among the next most common. In addition, gay and lesbian couples, with or without children, are increasingly demanding—and sometimes gaining—legal recognition as families.[11]

Then there are the complicated "recombinant" extended family networks created out of kinship, friendship, and the ex-kinship relationships left in the wake of divorce.[12] Meanwhile, families of all kinds coexist with a large and shifting population of singles, a group that most Americans are likely to be part of at least once in their lives.

Adding to the complexity are challenging questions about the meaning of parenthood raised by the new reproductive technologies. As one writer observes:

> It is now technologically possible to take sperm from any fertile male, an egg from any fertile female, join them by the *in vitro* fertil-ization process, and implant the resulting embryo in any womb. Af-ter birth, the child can be raised by any set of adults who may or may not have been participants in the child's conception and birth.[13]

It is little wonder that many Americans are anxious, confused, am-bivalent, "groping for a new paradigm of American family life"[14] yet looking back nostalgically at the "lost" family of the 1950s and seek-ing a villain to blame for its demise. Despite attempts to pin the decline of the family on peculiarly American forms of feminism or moral decay, on pathological defects in the American character, or on our government's social policies, our pattern of family changes has been repeated in all advanced industrial societies.[15] While lamentations about these developments may strike responsive chords in America, they only impede the kinds of pragmatic adjustments to family life in the modern age that have been made in other countries.

THE NEW RIGHT AND THE POLITICS OF NOSTALGIA

By the late 1970s, the startling shifts in marriage, fertility, and divorce rates that had occurred in the first half of the decade had leveled off. But by then the traditional family had been transformed, and with it our prevailing attitudes. All the signs seemed to show that the country was assimilating the changes and beginning to deal with the problems they had created. The 1980s, predicted Jessie Bernard, "will be a time of putting the pieces together to develop family structures suitable for this time and place, this day and age."[16]

Instead, of course, the country was on the brink of a decade-long attempt to turn back the clock and restore the traditional family. Like the passengers in Ogburn's bus, Americans as a nation spent most the 1980s backing into the future. President Reagan came to power promising to reinvent the America of the 1950s, with its breadwinner/housewife family, stable economy, and cold war consensus. But as we saw earlier, what appeared to be great changes in family life in the 1970s and 1980s was actually the resumption of long-term trends that had been interrupted during the deviant 1950s—so the attempt to resuscitate that strange decade was doomed to fail.

In retrospect, the conservative triumph in the election of 1980 seems far from inevitable. True, there was a backlash against feminism and sexual "permissiveness." But opinion data at the time and later revealed surprisingly little public support for specific conservative positions on abortion, women's rights, or sex education. Reagan owed his election less to the New Right social agenda than to the oil shortage, the hostage crisis, and double-digit inflation. "Without the economic troubles of the late Carter years," observes Dionne, "Ronald Reagan's presidency would have been impossible."[17]

Reagan himself was oddly cast in the role of champion of "traditional values" and a return to the Norman Rockwell family; a former Hollywood actor and the first divorced president, he was the son of an alcoholic father and a working mother. His relations with his children were often strained; one lived for a time, unmarried, with a rock singer, another became a writer for *Playboy*. He rarely attended church.[18] Carter, by contrast, was a born-again Christian with a close nuclear and extended family. He was a living example of the values Reagan espoused. Yet Carter was tolerant of the new attitudes and practices. Like the country itself, he embodied a mixture of tradition-alism and modernity.

Despite the lack of wide support for its positions on abortion and other issues, the New Right was able to mobilize its constituencies and seize the political initiative. The Moral Majority's Jerry Falwell and other right-wing Christian leaders were welcomed in the White House and courted by politicians. The pro-family New Right aimed to outlaw abortion; remove sex education from the schools and re-strict teenagers' access to birth control; restore school prayer; screen textbooks for references to "nontraditional" sex roles, evolution, and other ideas unacceptable to them; and dismantle the system of school busing for integration.

They believed that such measures would stem the threat to the traditional family represented by divorce, premarital sex, women in the workplace, single-parent families, and homosexuality. Along with Reagan, they believed that these reforms, combined with a military buildup and a renewed devotion to anticommunism, would restore the proud and dominant America of the 1950s.

Conservative pressure groups used their new political clout both locally and nationally to carry out these aims. Much of the conser-vative agenda was written into a legislative package called the "Family Protection Act," a measure repeatedly introduced into Congress, starting in 1979. Among other things, it would have narrowed the definition of child abuse by excluding corporal punishment on the part of parents or teachers, and denied federal funds for textbooks that "denigrated the role of women as it was traditionally under-stood"—one example of this "denigration" being a story that showed a young boy having fun cooking.[19]

But despite Reagan's close ties to the pro-family movement, he paid little more than lip service to their agenda and did not push the Family Protection Act or other New Right legislation through Con-gress. Nevertheless, he paid his debts to the social conservatives in-directly—through court appointments. When Reagan's term in office ended, he had left behind a series of "judicial time bombs"[20] that would continue to go off after he was gone. One of these was the *Webster* decision in the summer of 1989, allowing the states to restrict abortion. Ironically, this victory in the courts resulted in a number of conservative losses in the elections held in the fall of that year.

In the early 1980s, however, the "pro-family" conservative movement seemed to be more powerful than it actually was. The idea of
an America dominated by the Moral Majority was chilling to many
people; in 1985 Margaret Atwood's best-selling novel *The Handmaid's
Tale* captured this sense of dread in a frightening fantasy of religious
New Right principles carried to Orwellian extremes, a prospect that
at the time did not seem altogether farfetched.

Contrary to the claims implied by Falwell's name for his group, the
majority of Americans did not support the social agenda of the New
Right, even at the height of its political power.[21] Nevertheless, conservatives gave voice to widespread uneasiness about the sudden
changes in manners and morals. The new silent majority may have
supported abortion rights and feminist goals, yet they worried along
with the New Right about the erosion of family values. Uneasy about
the sexual revolution, drugs, and the increasingly explicit portrayals
of sex and violence in the media, they opposed the seeming normlessness and moral chaos that was widely seen to prevail in the wake
of the social upheavals of the 1960s and 1970s. Reagan's simple
themes resonated with much of the public; magically, he seemed to
embody these values even as his policies undermined them.

The religious New Right fell from political power as quickly as it
had risen. In the late 1980s, in a series of spectacular scandals as well
as some quieter defeats, it collapsed as a social movement.[22] Like the
fictional Elmer Gantry and certain real-life evangelists of the past,
Jim and Tammy Faye Bakker, Jimmy Swaggart, and a number of other
televangelists were undone by the old-fashioned sins of lust and greed.
And even Jerry Falwell, who had not been involved in any scandal,
became, according to opinion polls, one of the most disliked men in
America.[23]*

In the same year that brought about the downfall of the televangelists, Robert Bork lost his bid to become a Supreme Court justice.
The Senate debate on Bork's confirmation was the ideological turning point of the Reagan era; his defeat signaled a decline in conservatives' power to dominate the national debate on social issues. Both
his supporters and his opponents saw Bork's appointment as a way
to advance the New Right social agenda, from overturning *Roe v.
Wade* to returning religion to the public schools. With his distinguished record as a law professor, Federal Court of Appeals Judge

---

*One major reason for Falwell's negative public image was his vociferous support for
the government of South Africa at a time when the anti-apartheid movement was gaining
widespread support in America.

Bork seemed a candidate almost impossible for the Senate to reject. But his prolific writings proved to be his undoing.[24]

For example, Bork's opposition to the notion of a constitutional right to privacy had led him to reject not only the abortion decision but an earlier ruling that had overturned a state law banning the use of contraceptives by anyone, including married couples. This 1965 case, *Griswold v. Connecticut*, laid the groundwork for the reasoning in the abortion case.* In it, the Court ruled that the Constitution widely implies a right to privacy even if it does not explicitly state such a right. In his writings, Bork had attacked the Court's decision in *Griswold* and upheld the right of state legislatures to pass such intrusive measures as the Connecticut law. The revelation of these views in the Senate debate provoked alarm and did much to under-mine Bork's chances of confirmation.

Although the public remained uncomfortable with the legacy of the social revolution of the 1960s and 1970s, it was not willing to undo the rights that had been gained during those years. The threat that *Roe v. Wade*—or, worse yet, *Griswold*—might actually be over-turned, or that the clock might be turned back on racial and gender equality, proved sufficiently worrying to produce a ground swell of opposition to Bork. Even a number of Republican senators, unwilling to reopen debates on abortion and civil rights, voted against him. When the next Supreme Court vacancy appeared, it was clear that the political landscape had been significantly altered.

REVISING THE DREAM

If David Souter's "stealth candidacy" revealed how much the politics of abortion had changed in recent years, another issue surrounding his suitability was equally revealing about the national mood. Souter does not have a wife or children, a fact that occasioned general sus-picion of the man, more from liberals than conservatives. Could a bachelor Supreme Court justice understand the complexities of or-dinary family life, or issues faced by women?

*Griswold was the executive director of Planned Parenthood in Connecticut; he and its medical director were convicted as accessories for prescribing contraceptives to a mar-ried woman. The debate in the case centered around whether a married couple could be sent to jail for using contraceptives. In fact, the state did not try to enforce the law against married couples. It did, however, prevent birth control devices from being pre-scribed by doctors in their offices or in clinics and from being sold in stores. For details on the case, see Tribe 1978.

Since Gary Hart's fall from grace after his affair with Donna Rice, a political candidate's sexual habits, once viewed as a private matter, have come to be seen as clues to his or her fitness to hold public office. The debate over Souter's family status in the summer of 1990 suggested that the standard of political fitness was being narrowed still further. Some commentators wondered whether a new standard of qualification for public office was emerging: married, with children.

The public debate over Souter's personal life was eclipsed after Saddam Hussein invaded Kuwait. "Perhaps the only benefit we have reaped from Iraq's aggression," remarked Robert Bork, "is the sudden disappearance of opinion pieces by law professors who think that if a man is a bachelor and lives in a small town he cannot have the proper sensitivities ... on women, minorities, and the poor."[25]

The debates over the Souter nomination reveal the unsettled state of public discourse about the family in the late 1980s and early 1990s. This discourse, and family life itself, continue to reflect the three cultural eras of the recent past: the culturally constrained familistic 1950s; the era of political protest, cultural revolt, and domestic upheaval; and the era of nostalgia and conservative backlash that ushered in a war over the family as well as an ecumenical celebration of family values.

If Rip Van Winkle had gone to sleep in the 1950s and awakened three decades later, he would have found some aspects of the social landscape familiar. The 1950s American family dream, immortalized in the family sitcoms of the era, continued to have a strong hold on the hearts and minds of middle-class Americans. Indeed, he could catch up again with the same programs, in reruns. What's more, he could watch a new wave of close-knit, happy television families; Bill Cosby's hugely successful show led to so many warm family comedies that the industry coined a new term—"warmedies"—to describe them.[26]

Taking a tour of certain American neighborhoods—the kinds labeled by one market research firm as Blue-Collar Nursery, Young Suburbia, Furs and Station Wagons, Blue-Chip Blues, and Shotguns and Pickups[27]—he would have found middle-class and blue-collar communities filled with children, many of the homes with full-time homemakers. Confounding the predictions of demographers, the birthrate rose sharply toward the end of the 1980s. According to the Census Bureau, more babies were born in 1989—more than four million—than in any other year in our history. The fertility rate—

the number of children per woman—also rose to approximately 2, just below the replacement level of 2.1. Much of the increase was due to the large population of baby boomers deciding to have children. In a survey carried out by Peter Hart and associates for *Rolling Stone*, 92 percent of those interviewed were parents or wanted to be. Gallup reported a similar passion for parenthood. "One thing is clear," observed a report on the Hart survey, "this generation is desperate to have kids. . . . It is one of the most striking findings of the survey."[28]

But the social movements of the 1960s and 1970s and the revolutions in private life have also left their mark. Support for feminist goals remained strong throughout the 1980s, although a majority of women did not choose to label themselves feminists. Moreover, feminist principles such as careers for women, men's sharing in child care, and sexual autonomy became woven into the fabric of American lives. Meanwhile, gay and lesbian couples, unmarried heterosexual couples, and single mothers were commonplace challenges to older definitions of family.

One measure of change was the gradual fading of the term "illegitimate child." As soon as it became acceptable for an unmarried middle-class woman to keep a child she had conceived accidentally, growing numbers of middle-class women in their thirties and forties deliberately set out to become pregnant and bear children on their own.[29]

To a surprising degree, both the public and the law have been willing to grant recognition to variant family patterns. In the summer of 1989, New York State's highest court held that the partner of a gay man who had died retained the legal rights to the apartment they shared, just as a widow or widower would. The court used several factors to define a family, including the "level of emotional and financial commitment." Above all, "the totality of the relationship as evidenced by the dedication, caring and self-sacrifice of the parties" should determine what constitutes a family.[30]

It seemed a perfect melding of the gay liberation values of the 1970s and the traditional family values of the 1980s. Indeed, a "conservative defense" of gay marriage appeared in *The New Republic*; instead of assigning judges the task of defining what is and is not a family, Andrew Sullivan argues in the interests of promoting deeper personal commitments and social stability, gay marriage should be legalized.[31]

While the prospect of marriage licenses for gays seems unlikely anytime soon, many gay and lesbian couples are having informal and even church weddings. And courts and local governments around the country are giving increasing recognition to "domestic partnerships" and other nontraditional families. Further, to a surprising degree, although they do not favor granting unmarried couples the same legal rights as married ones,[32] Americans, like the New York judge in a rent-control case, define family and family values in terms of the nature and quality of relationships. For example, in a study conducted for the Massachusetts Mutual Insurance Company that asked respondents to choose among several definitions of family, three-quarters rejected the more traditional versions, picking instead "a group of people who love and care for one another."[33]

But, although these specific instances seem to suggest an embrace of the revised family dream, American attitudes toward the vast changes that have overtaken personal life since the 1960s are best described overall as ambivalent and paradoxical. Americans remain torn by their reverence for the traditional nuclear family as it was, or seemed to be, and their acceptance of the new. This deep ambivalence has been turning up in polls and surveys for years. A 1987 Gallup poll found that 87 percent of those surveyed claimed to have "old-fashioned values about family and marriage." Yet more than two-thirds repudiated the idea that "women should return to their traditional role."[34]

When asked for their views on divorce, Middletown women interviewed in the mid-1970s deplored what they saw as skyrocketing divorce rates, blaming them on "moral decay"—selfishness and irresponsibility. Yet they expressed little disapproval of specific people they knew who were divorced. Further, reported the researchers, "Middletown's wives resented the idea that a woman might be forced to endure a cruel husband or a miserable marriage because she had no other means of support."[35]

Perhaps the most contrary attitudes of all are held by the generation that played the starring role in overturning traditional social mores. The 1988 Rolling Stone survey revealed a generation "at odds with itself" over the recent changes in American life. Although they are glad they are no longer bound by the constraints of the traditional family, these young adults still revere the homilies of the Nelsons, the Andersons, the Cleavers, and the Huxtables, and yearn for the certainties and security their parents knew. "I don't think we're emotionally equipped to live with so many options," said one woman in the survey.[36]

In short, the generation that once celebrated sex, drugs, and rock and roll now has second thoughts. Two-thirds of those surveyed had had premarital intercourse and 30 percent had lived with a member of the opposite sex; but, although only 8 percent regretted these ex-periences, 59 percent of the total sample, and two-thirds of those with children, said permissive attitudes toward sex had been a change for the worse. The same was true for drugs. "What it comes down to is this," said the pollster Peter Hart. "These people did a lot, regret very little, and don't want their kids to do any of it."[37]

Perhaps the most dramatic evidence of the profound hold mar-riage and family life retains on American hearts and minds is the tale of what came to be known as the Harvard-Yale study. It began with a scholarly study of the marriage probabilities of black and white women with varying levels of education. Some of the study's conclu-sions were published in a small Connecticut newspaper, setting off a public and media uproar that reached a climax when *Newsweek* pub-lished a cover story on the study. The graph on the magazine's cover showed, in *Newsweek*'s notorious words, that a forty-year-old woman's chances of getting married were so low that she was "more likely to be killed by a terrorist."[38]

What the results of their analysis implied, according to the three researchers who carried out the study, was that white women college graduates who were still single at age thirty had only a 20 percent chance of marriage; those who remained single at thirty-five a 5 per-cent chance; and, at age forty, the chances dropped to 1 percent. A Census Bureau researcher disputed these estimates, and eventually the Yale and Harvard researchers themselves backed away from them. Since the estimates are essentially predictions about the future lives of young women now in their twenties and thirties, we won't know which projections are most accurate until after the turn of the cen-tury.[39]

The last part of the story concerns the lessons drawn from the whole episode. For many feminists, the affair was a media-concocted attempt to resurrect the old stereotype of the single, educated woman as a lonely old maid. It was also, feminists believed, a slap at the movement, an attempt to show that feminism had misled women into believing that they could "have it all"—a successful career and a happy family life. For social scientists, the episode pointed to the pitfalls of making predictions about human behavior during periods of massive social change.

But the chief significance of the episode was the profound public reaction to the supposed findings. The study's projections may have been off the mark, the media accounts of the study may have been biased, and many women may have been quite content to live the rest of their days unmarried—but a vast number of women were shaken by a new finding that seemed to tell them that, in delaying marriage, they had given up their chances of ever marrying. "It was surprising to find," observes Andrew Cherlin, "that in a society in which sexual relations among unmarried adults are accepted, cohabiting unions are common, and nearly one fourth of all children are born to unmarried mothers, so many people cared about the probability of marriage."[40] But the marriage they cared about was a new, more symmetrical ideal—a revised version of companionate marriage rather than the old breadwinner/homemaker model.

THE REVISED COMPANIONATE IDEAL

The new model of marriage attempts to resolve the central contradiction of companionate marriage in both its Victorian and twentieth-century versions: the egalitarian ideal of husband and wife as friends versus the inequalities of gender roles. The new model portrays husband and wife not just as companions but as best friends, emotional intimates, and fulfilling sexual partners. It has been infused with feminist as well as "therapeutic" sensibilities, emphasizing the husband's participation in child care as well as emotional candor and talk about feelings.[41] Despite the high divorce rate and the gulf between the ideal and the realities of family life, the companionate notion of marriage, in its revised version, seems to be as strong as ever.

It can be found not only on contemporary television shows like "Thirtysomething" and even "Roseanne," but in unexpected places, such as fundamentalist Christian writings and preaching about marriage[42] and the accounts of divorced people describing why their marriages broke up. Indeed, believing strongly in the companionate ideal constitutes the great expectations for marriage that set the stage for disillusion and divorce. "[T]he ideal of a 'marriage of companions' persists in the imaginations of people," observes a study of the recently divorced, "despite a reality that often contradicts it. . . . Individuals justify their divorces on grounds that the ideal's central components—emotional intimacy, primacy and companionship, and sexual fulfillment—were lacking."[43]

Despite gender and class variations, the new companionate ideal of marriage has spread to both sexes and to the working class, as did the middle-class Victorian ideal before it. The new vision was already awakening in the early 1970s when Lillian Rubin carried out her well-known study of working-class families, published as *Worlds of Pain.* When asked what they value most in their husbands, many women still answered as their mothers might have: "I guess I can't complain. He's a steady worker; he doesn't drink; he doesn't hit me." Not a single middle-class woman gave that response. But Rubin found that working-class expectations for marriage were changing: "Suddenly, new dreams are stirring. *Intimacy, companionship, sharing*—these are now the words working-class women speak to their men, words that turn *both* their worlds upside down."[44]

One can argue that this new, highly romanticized image of marriage and family life loads an impossible burden of expectations onto family life. Writing of the Victorian ideal of the home as a loving "Edenic retreat" from the horrors of the larger society, the historian Kirk Jeffrey claims that the "implacable perfectionism" of the ideal may have, ironically, "exacerbated the compulsive self-examination of many Protestant, middle-class husbands and wives and enormously increased the burdens of anxiety and guilt which they bore."[45]

On the other hand, a surprising number of relationships do live up to the companionate ideal, or at least approach it on their own terms. A classic study of successful middle-class marriages carried out in the early 1960s found that, contrary to Tolstoy's aphorism, happy marriages are not all alike. While some couples did seem to fulfill the companionate ideal, others were content with marriages that fell far short of it. "Conflict-habituated" couples, for example, battled continually but were nevertheless devoted; other couples were content with marriages lacking companionship and intimacy.[46] While fewer middle-class couples would tolerate such relationships today, marriage can still be "good enough" without being perfect.

In my own studies of the Berkeley longitudinal study members, carried out in the 1970s and early 1980s, I found that marital satisfaction was linked to a couple's strong emotional attachment.[47] A surprisingly large proportion of this middle-aged, middle American population had emotionally gratifying marriages. This companionate component of marriage was relatively independent of other aspects of marriage, such as amount of time spent together or how much of a social life the couple had. And in this "feminine mystique" generation, the emotional component of marriage was independent of sex role traditionality—a husband and wife could be traditional or egal-

itarian, but each had to be in accord with the other. The happy couples did not have perfect marriages, however. In fact, many of the
people who rated their marriages "unsatisfactory" had no more problems than did happier couples; the emotional bonds were simply not
strong enough to offset the grievances and complaints. Jessie Bernard
has said that every marriage is really two marriages—his and hers.[48]
I would add that every marriage also consists of the good marriage
and the bad marriage.

In many ways, however, the new, more feminized and symmetrical
ideal of marriage has ratcheted up the demands on family life still
higher—out of the reach of many men. The 1990 Virginia Slims Poll
found that women's expectations have outpaced the changes in men's
behavior. Conducted six times since 1970, the poll provides striking
evidence of change in both men's and women's attitudes. Men have
supported women's improved status, opposed sex discrimination in
the workplace, and agreed that they could help women balance jobs
and family by taking on more of the household chores.

But the poll also found that men's failure to live up to the ideal of
shared responsibility is a major cause of resentment. Seventy percent
of the women said that more help from their husbands is the single
biggest factor that allows a manageable balance between work and
family; 52 percent cited the lack of such help as a problem. Not surprisingly, the poll also found that women think less of men today
than they did in 1970, with the majority agreeing that men are too
absorbed in their outside lives and driven by their egos to keep
women down.[49]

In her recent study of two-job couples, Arlie Hochschild showed
how these dilemmas play out in daily life. Specifically, in examining
the effects on love and intimacy of "the second shift"—the work of
caring for children and keeping house—she revealed the issue of who
does what as a central yet often hidden struggle in most of the marriages she studied. The happiest two-job couples were the 20 percent
of the sample who shared the second shift and did not devalue chores
like picking up children at school or remembering the grocery list.
In the majority of the couples studied, women whose lives are very
different from their mothers found themselves living with men only
slightly different from their fathers.

Many of these couples were trapped in a painful dilemma: the men
perceived themselves as doing more around the house than their
fathers had, and more than other men did. Women, with a more
egalitarian standard in mind, were resentful of their double burden,

yet tried to stifle such feelings in order to preserve their marriages. This strategy took its toll on love and intimacy. As Hochschild puts it, "the most important injury to women who work the double day is not the fact that they work too long or get too tired. That is only the obvious and tangible cost. The deeper problem such women face is that they cannot afford the luxury of unambivalent love for their husbands."[50]

The wonder is not that divorce rates are so high today, but that so many marriages and families and relationships survive and even thrive. The proliferation of marriage counseling, family therapists, and support groups in recent years testifies both to the troubles people are experiencing in their personal lives and to the efforts they are willing to go to repair their relationships. The new notion that marriage and relationships need to be "worked on" may help to modify the gap between the intimate and symmetrical version of the companionate dream and "the rough realities of married life, with its critical in-laws, cranky children, disabling sickness, and the frustrating day-to-day grind of intimate cohabitation."[51]

As the sociologist Ann Swidler observed in interviews with married couples in the late 1980s, people still use elements of the traditional romantic love myth in describing their marriages. But the heroic struggle to marry that plays such a large role in the old tales of love has largely disappeared from their accounts. She notes:

> It has been replaced by another powerful heroism—the heroic effort people view as necessary to keep their relationships going. They insist that one must "work at" a relationship. But even more, they insist that a whole range of virtues—from honesty and a willingness to face change to stamina and a willingness to stick by one's commitments—are necessary to preserve a modern marriage.[52]

Mirroring shifts in the wider culture and in their clients, marriage counselors today have turned away from their concern in the 1970s with saving the spouses, not the marriage. One therapist observed that people used to come to her with their minds set on divorce— " 'We fight all the time, we're miserable, it's impossible.' " She still hears that, but less often: "Now couples come in saying 'When we got married, we thought we'd be more intimate, closer. But we're not. We wonder what we can do.' "[53]

The idealized notion of marriage embodied in the companionate ideal is not simply a myth that can be easily discarded. While modern societies encourage autonomy and individualism, they generate an equal and opposite need for intimacy and attachment. As Talcott Parsons pointed out in the 1950s, when the family's role in production declined, it became a more specialized institution: ministering to the psychological needs of its members, socializing children, "stabilizing" the personalities of adults. Its task was to provide nurturance and comfort in a harsh, competitive world.[54]

In the past, intimacy in the daily interaction with familiar people was a by-product of the family economy. With the separation of home and work that took place in the Industrial Revolution, people began to experience both a public self, which they presented to the world in their roles as workers, shoppers, and neighbors, and a private self. This new distinction created the need for intimacy, for a "backstage" world where we can relax and just be "ourselves." Thus, although it may seem that in modern societies family and family-like ties have withered away, they have actually become more important psychologically than they were in the past.

Parsons erred in assuming that the 1950s version of the family was a timeless "functional necessity" of society. He also erred in assuming that family could meet the demands placed on it. Instead, the concentration of so much emotional energy in family life makes it a highly charged source of tension and conflict. Further, the need for a special kind of intimacy helps make marriages unstable. A variety of studies have shown that marital satisfaction is the most important single factor in psychological well-being; people whose marriages are unsatisfactory or failing are extremely vulnerable to stress, depression, anxiety, and loss of self-esteem. As the sociologist Robert Weiss observes:

> Our primary sources of sympathy and support are our spouses. We are consequently both bruised and bereft when our spouses turn from allies to critics.... With marital support so important, a spouse's slight can easily be felt to be a grievous injury, and what might appear to an outsider to be an unimportant misunderstanding can give rise to feelings of intolerable misuse.[55]

In short, the essential insight of Parsons and others was correct: modern society generates intense needs for psychological support. The more complex, impersonal, and large-scale the public world, the more intense the need for a small-scale, intimate, private small world rich in the very qualities lacking in the world at large—love, concern, tenderness, nurturance. Or, as John Naisbett put it, "high-tech" generates a need for "high-touch."[56]

CONCLUSION

As the 1980s came to an end, the attitudes that defined those years had run their course. The decade that had begun with an emphasis on old-fashioned virtues came to be seen as an era of greed and corruption. "Supply-side economics" had cut taxes for the very rich but increased them for everyone else; the extremes of wealth and poverty at the end of the 1980s had turned America into something like a Third World country. The Reagan years, argued the Republican political strategist Kevin Phillips, had produced "one of America's most striking concentrations of wealth even as the American dream was beginning to crumble not just in inner-city ghettos and farm townships but in blue collar centers and even middle class suburbs."[57]

The cultural politics surrounding the family remained unresolved. Social conservatives still railed against the values of the 1960s, but the positions they attacked had few defenders. Virtually no one disputed the importance of family as a source of intimacy and comfort, a refuge from marketplace values and a lonely autonomy. Indeed, pro-family sentiment was so widespread across the political spectrum that the image of family life grew warm and fuzzy; the insight that normal families can be sources of pain and conflict as well as love and care was in danger of being lost.*

But it was also clear that the attempt to restore the family patterns of the 1950s had failed. At the beginning of the Reagan years, conservatives had portrayed the working mother as either a selfish feminist or a housewife driven into the workplace by Jimmy Carter's inflation. By the end of the 1980s, there was still widespread uneasiness about the difficulties of combining work and parenthood, but women were clearly in the workplace to stay. Further, feminism was no longer seen as the antithesis of "family values."

With feminists and liberals calling for child care, prenatal care, parental leave, and other items on a family policy agenda, conservatives had to share the pro-family label they had wrested away from their foes in the late 1970s. In a sense, we had come full circle, back

---

*The popularity of the term "dysfunctional family" reflects this new idealization; once used to describe families with severe problems, such as child abuse or neglect, the term now seems to be applied to any family that departs from a standard of perfect harmony.

to the pragmatic efforts of the Carter era to come to terms with family change, efforts that had been sneeringly dismissed at the time by both radicals and conservatives.

There was a general sense that the country was on the brink of another cycle of reform, to address not only family issues themselves but a mounting array of problems in America's social and economic infrastructure with profound effects on family life: the health care system, the schools, poverty, and unemployment. Yet even after the decade ended, the political process remained mired in the divisive ideological battles of the 1980s. It seemed inevitable that a new pol·itics would sooner or later emerge to address the predicaments be·setting the family and the country, but there was no telling when the inevitable would happen.

C H A P T E R   8

The State of the
American Family

The American family does not exist. Rather, we are creating many American families, of diverse styles and shapes. . . . We have fathers working while mothers keep house; fathers and mothers both working away from home; single parents; second marriages bringing together people from unrelated backgrounds; childless couples; unmarried couples, with and without children; gay and lesbian parents. We are living through a period of historic change in American family life.   —"The 21st Century Family"
Newsweek (1990)

The feminist revolution of this century has provided the most powerful challenge to traditional patterns of marriage. Yet paradoxically, it may also have strengthened the institution by giving greater freedom to both partners, and by allowing men to accept some of the traditionally female values.
—Helge Rubenstein
The Oxford Book of Marriage

The debate about whether the family in America is falling apart, here to stay, or better than ever has continued unabated since the 1970s, like an endless cocktail party conversation. There is of course no way of resolving the issue. "Most of us," observes Joseph Featherstone, "debate these matters from our general instinct of where history is tending, from our own lives and those of our friends. . . . One of the

199

difficult things about the family as a topic is that everyone in the discussion feels obliged to defend a particular set of choices."[1]

While the argument shows no signs of reaching a resolution, some of the debaters have wandered away. Others have switched sides. Most of the radical voices who celebrated the death of the family have disappeared. Those who denounced the family as an oppressive institution and lamented its persistence have also passed from the scene, although continuing critical attacks have granted them a kind of immortality. Meanwhile, the ranks of the optimists who think the family is alive and well have thinned considerably. Recently, one family researcher did publish a book entitled *The Myth of Family Decline*, but generally there is less talk of family decline and decay in the media and more of it among social scientists.[2]

There is no doubt that the family transformations of recent times have left a great deal of disruption in their wake. But those who lament "the decline of the family" lump together an array of serious problems, as well as changes that are not necessarily problems at all: divorce, the sexual revolution, working mothers, the rising age of marriage, teenage pregnancy, abortion, childhood poverty, child abuse, domestic violence, the economic effects of no-fault divorce for women and children, the failure of many divorced fathers to pay child support and maintain contact with their children, an increase in the percentage of people living alone, young people "postponing" adulthood and refusing to leave home, latchkey children, the "dysfunctional family," drug use in the ghettos and suburbs, problems of minority families.

Wrapping these issues in one big package labeled "decline of the family" muddles rather than clarifies our understanding of family change. Some of these problems arise out of the old plague of poverty, which has grown worse over the past decade; others are byproducts of an American economy afflicted by recession, inflation, and industrial decline and dislocation.

Still other difficulties are a result of the mismatch between the new realities of family life and social arrangements based on earlier family patterns. For example, the problem of "latchkey children" could be remedied if we had the will to do so—through afterschool programs, or a lengthening of the school day, or flexible work schedules for parents. And at least some of the painful consequences of divorce are products of the legal policies and practices governing the dissolution of marriage. No-fault divorce is a classic case of unintended consequences: what looked like reform of an unfair, degrading way of dealing with marital breakdown turned into an economic disaster for older homemakers and mothers with young children. Yet here, too, the worst features of the system can be remedied—for example, by postponing the sale of the family home until children are grown.

Moralistic cries about declining families and eroding values hinder public discussion about the kinds of modifications that can be made in other social institutions to alleviate current strains in family life. Framing the issue in terms of "the declining family" also leads to an overemphasis on personal and moral failings as the source of family and social problems, and draws attention away from the social sources of family change that have been discussed throughout this book: the economic and demographic factors that have drawn women into the workplace, the life-course revolutions that have reshaped families as well as the processes of growing up and growing old, and so on. The popularity of recent critiques of individualism reflects a strong American tradition of blaming serious social problems on individual moral character rather than on institutions and economic structures. For example, there was a tendency in the early 1930s—given voice by F. Scott Fitzgerald—to blame the Great Depression on the hedonism and immorality of the jazz age.

Without an economic catastrophe or government takeover by religious extremists, as in *The Handmaid's Tale*, women are not going to return to full-time domesticity, and unhappy couples will seek to remedy their unhappiness through divorce. Most people no longer feel there is a conflict between the family and the feminist search for equality. We need less hand wringing and more social ingenuity to help the families we do have work better. As E. J. Dionne has recently suggested, the American public is ready for a new "center" that makes peace between the liberal values of the 1960s and the work and family values of the 1980s.[3]

INDIVIDUALISM VERSUS ATTACHMENT

It is not clear why social scientists have become so much more pessimistic than they used to be. The deepening gloom does not correspond to marked shifts in demographic trends. In the 1980s, for example, such vital indicators of family life as divorce rates and birthrates, which had changed sharply in the 1970s, leveled off. Toward the end of the 1980s, new births reached baby-boom levels, confound-

ing the expectations of demographers. As a 1990 review of trends in
family life put it, "Predictions of childlessness and large-scale aban-
donment of family life for this generation, a generation supposedly
obsessed with individual fulfillment and achievement, will not be realized."[4]

Some family scholars may have been reacting against their overly
optimistic assessments of family change in the 1970s. Responding to
alarm about the impending "death of the family," many researchers,
pointing to demographic and survey evidence of persisting commitments to family life, argued that the family was "here to stay." Emphasizing the benefits of recent trends—more freedom from the
constraints of sex roles, greater opportunities for women, closer and
more satisfying marriages—they tended to downplay the costs and
hardships that come with changes. As if to compensate for that optimism, in the 1980s they stressed the negative.

But family scholars in recent years also seem to have been influenced by the pessimistic views of American character and culture that
began to dominate intellectual discourse in the mid-1970s. The landmark work in this genre during the 1980s was the widely acclaimed,
widely discussed, best-selling book *Habits of the Heart*, by Robert Bellah and his colleagues. Six years after *The Culture of Narcissism*, this
new work continued the critique of individualism that had become
prominent in the 1970s.

A work of interpretive social science based on interviews with
mostly middle-class people in California and elsewhere, *Habits of the
Heart* presents a far gentler and more complex picture of Americans than had Lasch's blighted portrait. Indeed, Bellah and his
co-authors reported that "if there are vast numbers of a selfish, narcissistic me-generation in America, we did not find them." The complaint is more subtle; instead of applying a psychiatric diagnostic
label to an entire population, the book takes issue with American
individualism in its contemporary version. While observing that "individualism lies at the very core of American culture" and that it is
closely linked to "[o]ur highest and noblest aspirations, not only for
ourselves, but for those we care about, for our society and the world,"
Bellah and his colleagues criticize both "utilitarian individualism"—
the pursuit of self-interest and success—and "expressive individualism"—the pursuit of happiness, the belief in each person's "unique
core of feeling and intuition."[5] The book argues that the two kinds
of individualism have perniciously combined to form the therapeutic
ethos, which forms the model for many relationships. Yet the authors

portray Americans not as asocial loners, devoid of family ties and community spirit, but merely as lacking a moral language to justify the commitments they do have.

Speaking to widely shared anxieties about social and cultural change, the book has played a surprisingly large role in the newly pessimistic discourse about the family on the part of social scientists. It is not uncommon to find works presenting hard statistical data on family trends that cite *Habits of the Heart* as evidence for a corrosive new individualism that can explain the trends.

Yet, as a number of critics have pointed out, the book's analyses are variations on older themes in the critique of modernity, such as the decline of community, the isolation of the self, the loss of religious certitude. Its criticism of "lifestyle enclaves"—communities of people who are socially or economically similar, as opposed to the "genuine" communities of the past—resembles the attack on suburbia in the 1950s. Like those earlier critiques, it contrasts a romantic vision of the past with a jaundiced vision of the present. Above all, *Habits of the Heart* represents the latest addition in an ongoing pessimistic discourse on the self, that, along with its optimistic counterpart, has been a persistent but largely unnoticed feature of American cultural life.[6]

The fact that these recent attacks on individualism strike such responsive chords in the American public suggests that moral and communitarian values are alive and well. American culture has always been marked by an ambivalent yearning for autonomy on the one hand and attachment to family and community on the other.[7] It is not simply that Americans are individualistic or communitarian, but that the tension between these impulses is a central theme in American culture. Yet most writings on American character ignore this duality and the psychological and social tensions it creates. And aiming criticism at personal and moral failings not only is in keeping with American religiosity—we are the most religious of Western countries,[8] in both belief and churchgoing—but promises that we can solve our problems through changes of heart rather than through the difficult and divisive route of political and social change. But the problems of family life are located less in the realm of personal defects and declining values and more in the difficulties of making and maintaining families in a time of sweeping social change, in a society that is neglectful of families and their needs.

The most recent extended argument for the decline of the family from a family scholar has been put forth by David Popenoe. Popenoe is precise about what he means by "family decline." Since the 1960s, he argues, four major trends have signaled a "flight" from the traditional nuclear family as both ideal and reality: declining birthrates, the sexual revolution, the movement of mothers into the workplace, and the divorce revolution. Citing *Habits of the Heart*, Popenoe suggests that the trends toward expressive individualism and the therapeutic attitude have contributed to family decline. He is also precise about what he means by "traditional nuclear family": it is "focused on the procreation of children" and consists of "a legal, lifelong, sexually exclusive, heterosexual, monogamous marriage, based on affection and companionship, in which there is a sharp division of labor (separate spheres) *with the female as full-time housewife and the male as primary provider and ultimate authority*" (italics added).[9]

Popenoe's argument illustrates that the debate over the declining family is often not so much about the decline of family life as about preference for a particular pattern of family and gender arrangements. He is certainly correct in claiming that what he defines as the traditional nuclear family is no longer dominant. Yet his definition is an essentially nineteenth-century portrait of family and gender roles, today favored by conservatives and the New Right but no longer shared by a majority of Americans. Clearly, the two-worker nuclear family is becoming the new cultural norm, and, while most people describe themselves as strongly pro-family, they favor a more symmetrical version of marriage.

Traditionalists like Popenoe place too much emphasis on family structure and not enough on the emotional quality of family life. Structural characteristics like divorce or maternal employment, as another researcher observes, "are weak predictors of the consequences most of us really care about: personal and family well-being, economic mobility, educational attainment, children's health."[10]

THE OZZIE AND HARRIET DEBATE

While Popenoe mourns the decline of the traditional nuclear family as he defines it, another family researcher has recently complained that it is more common than generally assumed and ought to be given more recognition.[11] David Blankenhorn argues that reports of the deaths of Ozzie and Harriet have been greatly exaggerated. This debate is a prime example of the family as a "great intellectual Rorschach blot."[12]

Since the 1970s we have been hearing that the kind of family that dominated the family imagery of the 1950s now constitutes only about 10 percent of American households. Conservatives, liberals, and radicals all use that figure to document the decline of the family—but it is both true and extremely misleading. For example, as we have seen, because of lengthening life spans and smaller families, the share of adult life devoted to raising children has become much smaller. Such statistics have been used to overemphasize the changes in American families, as Blankenhorn observes. In 1987, he points out, the "workadaddy-housewife family" constituted more like 33.3 percent of families with preschool children and 35 percent of all families with children under eighteen.[13]

The 10 percent figure comes from estimating the proportion of dependent children/breadwinner/housewife families out of all 89.5 million households in America in 1987. These households include families not yet or no longer living with children under eighteen, such as honeymooners and empty-nesters, as well as nonfamily households: people who live alone, students who room together, and the like. In the 1950s, the heyday of the Ozzie and Harriet family, this method of calculation would have shown only one-third of households to be made up of traditional families.

Blankenhorn's concern is that the 10 percent figure tells "traditional" families that they are "old fashioned, outmoded, irrelevant." Although he correctly points out that statistics have often been misused to generate a sense of crisis or to score ideological points, Blankenhorn is also guilty of massaging the data to make his points. For example, he criticizes those who count as "working mothers" women who are employed part-time, claiming they categorize working mothers this way in order to "diminish the importance of stay at home mothers." His solution is to combine part-time employees with mothers who do not work at all, arguing that "well over half" of mothers of preschoolers are employed either part-time or not at all. To make the numbers of at-home and part-time-worker mothers add up to more than half, Blankenhorn adds the 7 percent of Ozzieless families—those with preschoolers headed by a single mother not in the work force.[14]

If combining mothers who work full-time and part-time obscures the differences between two different life-styles, combining part-time employment with full-time mothering obscures still more. Part-time workers have many of the same needs and face many of the same pressures and tensions as full-time workers, but to a lesser degree:

finding good child care, dealing with a sick child, being pulled between the demands of work and the needs of the family. For social
policy purposes, it makes good sense to consider part-time employees
as working parents.

Further, what looks like an Ozzie and Harriet family in the 1980s
and 1990s may not truly reflect the 1950s model in either ideal or
reality. In the 1950s women were assumed to be housewives and
mothers almost by definition, and most women did define themselves
as such. Today's stay-at-home mother may still think of herself as a
high-powered professional. Many career women choose to stay home
while their children are small. By and large today's women consider
paid work as one of their roles in life, even if they are not working
at the moment.

We need take to take a life-course perspective. If we define "the
family" as existing only during that short time of life spent as a married couple with children under eighteen, we are ignoring the lives
of the vast majority of Americans. Although virtually all people live
in family households early in life and the vast majority live in family
households as adults, many of us will experience significant periods
of living apart. The prevailing family types are variants of the nuclear
family that have been around for a long time, if not in great number.
The current Ozzie and Harriet debate reveals that the meaning of
statistics on family life is not straightforward. In a highly charged
atmosphere, statistics can easily become ideological weapons. At best,
it is often difficult to make sense of the trends.

THE STATE OF THE CHILDREN

Anxiety about the state of the family often focuses most intensely on
the young. Children are not only profoundly vulnerable to any trouble in the family; they also embody the future for both their parents
and the society. Thus people worry about their own children as well
as other people's children. Today the vast majority of people—nearly
three out of four in one survey, both parents and nonparents—
believe that the quality of life for America's children has declined
since their own childhood.[15]

Yet this worry, like worries about the declining family in general,
is often built on a muddled mixture of issues. With the huge increase
in working mothers, divorce, and single-parent families, today's children certainly grow up in very different circumstances than did chil-

dren only a few decades ago. Most have working mothers, fewer brothers and sisters, and a good chance of spending time in group care. By the time they reach adulthood, at least half of American children, according to current estimates, will spend some time living in a single-parent family.[16] How children are faring under these circumstances is an issue with profound implications for the future of our society.

Yet many of problems afflicting children that came to public attention in the 1970s and 1980s—physical and sexual abuse, for example—had long histories. Further, a good deal of our current anxiety focuses on issues that are not directly part of family life: the state of children's health, the failings of our educational system, sex and violence in the media, drugs, unsafe schools and streets.

Alarming stories about the state of children and young people have become a media staple in recent years. We hear of "epidemics" of teen pregnancy, suicide, and drug use, and of the increasing poverty of children, the dire effects of divorce, the plight of latchkey children. We also hear of child abuse, incest, and sexual molestation. Pictures of missing children appear on milk cartons all over the country. Many of the changes in children's lives should indeed cause us concern, but many claims about threats to children are wildly exaggerated.[17]

To put today's anxieties into perspective, it is useful to recall that the supposed golden age of family life, the 1950s, was beset by a number of crises concerning children and youth. Shocking reports of juvenile delinquency, gang fights, all-night drinking parties, and sex clubs in teenage suburbia appeared in the mass media.[18] In the professional literature, sociologists and psychologists analyzed the problems of alienated youth and the decline of parental authority. Congress held hearings on the corrupting influence of comic books on the nation's children. In 1955, a book entitled *1,000,000 Delinquents* correctly predicted the number of adolescents who would be brought to court the following year.[19] "Teenagers on the Rampage" was the title of a *Time* magazine report on violence in the nation's high schools. Meanwhile, a widely proclaimed educational crisis for schoolchildren of all ages alarmed Americans.[20] A 1955 best-seller, Rudolph Flesch's *Why Johnny Can't Read*, described America as a nation of illiterates.

To point to the hysteria of an earlier time is not to minimize the difficulties facing today's children and young people. But cries of alarm and doom need to be subjected to serious scrutiny. Making sense of the changes in children's lives in recent years is more complicated than most people assume. Several family researchers have recently published comprehensive assessments of the state of children and young people in America.[21] In general, these reports show that, while the well-being of children has worsened in some ways, not all of the news concerning America's children is bad—in fact, some of it is good.

These studies generally agree that it is not useful to take one indicator—say, teenage suicide or SAT scores—as a general measure of child welfare. As Nicholas Zill and Carolyn Rogers point out, children's well-being is a "multifaceted phenomenon." Analyzing trends in indicators of children's economic, physical, and psychological well-being since the 1960s, Zill and Rogers challenge the widespread assumptions that the overall condition of children is deteriorating.

Taken together, these studies present a mixed picture of children's prospects. On the plus side, the average American child's physical health has improved dramatically since the 1960s. Although our infant mortality rates are higher than those of most other industrial societies, both our infant and child mortality rates have dropped considerably. Declining family size has increased most children's share of the family's material resources, even though overall family income has declined since the 1970s. The educational level of most parents has risen since the 1950s, a gain that has been most striking among black women.

On the other side of the ledger, troubling social behavior on the part of young people—delinquency, drug use, early sexual activity—has increased over the past several decades. But many of these trends leveled off or declined in the 1980s. Teenage suicide is frequently cited as an indicator of the emotional well-being of American youth in general, and its recent rise blamed on changing family patterns. (Teenage suicide rates more than doubled between 1960 and the mid-1980s.) But suicide rates are notoriously slippery; changes in reported rates could reflect fluctuating practices in reporting deaths as suicides, or the greater availability of lethal weapons. The number of suicide attempts is much larger than the number of completed suicides, but statistics on attempts are not as reliable.

Suicide may therefore not be a valid indicator of the overall psychological well-being of a population. As Zill and Rogers observe, some groups in the population have relatively low rates of suicide and, at the same time, relatively high rates of depression. Despite the rise in suicide rates, the vast majority of children do not seem to be depressed, unhappy, or alienated, and survey measures of children's life satisfaction and emotional well-being have not changed in recent years.

Now, as in the past, many of the difficulties facing children arise out of economic factors. During the 1980s overall poverty rates increased, and children became the poorest segment of the population; since 1988, one out of five children has lived below the poverty line. Several factors have led to the large increase in child poverty in recent years. One is the general decline in wages, especially for younger men in their peak child-rearing years. The enormous growth of poverty among working people *not* living in inner-city underclass communities is one of the untold stories of the 1980s. A second source of child poverty is the rise of single-parent families due to divorce and out-of-wedlock births. The impact on children of both of these trends has been worsened by shortsighted government policies— cutbacks or inadequate investments in housing, health care, child care, and other social supports.[22]

Other stresses arise out of the time pressures parents experience and other dilemmas of balancing work and family. Although there is little that government or business can do directly to reverse trends in family structure, policy choices such as child care, parental leave, opportunities for both parents to work part-time while children are young, and measures to fight poverty and joblessness can alleviate some of the current strains on families.

Surprisingly, the evidence linking family changes such as divorce and maternal employment to declines in children's well-being is weaker than most people think. In 1986, a widely discussed article by Peter Uhlenberg and David Eggebeen argued that the condition of American teenagers had steadily worsened in recent decades.[23] This decline, they said, was linked to recent changes in family structure.

Later, more detailed studies of trends in various measures of child and adolescent well-being do not, however, support a familial explanation of negative trends such as drug use, crime, or declining academic achievement. For example, many negative indicators leveled off in the late 1970s and 1980s, at a time when the family-disintegration hypotheses would have predicted increases. Further, as the sociologists Frank Furstenberg and Gretchen Condran point out, the worrisome behavioral trends among youth in the 1960s and 1970s were also found among people in their twenties and thirties.[24] Since these young adults had grown up during the years of postwar family stability, their problem behavior cannot be attributed to changing family patterns.

Much public concern and recent research has focused on the effects of maternal employment on young children. But despite the
widespread belief to the contrary, the research literature shows that
children whose mothers work are no more likely to suffer from developmental problems or behavioral difficulties than are children of
stay-at-home mothers.[25] Maternal employment alone reveals little
about the well-being of a child. A working mother's attitudes, the
amount of emotional and practical support she receives, and the
quality of available child care play a tremendous role in her morale
and the functioning of the family. The most depressed mothers are
those who want to work and can't, and those who would like to be
full-time homemakers but must work. A recent review of the research
literature on working mothers in two-parent families concludes:

> Where this pattern itself produces difficulties, they often seem to
> stem mainly from the slow pace with which society has adapted to
> this new family form. . . . It is the disequilibrium of social change
> that creates problems; the typical American family is a dual-wage
> family, but neither social policy nor social attitudes are in synchrony
> with this fact.[26]

The evidence on divorce is more mixed. Few would deny that it is
often a stressful experience for children or that children are best off
with two parents in a good marriage. Even most children whose parents have a bad marriage would probably prefer to have them stay
together. Yet we know surprisingly little about the long-term effects
of divorce on children. Is it uniformly devastating to all children who
go through it? Does it create deep psychological wounds that never
heal?

A relatively small number of largely middle-class white children has
served as the basis for much current research about the impact of
divorce on children. In 1989, Judith Wallerstein and Sandra Blakeslee
published *Second Chances*, a book describing the lives of a sample of
131 children of divorce whom Wallerstein had been studying for the
previous fifteen years. The detailed psychological portraits of these
now-grown children were poignant, and the conclusions of the book
disturbing.

Wallerstein and Blakeslee state that almost half of the young men
and women in the study were worried, underachieving, self-
deprecating, and angry. This bad news about divorce was widely publicized; reports on the book in the media elicited many comments

from adults who retained painful, vividly detailed memories of their parents' divorce. Yet other divorce researchers, while respectful of the book's clinical insights, suggest that it exaggerates the extent of the long-term harmful effects of divorce.[27]

There can be little doubt, though, that the time around the breakup of a marriage is a crisis for all concerned. The experiences associated with divorce and remarriage often increase a child's risk of developing problems of various kinds—psychological, social, and academic. But clearly not all children whose parents divorce develop such problems. Researchers in recent years have begun to focus on differences in children's responses to divorce and the conditions that influence whether they do well or poorly. One factor is the child's own temperament. Some children are more vulnerable than others to adversity and change; "difficult" children are especially likely to become targets of a stressed parent's anger.[28]

The major factor influencing a child's long- and short-term well-being after divorce is the relationship with the parents, especially with the custodial parent, usually the mother.[29] A child who can maintain a warm, supportive relationship with one or both parents, or with a grandparent or other adult, has a much better chance of dealing successfully with the stresses of divorce.

Most researchers now regard divorce not as one event but as part of a long process in which the divorce itself may not be the critical variable. It is not always easy to separate the effects of divorce from the effects of the circumstances that accompany it: conflict between the parents before and after separating; economic loss as a result of the divorce; disruptions in the child's life due to losing the family home, changing schools, and so forth.

There is increasing evidence that parental conflict, whether in the form of shouting or hitting or cold hostility, which may exist in both intact and divorcing families, is a key factor in children's psychological well-being.[30] Yet studies of the effects of divorce rarely compare divorced families to intact families with high levels of conflict. A 1986 study found some children, long before their parents separated, already showing the kinds of behavioral problems that have been viewed as effects of divorce.

In 1968, the psychologists Jeanne and Jack Block began a study of three-year-olds and assessed them periodically for years afterward. When the children were fourteen, the researchers looked back at their data and discovered that those children, especially boys, whose parents would later divorce were rated long before the marriage ended as more aggressive and impulsive and more likely to be in conflict with their parents.[31] Of course, we don't know whether parental conflict led to difficulties for these children, or whether difficult children were creating problems for their parents' marriage. But it is clear that these children's problems did not result from the divorce itself. Recently, a large-scale before-and-after study of the effects of divorce found similar results as had the Blocks in their small sample; a British study of 17,000 families found that many of the problems children exhibited after divorce had existed earlier.[32]

The economic disruptions of divorce often compound the emotional problems. Large numbers of children lose not only their father's presence in the home but his financial support. Their standard of living declines dramatically, and they must adjust to a new home, a new school, new household routines. Policy changes in the economic arrangements following divorce could greatly reduce the stress and disruption children experience.

If we care about children, we need to focus less on the form of the families they live in and more on ways of supporting their well-being in all kinds of families. We need to accept the fact that while the family is here to stay, so are divorce, working mothers, and single-parent families. As the anthropologist Paul Bohannon suggests, we need cultural models of the successful divorce and the successful postdivorce family—one that does the least harm to children and leaves them with good relationships with both parents.[33]

The impact of divorce on children's lives seems to be more harsh in America than in other countries. The United States has been less careful than others to ensure that children are provided for after their parents' marriage ends. As the economist Sylvia Hewlett points out, there are two models of divorce reform in Western Europe. In France, for example, no-fault divorce requires that the father continue to support the wife and children in their current life-style. In Sweden, child support is publicly provided, and tailored to the needs of one-parent families. In the United States, however, we have failed to provide either public or private supports for children in the wake of divorce.[34]

American society is prepared to deplore the plight of children and to exhort parents to fix it. It is less willing to make the kinds of investments in children's well-being that other advanced nations do. Our empty calls for parental sacrifice, "lovingly packed lunchboxes,"[35] and a return to the traditional family will do little to improve the quality of children's lives.

"A HIGH RISK AND
HIGH STRESS SOCIETY"

In the early 1980s three American corporations asked a group of British scholars to make reliable projections about the social, economic, political, and cultural trends that would shape America in the next ten years. The portrait of the emerging American society they produced was not flattering. America, they argued, was becoming "a high risk and high stress society."[36]

The future these researchers foresaw offered less economic opportunity, greater risks of downward mobility, fewer public efforts to respond to social needs, and a widening gap between haves and have-nots. Under these circumstances, people would experience greater stress and anxiety than at any other time in America's postwar history. Americans, they predicted, would also be torn between the competing goals of success at work and family happiness.

Increasingly, people would turn to marriage and the family to make life worthwhile, looking for intimacy, personal fulfillment, and a haven from the high-stress world. Yet, tensions and instability would remain high in the very place to which people would turn for security. Strains arising out of changing family relationships would be intensified by increasing poverty and falling standards of living.

In the 1970s and 1980s two kinds of economic changes had profound effects on families—the structural shifts that came with the move to a postindustrial society, and a downturn in the economy that ushered in a prolonged period of low growth; one economist labeled it a "quiet depression."[37] The cyclical change exacerbated the dislocations resulting from the decline of manufacturing and the loss of blue-collar jobs. In the 1980s, government policies and social program cuts made them even worse. Obviously, economic change cannot explain all of the structural changes in family life, but it has played a much larger role than is generally acknowledged. Meanwhile, the celebration of "traditional family values" masked the decimation of the American family dream.

Haves and Have-nots

By the late 1980s, the economic inequality produced during the Reagan years had become increasingly evident. As Kevin Phillips pointed out, "shifts of 3 to 5% of national income from the grass roots to the top 1% of the population have hurt the bottom half of Americans by effects ranging from small-town decay to urban crime, weakened families, and lost economic opportunity for the unskilled."[38] While it is possible to quibble with these percentages, the most dramatic effects were plain to see: homelessness and the growth of an underclass in the nation's ghettos. Economic change also turned once-thriving industrial regions into Rust Belts, while farm states like Iowa witnessed a replay of the Great Depression, with boarded-up small towns and farm families packing up their belongings and heading west. In 1988 the *Wall Street Journal* observed that the United States "is in the midst of a coast to coast, border to border collapse of much of its rural economy," involving about a quarter of the nation's population.[39]

For most of the 1980s, these harsh changes were disguised by the paradox of a growing economy. Supporters of Reaganomics could point to twenty million new jobs (mostly low-paying, low-benefit positions in sales and service), a host of other favorable economic indicators, and the many visible signs of an uneven prosperity, such as rising sales of luxury goods like Mercedes-Benzes and BMW's. While large numbers of middle-class Americans were slipping down the economic scale, or barely clinging to middle-class living standards, large segments of the upper middle class were prospering, especially two-earner professional families.

"We knew that something was wrong," observed the economist Frank Levy in 1987, "but we lacked the language to describe it."[40] Conservatives dominated national debates on the both the family and the economy. Blaming the growth of "the welfare state" during the 1960s and 1970s for the nation's economic problems and for undermining poor families, they attributed the widening gap between rich and poor to the increase of single-parent families. For their part, many left-leaning social critics continued to fight the cultural battles of the 1970s, ignoring the growth of economic inequality and railing against consumerism and narcissism, especially as personified by the yuppie.

Conservatives blamed increasing poverty rates on changes in family structure. Yet the widening gap between rich and poor could not be attributed solely to the increase in single-parent families— unmarried women and their children. Moreover, recent research supports the view that among the persistently poor, family breakups and teenage childbearing are largely a response to, rather than a cause of, persistent poverty.[41] Further, while married-couple families tended to fare much better in the 1980s than did other kinds of households,

the growth of inequality also showed up strikingly among intact families and among working Americans. Of the twenty million people
who fell below the Census Bureau's poverty line in 1987, nearly 60
percent were from families with at least one member working full-
time or part-time.[42] Throughout most of the postwar era, poverty was
almost synonymous with being unemployed. The 1980s saw the rise
of the working poor; by mid-decade the salary offered by nearly one-
third of full-time jobs could not keep a family of four above the
poverty line.[43]

The Myth of the Yuppie

The 1980s were particularly hard on young people, women, minorities, blue-collar workers, the unskilled, and those without a college
education. Young adults across the range of social classes devised
a number of strategies to cope with declining real earnings. According to one study, "they postponed marriage, both spouses entered
the labor market, they had fewer children, and they went into debt."[44]
The same four strategies were undertaken by the much-maligned
yuppie.

Yuppies formed one piece of the confused media imagery of the
baby-boom generation, the leading edge of whom was thirtysomething as the 1980s began. The yuppie stereotype took on a life of its
own. A variant of the myth of narcissism and the earlier myth of
suburbia, the yuppie presented a more acceptable target of resentment than the truly rich millionaires who were the real beneficiaries
of Reaganomics. Yet the yuppie was a misleading symbol of the baby-
boom generation and the national economy. There were no more
young families with incomes over $35,000 than there had been in the
early 1970s (in constant dollars). Moreover, back then, more families
attained this level of income with only one earner.[45]

The generation that followed the baby boomers fared still worse in
the 1980s. According to a 1988 study by the William T. Grant Foundation, the economic changes of the 1980s fell hardest on children,
youths in their teens and twenties, and young families. Media images
of "a generation on the skids," the report argues—unstable and irresponsible, unwilling to grow up and make commitments to family
and work, beset by drugs, crime, and out-of-wedlock pregnancy—are
harmful and misleading. The majority of young people are staying
in school, working in one or more jobs, saying no to drugs, and

avoiding premature marriage and childbearing. To the extent that problems do exist, they cannot be blamed on "moral decay": *"The primary problem lies with the economy, and the paths for youth who enter it, rather than with the youth themselves. Education can certainly help, but it is no cure-all for massive changes in the labor market"* (italics in original).[46]

A Growing Underclass

The most malignant effects of the declining fortunes of the young have fallen on those who are both poor and members of minorities. In the 1970s and 1980s there was a decline in marriage rates among black women and a dramatic rise in black female-headed households. Many African-American observers agreed that there was indeed a crisis in the black family. In contrast to what many feared, however, changes in black families were not "leading indicators" of future changes in white family life; rather, the family patterns of the two groups were moving farther apart than they had ever been in this century.[47]

While not all differences between black and white families could be explained by spreading poverty, many of the more disturbing changes associated with the rise of a ghetto underclass were linked to the economic changes of recent years. A number of scholars, most notably William Julius Wilson, have argued that the social pathologies that have emerged in inner-city black neighborhoods over the last twenty years are a response to powerful economic forces. Manufacturing declined or moved to the suburbs, eliminating many well-paying, unskilled jobs. High unemployment led to more persistent and concentrated poverty and a set of mutually reinforcing problems—increased welfare dependence, high rates of family disruption, high crime rates, drug use, and so on.

Further, the growth of a population of unemployed and unemployable young men reduced the pool of potential marriage partners, leading to a decline in marriage rates and an increase in the number of unmarried mothers. Growing numbers of young women, suspecting that they will never find a husband able to help support a family, see no advantage to marriage or waiting to have a child.

One ethnographic study of a poor black community in the late 1980s describes teenage childbearing as an alternative life-course strategy adopted in response to economic and social constraints. Faced with limited prospects of an economically viable marriage,

young women invest in a vertical kin system, relying on female relatives for emotional and practical support. As one fourteen-year-old
mother explained: "Ever since I can remember I always expected to
have a baby when I was 15 or 16 but I never believed I would ever
have a chance to get a husband. One of the things my grandmother
always said, 'Pay your dues to your kin because they will take care of
you.' "[48]

Although various aspects of Wilson's analysis have been challenged, his overall argument that unemployment, underemployment,
and poverty have profound effects on family life are indisputable.
Glen Elder's studies of children and families in the Great Depression,
and Katherine Newman's recent study of job loss and subsequent
downward mobility in the 1980s, provide vivid portraits of what happens when families get caught in the undertow of economic decline.[49]

During the 1980s conservative arguments dominated debates about
poverty and the underclass: people were poor because of flaws in
their attitudes, values, and behavior; because a "culture of poverty"
was passed along from generation to generation, untouched by external circumstance; and because government social policies created
perverse incentives. Conservative critics such as George Gilder and
Charles Murray made "welfare" the key to the many troubles that
beset America in the 1970s and 1980s—economic stagnation, high
taxes, crime in the streets, moral decline.[50] These arguments fit the
mood and intuitions of the public during the Reagan years. Poverty
in America was typified by Reagan's image of the Cadillac-driving
"welfare queen" and the strutting black stud who appeared on a Bill
Moyers television documentary on the crisis of the black family and
boasted of how many babies he had made.

In the early 1990s, poverty and its attendant ills are still being
defined as moral and personal, but the rhetoric has begun to shift.
There is a little less talk of declining cultural values, a little more
about reordering national priorities. The appearance of homeless
people all over America in the mid-1980s has transformed American
cities; homelessness—especially homeless families, women, and children—signify a kind of poverty that few can defend. Slowly, a consensus has begun to grow among liberals and conservatives, especially
on the part of American business, that destitution and rampant social
pathology, whatever their sources, are not good for the country and
will in the long run be costly to taxpayers.

DEFYING THE "LOGIC OF
INDUSTRIALISM"

America is not the only country to have experienced a historic change
in family life in recent years. As I discussed earlier, other societies
have seen similar changes in sex roles, divorce rates, and family structure—but their public policy responses have been very different. By
the end of the 1980s there was increasing awareness in the media
that America lagged far behind other industrial nations in family and
social policy. Stories appeared about French prenatal care and pre-
schools, the Canadian health care system, German apprenticeship
training, and the like.

The gap between rhetoric about family values and American willingness to address the needs of families may have stretched in recent
years, but it is not new. Since the nineteenth century, Americans have
looked to the family as the source of individual and social salvation.
Europeans, by contrast, have looked at the family as a fragile institution in need of support from the wider society.

Most European countries conceive of family policy as something
required by the "logic of industrialism"—the need of families no
longer living on the land, dependent on wages and salaries, for help
in dealing with unemployment, major illness, the dependencies of
old age.[51] Hence the unquestioned role of governments in virtually
all industrial countries in supplying a considerable array of family
supports—health care, child allowances, housing allowances, support
for working parents with children that includes child care, parental
leave, short work days for parents—as well as an extensive array of
services at the other end of the life cycle, for the aged.

In a study of family policy in eighteen "rich democracies," the sociologist Harold Wilensky found some striking differences in the politics of the family as well as in family policies.[52] Americans debate
endlessly about emotionally charged moral issues like abortion, sex
education, and gay rights, while in Europe, family policy is part of
general economic policy. Support for children and families in America has been generally based on the assumption that families are
inadequate if they are not self-sufficient. Other countries provide a
range of supports for children and families across income groups,
not just for the poor, with no stigma attached to them.

Several factors, according to Wilensky, seem to account for inno-
vative and expansive social policies in other countries. Among these
are the extent of industrial development, high levels of women in the

labor force, and strong Left and Catholic parties, both of which share a strong interest in supporting families, despite differences in ideas about women's place. A large aging population is also a factor. Older people are strong supporters of family policy, including support for child care, in the United States as well as other countries.[53] There is little evidence for the generational war that some commentators have described. Framing policy issues in terms of young against old is a deceptive and politically opportunistic way of avoiding more funda-mental issues of economic inequality in America.

Paradoxically, Americans have a stronger sense of both familistic values and family crisis than do other advanced countries. We have higher marriage rates, a more home-centered way of life, and greater public devotion to family values, yet also greater rates of instability—divorce, single-parent families, and teenage pregnancies—than other countries.

Eventually, despite our unique cultural and political traditions, it seems likely that the logic of industrialism will prevail, and America will converge with other countries in providing support for families. The proportion of old people rising and will leap to new heights when the baby-boom generation ages. The proportion of women at work is also likely to remain high or even increase. Today's policy debates over child care, parental leave, health insurance, and care for the elderly are a preview of the future.

The current "stalled revolution" (in Arlie Hochschild's phrase) in family life is not likely to last indefinitely. In the 1980s a concern for family values was harnessed to a conservative drive to dismantle the already fragmented and relatively ungenerous systems of public pro-vision that had grown out of the New Deal and the Great Society. In the 1990s, family values might be harnessed to revitalize a new thrust for public and private sector policies in support of children and fam-ilies.

RECONSTRUCTING THE DREAM

After almost three decades of social upheaval and cultural civil war, there are signs that the family debate in America has entered a new stage. By the early 1990s, the polarized political climate that had pre-vailed for more than a decade seemed to be fading and the contours of a new consensus began to emerge. Most Americans, according to survey data and in-depth studies of attitudes, have already made peace

between the liberal values of the 1960s—self-fulfillment, equal opportunity for women—and the traditional work and family values of
the 1980s.[54] The most dramatic evidence of such a shift was the formation in 1991 of an unusual alliance of a group of well-known liberals and New Right conservatives; disregarding the issues that
continue to divide them, such as abortion, they joined forces to press
for specific family support issues on which they could agree.[55]

Further, despite continuing talk of family decline, the outlines of
a new American family are beginning to be seen. It is more diverse,
more fragile, more fluid than in the past. The image of a vast, homogenized middle class that was mythologized in the 1950s applies
even less to today's realities than it did then. Yet contrary to some
critics, the middle class, and middle-class aspirations for family life,
have not disappeared. Although there is much more tolerance for
variation, lifelong heterosexual marriage, with children, remains the
preferred cultural norm.[56]

The New American Dream mixes the new cultural freedoms with
many of the old wishes—marital and family happiness, economic security, home ownership, education of children.[57] But the new dream
is more demanding than the old, and even the basics—a secure job,
a home, health care, education—are becoming more difficult to
achieve. The new life course has more twists and turns than it did in
the past; it offers greater opportunities for autonomy, but greater
risks of loneliness. Further, even the middle class faces more travails
than in the past: divorce, time pressures, and the dilemmas of raising
children in a world that has grown more dangerous, competitive, and
uncertain.

The meaning of other aspects of family change can also be debated
endlessly, but the argument obscures a complex reality: the glass is
both half full and half empty. It is possible to be optimistic about the
future of the family and still be concerned about the number of children who live in poverty, the disruptions of divorce, the difficulties
of balancing work and family.

On one issue, however—the centrality of family in the lives of most
Americans—the optimists are surely correct and the pessimists wrong.
For better or worse, family life, and an idealized image of what the
family should be, remain at the source of our greatest joys, our deepest worries, our most painful hurts.

It is possible to build a convincing case for either the optimistic or
the pessimistic view of recent changes. Pessimists point to high divorce rates as evidence that the family is falling apart and that people

are no longer capable of deep and lasting commitments. Optimists argue that getting divorced is not the same thing as rejecting marriage. Besides, they point out, three-quarters of divorced people remarry, and higher rates of divorce only indicate that marriage has become so important that people are no longer willing to put up with the kinds of unsatisfying, conflicted, or "empty-shell" marriages earlier generations tolerated.

When people are polled about the most important elements in a good life, they place family values—"a happy marriage," love, and emotional support—at the top of the list.[58] Through all the years of dramatic changes in the leading family indicators, surveys have shown that about 90 to 95 percent of young men and women—the alleged Me generation—have planned to marry. National surveys also show that, once married, the vast majority of people report being "very satisfied" or "very happy" with their marriages. But the pollster Lou Harris recently reported that while 87 percent of men say they would remarry their wives, only 76 percent of women say they would remarry their husbands.[59] And contrary to notions of a male "flight from commitment," a greater proportion of men than women marry and remarry.*

Not only have young people continued to value marriage but they expect to have children. Between 1971 and 1979, despite the supposed Me Decade, less than 1 percent of young women considered having no children as the "ideal family situation."[60] Similarly, surveys of both sexes during the 1980s revealed that young adults felt a near-universal urge to have children.[62] In one study of parents and children, 88 percent of the parents said they would choose to have children again, and 71 percent described their families as "close and intimate."[63] Needless to say, what people say to polltakers may not reflect the realities of their family lives; we may not wish to bare our souls or air the family's dirty linen when the survey researcher comes to call. Still, the upbeat answers reveal what people see as the prevailing cultural values.

Further, numerous surveys show that despite talk about the disap-

---

*The "male flight from commitment" is the subject of Barbara Ehrenreich's book *The Hearts of Men*. She argues that a "playboy" ethic led men to reject the breadwinner role in favor of a fun-filled bachelor life. The notion that men today are reluctant to marry and take on family responsibilities fits with the experience of large numbers of women. And certainly, many men have fled responsibilities for their children after divorce. Yet, as Lillian Rubin points out, "something is wrong with the picture as drawn." It leaves out the vast majority of men who do make a commitment to marriage, kids, mortgages, and the like. Most men can't afford the affluent bachelor life, and those who can are less likely to remain single than those at the bottom of the income scale.[61]

pearance of the extended family, family ties beyond the nuclear family persist. Regardless of mobility, most Americans had ready access
to members of their family, nearly 90 percent having at least one
household of relatives living nearby. Sixty percent of these people
saw nearby relatives at least once a week. Those with no relatives
nearby, or who saw nearby relatives less often than once a month,
comprised about 30 percent of the population.[64] It seems likely that
most of these people were in touch with their families by mail and
phone, visited on holidays, and mobilized to help one another during
emergencies. Clearly, the image of contemporary Americans as isolated, rootless loners is far from reality.

How, then, to account for the widespread belief in the isolated
nuclear family and the lack of kin ties in contemporary society? Part
of the answer may be that the highly educated (especially professional) middle class is more geographically mobile than other segments of the population, and less involved with kin on a daily basis.[65]
For the less educated, the working class, and lower middle class, as
well as some ethnic groups, social life largely revolves around relatives. Since social critics tend to be members of the upper middle
class, in their discourse on the excesses of individualism they are
likely to be projecting their own life-styles onto the population as a
whole.

Whatever the reasons, it is clear that a certain cynical stance toward
marriage and family, once considered sophisticated and modern, now
seems old-fashioned. As a sign of the times, big weddings are back in
style. Even feminists are more likely to choose a traditional wedding
with all the trappings: a long white gown, a reception for a hundred
relatives and friends, a honeymoon.[66] This shift in the emotional and
intellectual mood has permeated popular culture.

In the 1950s it became almost a convention for Broadway and Hollywood to portray marriages as unhappy, especially if the spouses
were middle-class or middle-aged. *Who's Afraid of Virginia Woolf?*—
both the play and the film—is a prime example of the genre. Joseph
Heller's best-selling 1974 novel *Something Happened* was one of a number of novels that offered a similar message at the time. A depressing
family saga, the book presented in a more naked way a message common to many literary works of the period. Its "hero," Slocum, is totally disaffected from both his corporate job and his suburban family.
In both places, but especially the home, the prevailing emotions are
boredom, indifference, isolation, and unhappiness, punctuated by
anxiety and hatred.

By the end of the 1970s, such a view of middle-class life had begun to seem stale. After the upheavals of the 1960s and early 1970s, the problem seemed to shift from too much social order to too little, from a stifling, seemingly all-powerful system to a sense of chaos and social disintegration. People across the political spectrum groped for symbols of stability and yearned for attachment, roots, tradition.

During the 1980s, these longings fastened on the family. Once again, family and children came to be reinvested with deep-seated values, in an almost religious revitalization easily exploited by politicians and advertisers. The family had arisen like a phoenix from the challenges of ideological assault and demographic upheaval to reclaim its status as a sacred symbol, affecting even those who had been at the forefront of cultural and political revolt. "The new consensus," observed one feminist critic, "is that the family is our last refuge, our only defense against universal predatory selfishness, loneliness, and rootlessness; the idea that there could be a desirable alternative to the family is no longer taken seriously."[67]

The new familistic mood even penetrated into the avant-garde. Woody Allen's films trace the transition from the celebration of liberated sex (*Play It Again, Sam* in 1972) to the search for "relationships" (*Annie Hall* in 1977) to the celebration of family bonds, family rituals, and children (in the recent *Hannah and Her Sisters*, *Radio Days*, and even the dark comedy *Crimes and Misdemeanors*). The work of the avante-garde playwright Sam Shepard has followed a similar odyssey. Shepard himself went from being an East Village bohemian to becoming the embodiment of the all-American hero in his film portrayal of the test pilot Chuck Yeager (*The Right Stuff*). His stormy dramas of the 1960s and 1970s portrayed fractured, alienated families like those of O'Neill, Williams, and Albee; his later plays portray versions of the same vaguely autobiographical characters reuniting and reconciling. A recent play, observes one critic, "finds its mystery not in lies of the mind [the play's title], but in loves of the heart."[68]

Yet if the past has any lesson to teach, it is that inflated expectations for family life are a recipe for personal disenchantment and social neglect. The emphasis on the home as the source of both personal happiness and social order has been responsible for the recurring sense of crisis concerning children and the family that has afflicted American culture since the 1820s. For almost two centuries, social critics have been both singing the praises of the family and decrying its failures.

The vision of the family as an earthly paradise was a nineteenth-century invention. But the most vivid portrayals of the family have been profoundly ambivalent. In what could be called the "high tragic" tradition—including Greek drama and Shakespeare, as well as the Bible, fairy tales, and the novel—the family is portrayed as a power-fully emotional setting, seething with dark Freudian passions. To Freud, such figures as Cain and Abel, Oedipus and Medea, Hamlet and Lear, and the witches and ogres of fairy tales present disguised versions of the emotions of ordinary family life.

As Freud and others have recognized, ambivalence and conflict are woven into the fabric of family life; they arise from the intimacy and commitment that provide its distinct benefits. Nor is it simply the isolated nuclear family that is prone to accumulate tension and con-flict. A large body of anthropological evidence suggests that extended kin groups not only confer security and belonging but give rise to intense conflicts that cannot be openly dealt with, but may emerge in explosive form.

Rather than yearning for an elusive perfected family, we would be wiser to consider new social arrangements that fit the kinds of fami-lies we now have and the kinds of lives we now lead. We need both political will and social creativity in order to devise ways, for exam-ple, of living with divorce and of coming to grips with the implica-tions of living in history's first mass-longevity society. Our traditions have not prepared us for the long and fluid lives we live today. The current celebration of marriage and family does not take into ac-count that most of us will spend parts of our lives living apart from family. We need to think of how to supply substitutes for the com-forts and companionship of home.

We also need to think of how to encourage a broader sociability. Middle-class Americans have substituted a vision of the ideal home for a vision of the ideal city.[69] As a result, our lives are divided be-tween home and work, leaving us yearning for a broader sense of community. Yet what we may be missing is not the idealized small town of our imagined past, but that "third realm" of sociability and social cohesion beyond the home and the workplace—public spaces and informal meeting places—that our European counterparts take for granted as part of the good life.[70]

There are no quick, easy, or cheap fixes for the problems of family life today. And there is good reason to believe that we may never solve some of the dilemmas of family—our paradoxical needs for autonomy and attachment, for privacy and community, the ambivalence built into deep emotional bonds, the tensions stirred by intense intimacy, conflicts between genders and generations. But there is much that could be done to alleviate some of the major, outer sources of stress and strains; sooner or later, policy makers will translate rhetoric and genuine public concern about children and families into ways of addressing the new realities of family life.

Without minimizing our current troubles or our attempts to resolve them, we need to remember that many of the most vexing issues that confront us derive from the very benefits of modernization, benefits too easily forgotten in our yearnings for a lost past. There was no problem of elder care when most people died before they grew old; the problems of adolescence were unknown when work began in childhood; education was a privilege for the well-to-do; and a person's place in society was determined at birth. And when most people were illiterate and living on the margins of survival, only aristocrats could worry about sexual satisfaction and self-fulfillment.

However great the difficulties of the present appear, there is no point in giving in to the lure of nostalgia. There is no golden age of family life to long for, no past pattern that, if only we had the moral will to return to, would guarantee us happiness and security. Family life is always bound up with the economic, demographic, and cultural predicaments of specific times and places. We are no longer a nation of pioneers, Puritans, farmers, or postwar suburbanites. We must shatter the myths that blind us and find ways to cope with our present, the place where social change and family history have brought us.

N O T E S

Prologue

1. Lipsitz 1990, p. 80.

Introduction   A Cultural Earthquake

1. Cited in Mandel 1987.
2. Williams 1961, pp. 48–49.
3. O'Neill 1986; Diggins 1988.
4. Susman 1989.
5. Cited in Ehrenreich 1989, p. 19.
6. Klineberg 1984, p. 129.
7. Fishman 1987.
8. Taylor 1989.
9. Cited in "On and Off the Avenue," *The New Yorker*, December 12, 1977.
10. Spiegel 1971.
11. Birdwhistell 1966.
12. Bottomore 1966, p. 105.
13. LaBarre 1954, p. 104.
14. Tiger 1989, p. 17.
15. Cited in Moynihan 1986, p. xi.
16. Cited in Burns 1989, p. 601.
17. White 1988.
18. Cited in Levitan, Belous, and Gallo 1981.

19. Levitan, Belous, and Gallo 1981.
20. Caplow et al. 1982, p. 323.
21. See Levitan, Belous, and Gallo; 2nd ed. 1988; Glenn 1987.
22. Klatch 1987, p. 26.
23. Willis 1981, p. 164.
24. Paul Zweig, cited in Brugger 1981, p. 385.
25. Lasch 1976, p. 10.
26. Laslett 1976, p. 91.
27. Mintz and Kellogg 1988, p. xx.
28. Anderson 1980.
29. Wells 1982.
30. Gans 1967, p. v.
31. Cherlin 1981.
32. Smith 1985.
33. McLoughlin 1978.
34. This discussion is based on McLoughlin 1978; Smelser and Halpern 1978; and Smith-Rosenberg 1985.
35. Hunter 1987.
36. Davis 1988, p. 74.
37. Williams 1961.
38. Margolis 1984.
39. Ogburn 1950.
40. Hochschild 1989.
41. Kitson, Babri, and Roach 1985.
42. Uhlenberg 1980.
43. Wells 1982, p. 221.
44. Blythe 1979.
45. Sheehy 1976.
46. Clecak 1983.
47. Chafe 1986.
48. Gitlin 1987.
49. Mead 1987, p. 181.
50. Veroff, Douvan, and Kulka, 1981.
51. Ibid., p. 24.
52. Ibid., p. 25.
53. Bernard 1975.

Chapter 1   Sentimental Journeys: Making and Remaking the Modern Family

1. Goldberg 1987, p. 19.
2. Burgess and Locke 1945.
3. Brown 1987, pp. 19ff.
4. See, for example, Berger and Berger 1984; Lasch 1979.
5. Mintz and Kellogg 1988; Coontz 1988.
6. See Thornton and Frick 1987.

7. Smith-Rosenberg 1978.
8. For a useful discussion of the debates surrounding the concept of class and the evidence in support of the rise of a distinct middle class in nineteenth-century America, see Blumin 1989. Gay (1984) discusses diversity and conflicts within the European and American middle classes from the 1820s to World War I.
9. Gay 1984.
10. Fishman 1987.
11. Hajnal 1965.
12. Goode 1963.
13. See Anderson 1971; Hareven 1975.
14. Demos 1976, p. 10.
15. Wells 1982.
16. Cited in Gadlin 1976, p. 237.
17. Wall 1990, p. 127.
18. Shorter 1975.
19. Stone 1977.
20. Trumbach 1978.
21. Macfarlane 1986, p. 664.
22. Taylor, Charles 1989.
23. Shammas 1980, pp. 3–24.
24. Grossberg 1985, p. 6.
25. Quoted in Wall 1990, p. 133.
26. Fleigelman 1982, p. 127.
27. In Evans 1989, p. 63.
28. Cited in Woloch 1984, p. 93.
29. Greven 1977.
30. Mintz and Kellogg 1988.
31. Boydston 1991.
32. Welter 1966/1973.
33. Stone 1977, pp. 667–68.
34. Smelser and Halpern 1978.
35. Cited in Hellerstein, Hume, and Offen 1981; Tennyson himself may not have identified with these sentiments.
36. Welter 1966/1973.
37. Ibid., p. 225.
38. Boydston 1991.
39. Kessler-Harris 1982.
40. Modell and Hareven 1973.
41. McLaughlin et al. 1988, p. 18.
42. Poovey 1988.
43. Weeks 1985, p. 16.
44. Susman 1984.
45. Quoted in Jeffrey 1972, p. 29.
46. Wall 1990, p. 149.

47. Karen Lykstra (1989) makes the case for romantic love as a factor in social history.
48. Griswold 1982, p. 5.
49. Zelizer 1985.
50. Caldwell 1982.
51. Fass 1977.
52. Degler 1980; Gay 1984.
53. Demos 1976, p. 30.
54. Jeffrey 1972.
55. Smelser and Halpern 1978.
56. Bergmann 1986, p. 8.
57. De Tocqueville 1966.
58. Mintz and Kellogg 1988.
59. Gay 1984.
60. Cited in Wall 1990, p. 138.
61. In Frykman and Lofgren 1987, pp. 120–21.
62. Brenton 1966, p. 194.
63. Demos 1986, p. 23.
64. D'Emilio and Freedman 1988, p. 183.
65. Freud 1912, p. 207.
66. Coontz 1988, p. 222.
67. Fiedler 1962.
68. Demos 1976, p. 24.
69. LeVine and White 1987.
70. Baumeister and Tice 1986.
71. Coontz 1988.
72. Filene 1986, p. 40.
73. In Leuchtenburg 1958, p. 6.
74. Ibid., p. 178.
75. Norton et al. 1986, p. 540.
76. Zaretsky 1976.
77. Filene 1986, p. 134.
78. D'Emilio and Freedman 1988.
79. Cott 1987, p. 150.
80. Taft 1922.
81. Kinsey 1948.
82. Cott 1987, p. 149.
83. See Reiss and Lee 1988, p. 141.
84. Kinsey 1948.
85. Bailey 1988, p. 3.
86. Fass 1977, p. 262.
87. Cott 1987, p. 150.
88. Van Horn 1988, pp. 32–45.
89. Griswold 1982, p. 179.
90. Anderson 1980, p. 39.
91. Wall 1990.

92. Anderson 1980, p. 45.
93. Demos 1976, p. 30.
94. Harris 1983.

Chapter 2   "Trying Out the Dream": The Family in the 1950s

1. Rafferty and Powelson 1988, p. 46.
2. Discussed in Sheff 1988.
3. Mander 1969.
4. Conger 1981, pp. 1477–78.
5. Susman 1989.
6. Cherlin 1981.
7. Masnick and Bane 1980, p. 2.
8. Filene 1986.
9. Elder 1974.
10. O'Neill 1986, p. 42.
11. Van Horn 1988.
12. Haskell 1974, p. 235.
13. Cited in Chafe 1986, p. 11.
14. Hodgson 1977, p. 52.
15. Chafe 1986.
16. Hine 1986.
17. Quoted in Baritz 1988, p. 184.
18. Lekachman 1966, p. 190.
19. Harrington 1963.
20. Lynd and Lynd 1929, pp. 23–24.
21. Caplow et al. 1982.
22. Hodgson 1977, p. 53.
23. Inglehart 1977, p. 7.
24. Davis 1984.
25. Oakley 1986, p. 257.
26. Caplow et al. 1982, p. 25.
27. Gans 1967; Berger 1971.
28. Hirschman 1982, p. 25.
29. McKendrick et al. 1982; Campbell 1987.
30. Cited in Hirschman 1982, p. 43.
31. Riesman et al. 1950.
32. Whyte 1956.
33. Keats 1956; Gordon et al. 1961; Berger 1971.
34. Diggins 1988.
35. Cited in Donaldson 1969, p. 119.
36. Donaldson 1969, p. 119.
37. Best 1990; Brunvand 1981.
38. Brunvand 1981, p. 189.
39. Berger 1960; Berger 1971, p. 157.
40. Gans 1967, p. xvii.

41. Ibid., p. 409.
42. See Breines 1986 for an analysis of contradictions between social criticism and empirical observations of family life.
43. Gans 1967, p. 334.
44. Berger 1971; see also Donaldson 1969.
45. Berger 1971.
46. For a description of the kitchen debate, see May 1989.
47. Berger 1971.
48. Whyte 1956; MacDonald 1957.
49. Lears 1989.
50. Gans 1967, overleaf.
51. Hunter 1986.
52. Hewlett 1986.
53. Cherlin 1981.
54. Personal interview, 1988.
55. Easterlin 1980.
56. Chafe 1986, p. 12.
57. Quoted in ibid., p. 14.
58. Honey 1984, pp. 1-2.
59. Friedan 1963.
60. Honey 1984, p. 55.
61. Elder 1984.
62. Pleck 1985.
63. Rupp 1978, p. 151.
64. Honey 1984, p. 125.
65. May 1988.
66. Modell 1989.
67. Chafe 1986.
68. Cited in ibid., p. 83.
69. Eisler 1986.
70. *McCall's* (May 1954), cited in ibid., p. 207.
71. Cited in Hewlett 1986.
72. Wolfenstein 1955.
73. Sears et al. 1957.
74. Weiss 1977.
75. Zuckerman 1975.
76. Bronfenbrenner 1958.
77. Kagan 1977.
78. Levenson 1972.
79. Cited in Friedan 1963, p. 43.
80. Farnham and Lundberg 1947.
81. Ehrenreich 1983, p. 129.
82. Douglas 1982.
83. Eisler 1986, p. 18.
84. Diggins 1988, p. 219.
85. Bernard 1973.

86. O'Neill 1986, p. 42.
87. Footlick 1990.

Chapter 3   The "Burned-over" Decade: Public Disorder and
            Private Transformation in the 1960s

1. Kaiser 1988.
2. Ibid., p. 255.
3. Fitzgerald 1987.
4. Quoted in Baritz 1988, p. 230.
5. Dickstein 1977, p. 26.
6. Hodgson 1976, p. 307.
7. See, for example, Daniels 1989.
8. Cited in *Newsweek*, September 5, 1988, p. 24.
9. Lhamon 1990.
10. Schlesinger 1960, reprinted in Howard 1982, p. 45.
11. Ibid., p. 54.
12. Lears 1989.
13. Susman 1989.
14. Goldthorpe 1987, p. 80.
15. Krantz 1988.
16. Isserman and Kazin 1989, p. 225.
17. J. Skolnick 1969, p. 83.
18. Fraser and Gerstle, 1989, p. 2.
19. Jones 1980.
20. Keniston 1971.
21. Inglehart 1977.
22. Gitlin 1987, p. 19.
23. Ibid., p. 20.
24. Fraser and Gerstle, 1989, p. 16.
25. Seigel 1986.
26. Berger 1971.
27. Dickstein 1977, p. 19.
28. Fass 1977, p. 14.
29. Bailey 1988.
30. Cited in Rothman 1984, p. 298.
31. Cited in ibid., p. 298.
32. Petchesky 1984, p. 214.
33. Eisler 1986, p. 129.
34. Hunt 1974.
35. Haskell 1974, p. xii.
36. Reiss 1960.
37. Reiss 1966.
38. McLaughlin et al. 1988.
39. Terman 1938.
40. Sorenson 1973, p. 341.

41. Ehrenreich, Hess, and Jacobs 1986.
42. D'Emilio and Freedman 1988.
43. Reid 1978.
44. Ehrenreich et al. 1986.
45. Esman 1990.
46. Rothman 1984, p. 310.
47. Farber 1964.
48. Collins 1990, pp. 344–45.
49. Ibid.
50. See Lawson 1988.
51. Ogilvy and Ogilvy 1972, p. 83.
52. Kern 1981.
53. Jeffrey 1972.
54. Berger 1979.
55. Ibid.
56. Zablocki 1971, p. 309.
57. Speck et al. 1972, p. 9.
58. Zablocki 1980.
59. Zablocki 1971.
60. Berger 1979.
61. Aidala 1989.
62. Cited in Collins 1990, p. 489.
63. Schlesinger, in Howard 1982, p. 54.
64. Berger 1971, p. 216.
65. Yankelovich 1981, p. 43.
66. Robinson 1976, p. 3.
67. Gitlin 1987.
68. Dickstein 1977.
69. McLoughlin 1978.
70. Turner 1974; Wallace 1956, 1970.
71. Smith-Rosenberg 1985.
72. Ryan 1981; Smelser and Halpern 1978.
73. Berger 1979, p. 237.

Chapter 4   Half a Revolution: The Second Wave of Feminism and the Family

1. Cohen 1988, pp. 149–53; Echols 1989.
2. Filene 1986, p. 204.
3. Quoted in Cohen 1988, p. 153.
4. Gornick 1978.
5. O'Reilly 1972.
6. Ibid.
7. Filene 1986, pp. 205–6.
8. Cited in Hole and Levine 1971.
9. Ogden 1986, p. 209.

10. Fleming 1988.
11. Freeman 1975, p. 147.
12. Quoted in Astrachan 1988, p. 201.
13. Gornick 1978.
14. Gittelson 1972.
15. McLaughlin et al. 1988.
16. Cited in Degler 1980, p. 448.
17. Chafe 1986, p. 434; Fleming 1988.
18. Chafetz and Dworkin 1987.
19. Rosen 1987, p. 53.
20. McLaughlin et al. 1988, p. 179.
21. Degler 1980, p. 443.
22. Chafe 1987.
23. Aisenberg and Harrington 1988.
24. Weiner 1985.
25. Uhlenberg 1980.
26. See Stewart et al. 1985.
27. Chafe 1986, p. 126.
28. Chafe 1987, p. 210.
29. Filene 1986, p. 192.
30. Ibid., p. 193.
31. Chafe 1986, p. 127.
32. Davis 1988.
33. For a history of the "pin-money" myth and the reports debunking it, see Margolis 1985.
34. Chafe 1986, p. 127.
35. Rubin 1979, pp. 163–64.
36. Landis 1955.
37. Chafe 1986, p. 126.
38. In Diggins 1988, p. 217.
39. Miller and Swanson 1958.
40. See Breines 1986; Ehrenreich 1983.
41. Wylie 1942/1955.
42. Goodman 1961, p. 1.
43. Kimmel 1987.
44. Griswold 1988.
45. Lynes 1953, p. 51.
46. May 1988.
47. Skolnick 1981.
48. King 1987, p. 460.
49. Quoted in Mathews 1982, p. 410.
50. Friedan 1963.
51. Quoted in Diggins 1988, p. 215.
52. *Newsweek*, March 7, 1960, cited in Friedan 1963, p. 19.
53. Smith-Rosenberg 1978.
54. Friedan 1963.

55. Cited in King 1987.
56. Ibid.
57. Gitlin 1987.
58. *Roe v. Wade* 1973.
59. Rosenfelt and Stacey 1987.
60. Gornick 1969.
61. Morgan 1975/1987.
62. Cited in Hole and Levine 1971.
63. Chafetz and Dworkin 1987.
64. Luker 1984.
65. Mansbridge 1986.
66. Cherlin 1981.
67. Mathews 1982.
68. Ibid.
69. Fuchs 1983.
70. O'Reilly 1975.
71. Chafe 1986.
72. Belkin 1989; Destefano and Colesanto 1990.
73. Echols 1989, p. xv.
74. Solomon 1991.
75. Rosenfelt and Stacey 1987, p. 351.
76. Rubin 1990.
77. Sidel 1990.

Chapter 5   The 1970s and the Culture of Nostalgia

1. The quotes are from *An American Family*, 1973, prepared by Ron Goulart for Warner paperbacks.
2. Susman 1989, p. 6.
3. Smelser and Halpern 1978.
4. Smith-Rosenberg 1978, p. 220.
5. Zweig 1980.
6. Bernard 1981.
7. Steiner 1981, p. 13.
8. Steinmetz and Straus 1974, p. 3.
9. Steiner 1981, p. 205.
10. Lennard and Bernstein 1969.
11. Quoted in Framo 1972, p. 10.
12. Cited in Steiner 1981, p. 25.
13. Cited in Carroll 1982, p. xiii.
14. Cited in Phillips 1982.
15. Reich 1970. p. 2.
16. Barone 1990, p. 478.
17. Clecak 1983, p. 229.
18. Friedman 1990.
19. Morgan 1975.

20. Hunt 1974.
21. Rubin 1976, p. 120.
22. Levy 1987.
23. Caplovitz 1979.
24. Ehrenreich 1989.
25. Gans 1988.
26. Lipset 1982.
27. Bennett 1988, 1990.
28. Blumberg 1980, p. 239.
29. White 1988.
30. Phillips 1983.
31. See Jones 1980, chap. on "The Nostalgic Style." Also see Davis 1979.
32. The quotation is by Cawelti, in Ferraro 1989, p. 192.
33. Roiphe 1973.
34. Cited in Burns 1989, p. 601.
35. Wilkenson 1983, 1988.
36. The guest list included Christopher Lasch, Daniel Bell, and Robert Bellah. See Clecak 1983.
37. O'Neill 1977, p. 11.
38. Becker 1960.
39. Zweig 1980.
40. Wolfe 1982, p. 278. (Originally published 1976.)
41. Cited in Carroll 1990, pp. 142–43.
42. Lasch 1976.
43. Carroll 1990, p. 145.
44. Wolfe 1976, p. 31.
45. See Gans 1988.
46. Lasch 1976, p. 50.
47. Brugger 1981, p. 385.
48. Pulver 1986.
49. Rycroft 1968, pp. 94–95.
50. Cooper 1986.
51. Battan 1983, p. 211.
52. Lasch 1979.
53. Bane 1976, p. 35.
54. Bane 1976, p. 35.
55. Veroff et al. 1981.
56. Ibid., p. 105.
57. Preceding quotes and statistics from ibid., p. 138.
58. Preceding quotes and statistics from Yankelovich 1981, pp. 91, 5, 113.
59. Carroll 1990.
60. Katz 1989, p. 8.
61. Berger 1971, p. 159.
62. Wilkenson 1988, p. 16.
63. Long 1985, pp. 188–89.

Chapter 6 Changes of Heart: The Social Sources of Psychological Transformation

1. Blankenhorn 1990, p. 18.
2. Veroff, Douvan, and Kulka 1981, p. 25.
3. Inglehart 1977; Alwin 1988.
4. Giddens 1990.
5. Hagestad 1986.
6. Moroney 1980.
7. Blythe 1979, p. 4.
8. Preston 1976.
9. Cited in Hagestad 1986.
10. Wells 1982, p. 222.
11. Preston 1976.
12. Uhlenberg 1980.
13. Demos 1986.
14. Knapp 1987.
15. Zelizer 1985.
16. Langer 1972; Trexler 1973.
17. Kessen 1965.
18. Scheper-Hughes 1985.
19. Cited in Imhof 1986, p. 248.
20. Cited in Goldthorpe 1987, p. 71. (Original citation from Encyclopedia Brittanica, 1910.)
21. Kain 1990, p. 62.
22. Stone 1990, p. 410.
23. Ariès 1962, p. 128.
24. Linda Pollock (1983) has argued against the idea of cultural discontinuity implied in the invention of childhood, insisting that parental solicitude is invariant across human cultures. Pollock's work has been challenged on a number of grounds. See Bellingham 1988.
25. Demos 1986, p. 96.
26. Muuss 1962.
27. Hill and Monks 1977, pp. 14–15.
28. Kern 1974; Mintz and Kellogg 1988.
29. Demos 1986, p. 107.
30. Smith-Rosenberg 1978.
31. Baumeister and Tice 1986.
32. Hall 1904, p. xiii.
33. Ibid.
34. Eisenstadt 1956; see Fass 1977.
35. Baumeister and Tice 1986.
36. Abrams 1982; Greenberg 1977.
37. Esman 1990.
38. Grant Foundation 1988.
39. Esman 1990, p. 98.

40. Cited in Spacks 1981, p. 1.
41. Spacks 1981, p. 243.
42. Ariès 1962, p. 30.
43. Perun and Bielby 1979, p. 294.
44. Clausen 1990.
45. Baumeister 1986, pp. 212–13.
46. Marcus 1984, p. 187.
47. Laslett 1989.
48. Fitzgerald 1987.
49. Plath 1980, p. 1.
50. Hagestad 1987, p. 3.
51. Hagestad 1986.
52. Cited in Gerber et al. 1989, p. 24.
53. Demos 1986, p. 131.
54. Kohli 1986.
55. Ibid.
56. Chudacoff 1989.
57. Kohli 1986.
58. Ibid., p. 296.
59. Uhlenberg 1980.
60. Imhof 1986.
61. Modell et al. 1978.
62. Hareven 1982.
63. Goldin 1983.
64. Buchmann 1989.
65. Modell 1989.
66. Keniston 1971.
67. Furstenberg and Spanier 1987, p. 53.
68. Schnaiberg and Goldenberg 1989.
69. Friedman 1990.
70. Clecak 1983.
71. Bernstein 1964, 1970; Cook-Gumperz 1973.
72. Trumbach 1978.
73. Hellerstein, Hume, and Offen 1981, p. 4.
74. Alwin 1988.
75. Bernstein 1964, p. 59.
76. Kohn 1959, p. 351.
77. Sluzki and Eliseo 1971, pp. 398–99.
78. De Swaan 1981.
79. Clecak 1983.
80. De Swaan 1981, p. 376.
81. Gordon 1988.
82. De Swaan 1981, p. 373.
83. Estrich 1987, p. 41.
84. Caspi, Bem, and Elder 1989.
85. Hunter 1986, p. 88.

86. Giddens 1990, p. 43.
87. Gellner 1985, p. 11.
88. Ibid., p. 33.
89. White 1978, p. 55.
90. Trilling 1972, p. 19.
91. Taylor 1989.
92. Cited in Wrong 1976. (Lionel Trilling's story "Of This Time, Of That Place" was originally published in 1943.)
93. Hewitt 1989.
94. Melucci 1989, p. 116.
95. Gendlin 1987.
96. Stearns and Stearns 1986.
97. Barsky 1988.
98. Berger 1976; Marcus 1984.

Chapter 7   Backing into the Future

1. Dionne 1991, p. 8.
2. Wells 1982.
3. Cited in Edwards 1987, p. 355.
4. Gay 1984.
5. Smith 1985, pp. 911–14.
6. Margaret Mead once observed that social change makes us "immigrants in time." The reference to Ogburn is from a speech by Mirra Komarovsky reported in Komarovsky 1990.
7. Berthoff 1971.
8. Schlossman 1880, p. 3.
9. Cited in Chafe 1986, p. 450.
10. Dornbusch and Strober 1988.
11. Lewin 1990.
12. "Recombinant" family life is described in Stacey 1990.
13. O'Rourke, cited in Kay 1989, pp. 405–6.
14. Mintz and Kellogg 1988, p. xvii.
15. Cherlin and Furstenberg 1988.
16. Bernard 1981, p. 59.
17. Dionne 1991, p. 243.
18. Cannon 1982, p. 31; White 1988, p. 40.
19. Gutmann, 1989, p. 81.
20. Dionne 1991.
21. Lipset 1982.
22. D'Antonio 1989.
23. See Harris 1987; Dionne 1991.
24. Bronner 1989.
25. Bork 1990, p. A21.
26. *Newsweek*, November 24, 1986, p. 76.
27. Weiss 1988.

28. Sheff 1988, p. 62.
29. Merritt and Steiner 1984.
30. Gutis 1989b, p. B1.
31. Sullivan 1989.
32. *Newsweek*, Spring/Summer 1990, (special issue on "The 21st Century Family") p. 18.
33. "Most Regard Family Highly," *New York Times*, October 10, 1989.
34. Cited in Dionne 1991, p. 325.
35. Caplow et al. 1983, p. 131.
36. Sheff 1988, p. 48.
37. Cited in Goodman 1989, p. 360.
38. "Too Late for Prince Charming," *Newsweek*, June 2, 1986.
39. Cherlin 1990.
40. Ibid., p. 122.
41. See Cancian 1987.
42. See Stacey 1990.
43. Reissman 1990, p. 68.
44. Rubin 1976, p. 93; Reissman 1990, p. 120.
45. Jeffrey 1972, p. 30.
46. Cuber and Harroff 1965.
47. Skolnick, 1981.
48. Bernard 1982.
49. Fields 1990; Kelly 1990.
50. Hochschield 1989, p. 260.
51. Stone 1989, p. 15.
52. Swidler 1985.
53. Lear 1988, p. 63.
54. Parsons 1955.
55. Weiss 1979.
56. Naisbitt 1982.
57. Phillips 1990.

Chapter 8   The State of the American Family

1. Featherstone 1979, p. 22.
2. Kain 1990; Glenn 1987; Spanier 1989.
3. Dionne 1991.
4. Bianchi 1990.
5. Bellah et al. 1985, p. 290.
6. Wilkinson 1988; Hewitt 1989.
7. Ibid.
8. Lipset 1982.
9. Popenoe 1989, p. 1.
10. Orthner 1990, p. 34.
11. Blankenhorn 1989.
12. Featherstone 1979.

13. Blankenhorn 1989.
14. Ibid.
15. Mellman, Lazarus, and Rivlin 1990.
16. Bianchi 1990, p. 10.
17. Best (1990) examines the evidence underlying the claims about missing children, sexual abuse, molestation, Halloween sadism, and so on, and concludes that the emergence of these threats as public issues bears little relation to changes in "objective" risks to children.
18. Diggins 1988, p. 201.
19. Fine 1955.
20. Cited in Diggins 1988, pp. 201-3.
21. Statistics in the following paragraphs are based on Zill and Rodgers 1988; Furstenberg and Condran 1988; Bianchi 1990.
22. Bianchi 1990.
23. Uhlenberg and Eggebeen 1986.
24. Furstenberg and Condran 1988.
25. Bronfenbrenner and Crouter 1982.
26. Hoffman 1989, p. 90.
27. Furstenberg and Cherlin 1991.
28. Hetherington, Hagan, and Anderson 1989.
29. Furstenberg and Cherlin 1991.
30. Emery 1989.
31. Block, Block, and Gjerde 1986.
32. Brody 1991.
33. Bohannan 1985.
34. Hewlett 1991.
35. Ibid.
36. Oxford Analytica 1986.
37. Levy 1987.
38. Phillips 1990, p. 217.
39. Cited in ibid., p. 200.
40. Levy 1987, p. 193.
41. Bane, Fuchs: see Grant Foundation 1988, p. 81.
42. Census Bureau 1989, p. 65.
43. Stipek and McCroskey 1989, p. 416.
44. Grant Foundation 1988, p. 20.
45. Grant Foundation 1988, p. 20.
46. Ibid.
47. Cherlin 1989.
48. Burton 1990, p. 133.
49. Wilson 1987; Elder 1974; Newman 1988.
50. Katz 1989.
51. Weir, Orloff, and Skocpol 1988, p. 8.
52. Wilensky 1990.
53. Ibid.
54. Dionne 1991; see also Mellman, Lazarus, and Rivlin 1990.

55. Holmes 1991.
56. Orthner 1990.
57. Richman and Slovak 1990.
58. Campbell 1981; Mellman, Lazarus, and Rivlin 1990; Fischer 1982.
59. Harris 1987.
60. Borus et al. 1980.
61. Ehrenreich 1983; Rubin 1990, p. 142.
62. Sheff 1988; Gallup and Newport 1990.
63. Cherlin and Furstenberg 1988b.
64. Blankenhorn 1989.
65. Fischer 1982.
66. Gillis 1985, p. 308; Gelman 1990.
67. Willis 1981, p. 150.
68. Luedke 1986.
69. Hayden 1984.
70. Odenburg 1989.

BIBLIOGRAPHY

ABRAMS, PHILIP. 1982. *Historical Sociology*. New York: Cornell University Press.

AIDALA, ANGELA A. 1989. "Communes and Changing Family Norms: Marriage and Life-Style Choice Among Former Members of Communal Groups." *Journal of Family Issues* 10, no. 3, pp. 311–38.

AISENBERG, NADIA, AND MONA HARRINGTON. 1988. *Women of Academe: Outsiders in the Sacred Grove*. Amherst: University of Massachusetts Press.

ALWIN, D. F. 1988. "From Obedience to Autonomy: Changes in Traits Desired in Children, 1924–1978." *Public Opinion Quarterly* 52, pp. 33–52.

ANDERSON, MICHAEL. 1971. *Family Structure in Nineteenth Century Lancashire*. Cambridge: Cambridge University Press.

———. 1980. "The Relevance of Family History." In *Sociology of the Family*, 2nd ed, pp. 33–63. Edited by Michael Anderson. New York: Penguin Books.

ARIÈS, P. 1962. *Centuries of Childhood: A Social History of Family Life*. Translated by R. Baldick. New York: Knopf.

ASTRACHAN, ANTHONY. 1988. *How Men Feel: Their Response to Women's Demands for Equality and Power*. New York: Anchor Press/Doubleday.

ATWOOD, MARGARET. 1986. *The Handmaid's Tale*. Boston: Houghton Mifflin.

BAILEY, BETH L. 1988. *From Front Porch to Back Seat: Courtship in Twentieth-Century America*. Baltimore: Johns Hopkins University Press.

BANE, MARY JO. 1976. *Here to Stay: American Families in the Twentieth Century*. New York: Basic Books.

BARITZ, LOREN. 1988. *The Good Life: The Meaning of Success for the American Middle Class*. New York: Knopf.

BARONE, MICHAEL. 1990. *Our Country: The Shaping of America from Roosevelt to Reagan*. New York: Free Press.

BARSKY, ARTHUR J. 1988. "The Paradox of Health." *The New England Journal of Medicine* 318: 414–18.

BATTAN, JESSE. 1983. "The New Narcissism in 20th-Century America: The Shadow and Substance of Social Change." *Journal of Social History* 17: 200–213.

BAUMEISTER, ROY F. 1986. *Identity: Cultural Change and the Struggle for Self*. New York: Oxford University Press.

———, AND DIANE TICE. 1986. "How Adolescence Became the Struggle for Self: The Historical Transformation of Psychological Development." In *Psychological Perspectives on the Self*, vol. 3. Edited by Jerry Sulls and Anthony Greenwald. Hillsdale, NJ: Lawrence Erlbaum.

BECKER, H. 1960. "Normative Reactions to Normlessness." *American Sociological Review* 25: 803–10.

BELKIN, LISA. 1989. "Bars to Equality of Sexes Seen as Eroding, Slowly." *New York Times*. August 20, pp. A1, A16.

BELLAH, ROBERT N., RICHARD MADSEN, WILLIAM M. SULLIVAN, ANN SWIDLER, AND STEVEN M. TIPTON. 1985. *Habits of the Heart: Individualism and Commitment in American Life*. Berkeley: University of California Press.

BELLINGHAM, BRUCE. 1988. "The History of Childhood Since the Invention of Childhood: Some Issues in the Eighties." *Journal of Family History* 13: 347–58.

BENNETT, DAVID H. 1988. *The Party of Fear: From Nativist Movements to the New Right in American History*. Chapel Hill: University of North Carolina Press.

BERGER, BENNETT M. 1960. *Working-Class Suburb: A Study of Auto Workers in Suburbia*. Berkeley: University of California Press.

———. 1971. *Looking for America: Essays on Youth, Suburbia and Other American Obsessions*. Englewood Cliffs, NJ: Prentice Hall.

———. 1979. "American Pastoralism, Suburbia and the Commune Movement: An Exercise in the Microsociology of Marriage." In *On the Making of Americans: Essays in Honor of David Reisman*. Edited by Herbert J. Gans, Nathan Glazer, Joseph R. Gusfield, and Christopher Jencks. Philadelphia: University of Pennsylvania Press.

BERGER, BRIGITTE, AND PETER F. BERGER. 1983/1984. *The War over the Family*. Garden City, NY: Anchor Books.

BERGER, PETER. 1976. "The Socialist Myth." *Public Interest* 44: 3.

BERGMANN, BARBARA. 1986. *The Economic Emergence of Women*. New York: Basic Books.

BERNARD, JESSIE. 1972, rep. 1973. *The Future of Marriage*. New York: Bantam Books.

——. 1975. "Adolescence and the Socialization for Motherhood." In *Adolescence and the Life Cycle*, pp. 227–52. Edited by S. E. Dragastin and G. H. Elder. New York: Wiley.

——. 1981. "Facing the Future." In *Society* 18, no. 2: 53–59.

BERNSTEIN, BASIL. 1964. "Social Class and Psychotherapy." *British Journal of Sociology* 15: 54–64.

——. 1970. "A Socio-Linguistic Approach to Socialization." In *Directions in Socio-Linguistics*. Edited by J. Gumperz and D. Hymes. New York: Holt, Rinehart and Winston.

BERTHOFF, ROLAND. T. 1971. *An Unsettled People: Social Order and Disorder in American History.* New York: Harper & Row.

BEST, JOEL. 1990. *Threatened Children: Rhetoric and Concern About Child-Victims.* Chicago: University of Chicago Press.

BIANCHI, SUZANNE M. 1990. "America's Children: Mixed Prospects." *Population Bulletin* 45, no. 1.

——, AND DAPHNE SPAIN. 1986. *American Women in Transition.* New York: Russell Sage.

BIRDWHISTELL, R. L. 1966. "The American Family: Some Perspectives." *Psychiatry* 29: 203–12.

BLANKENHORN, DAVID. 1989. "Ozzie and Harriet, Alive and Well," *Washington Post,* June 11. Outlook sec., p. 3. See also "Ozzie and Harriet: Have Reports of Their Death Been Greatly Exaggerated?" *Family Affairs* 2, nos. 2–3 (Summer/Fall 1989): 10.

——. 1990. "American Family Dilemmas." In *Rebuilding the Nest: A New Commitment to the American Family*. Edited by David Blankenhorn, Steven Bayme, and Jean Bethke Elshtain. Milwaukee, WI: Family Service America.

BLOCK, J. H., J. BLOCK, AND P. F. GJERDE. 1986. "The Personality of Children Prior to Divorce: A Prospective Study." *Child Development* 57: 827–40.

BLUMBERG, PAUL. 1980. *Inequality in an Age of Decline.* New York: Oxford University Press.

BLUMIN, STUART. 1989. *The Emergence of the Middle Class: Social Experience in the American City, 1760–1900.* New York: Cambridge University Press.

BLYTHE, RONALD. 1979. *The View in Winter.* New York and London: Harcourt Brace Jovanovich.

BOHANNAN, PAUL. 1985. *All the Happy Families: Exploring the Varieties of Family Life.* New York: McGraw-Hill.

BORK, ROBERT. 1990. "At Last an End to Supreme Court Activism." *New York Times.* August 29, p. A21.

BORUS, M. E., J. E. CROWLEY, R. W. RUMBERGER, R. SANTOS, AND D. SHAPIRO. 1980. *Pathways to the Future: A Longitudinal Study of Young Americans.* Columbus: Ohio State University Press.

BOTTOMORE, THOMAS B. 1966. *Classes in Modern Society.* New York: Pantheon.

BOYDSTON, JEANNE. 1991. "The Pastoralization of Housework." In *Women's*

America: Refocusing the Past, pp. 148–61. Edited by Linda Kerber and Jane Sherron De Hart. Oxford and New York: Oxford University Press.

BREINES, WINIFRED. 1986. "The 1950's: Gender and Some Social Science." *Sociological Inquiry* 56, no. 1: 69–92.

BRENTON, MYRON. 1966. *The American Male.* New York: Coward-McCann.

BRODY, JANE. 1991. "Problems of Children: A New Look at Divorce." *New York Times.* June 7, p. B1.

BRONFENBRENNER, U.. 1958. "Socialization and Social Class Through Time and Space." In *Readings in Social Psychology*, 3rd ed., pp. 400–425. Edited by E. E. Maccoby, T. M. Newcomb, and E. L. Hartley. New York: Holt, Rinehart and Winston.

———, AND A. CROUTER. 1982. "Work and Family Through Time and Space." In *Families That Work: Children in a Changing World*, pp. 39–83. Edited by S. B. Kamerman and C. D. Hayes. Washington, DC: National Academy Press.

BRONNER, ETHAN. 1989. *Battle for Justice: How the Bork Nomination Shook America.* New York: Norton.

BROWN, PATRICIA L. 1987. "Long Live Victoria: Her Age Inspires Designs for 1980's." *New York Times.* June 25, p. 19.

BRUGGER, ROBERT J., ED. 1981. *Our Selves/Our Past: Psychological Approaches to American History.* Baltimore: Johns Hopkins University Press.

BRUNVAND, JAN HAROLD. 1981. *The Vanishing Hitchhiker.* New York: Norton.

BUCHMANN, MARLIS. 1989. *The Script of Life in Modern Society: Entry into Adulthood in a Changing World.* Chicago: University of Chicago Press.

BURGESS, E. W., AND HARVEY J. LOCKE. 1945. *The Family.* New York: American Book Co.

BURNS, JAMES MACGREGOR. 1989. *The Crosswinds of Freedom.* New York: Knopf.

BURTON, LINDA M. 1990. "Teenage Childbearing as an Alternative Life-Course Strategy in Multigeneration Black Families." *Human Nature* 1, no. 2: 123–43.

CALDWELL, J. 1982. *Theory of Fertility Decline.* New York: Academic Press.

CAMPBELL, ANGUS. 1981. *The Sense of Well-Being in America: Recent Patterns and Trends.* New York: McGraw-Hill.

CAMPBELL, COLIN. 1987. *The Romantic Ethic and the Spirit of Modern Consumerism.* Oxford: Basil Blackwell.

CANCIAN, FRANCESCA. 1987. *Love in America.* New York: Cambridge University Press.

CANNON, LOU. 1982. *Reagan.* New York: Perigee Books.

CAPLOVITZ, D. 1979. *Making Ends Meet*, vol. 86. Beverly Hills, CA: Sage Library of Social Research.

CAPLOW, THEODORE, HOWARD BAHR, BRUCE CHADWICK, REUBEN HILL, AND MARGARET HOLMES WILLIAMSON. 1982. *Middleton Families: Fifty Years of Change and Continuity.* Toronto: Bantam Books.

CARROLL, PETER N. 1982. *It Seemed Like Nothing Happened: America in the 1970's.* New Brunswick, NJ: Rutgers University Press.

———. 1990. *Keeping Time: Memory, Nostalgia, and the Art of History.* Athens, GA: University of Georgia Press.

CASPI, AVSHALOM, DARYL J. BEM, AND GLEN H. ELDER, JR. 1989. "Continuities and Consequences of Interactional Styles Across the Life Course." *Journal of Personality* 56: 375–406.

CHAFE, WILLIAM H. 1986. *The Unfinished Journey: America Since World War II.* New York: Oxford University Press.

———. 1987. "Social Change and the American Woman, 1940–1970." In *A History of Our Time: Readings on Postwar America.* Edited by William H. Chafe and Howard Sitcoff. New York: Oxford University Press.

CHAFETZ, JANET SALTZMAN, AND ANTHONY GARY DWORKIN. 1987. "In the Face of Threat: Organized Antifeminism in Comparative Perspective." *Gender and Society* 1, no. 1. New York: Sage.

CHERLIN, ANDREW. 1981. *Marriage, Divorce, Remarriage.* Cambridge: Harvard University Press.

———. 1983. "Changing Family and Household: Contemporary Lessons from Historical Research." *Annual Review of Sociology* 9: 51–56. Palo Alto: Annual Reviews, Inc.

———. 1989. "Marriage, Divorce, Remarriage: From the 1950's to the 1980's." Paper presented at the American Sociological Association. San Francisco, August 11.

———. 1990. "The Strange Career of the 'Harvard-Yale Study.'" *Public Opinion Quarterly* 54: 117–24.

———, ED. 1988. *The Changing American Family and Public Policy.* Washington, DC: Urban Institute Press.

CHERLIN, ANDREW, AND FRANK F. FURSTENBERG, JR. 1988a. "The Changing European Family: Lessons for the American Reader." *Journal of Family Issues* 9, no. 3: 291–97.

———. 1988b. "The American Family in the Year 2000." In *Current Issues in Marriage and the Family,* pp. 337–61. Edited by J. Gipson Wells. York: Macmillan.

CHUDACOFF, HOWARD P. 1989. *How Old Are You?: Age Consciousness in American Culture.* Princeton, New Jersey: Princeton University Press.

CLAUSEN, J. A. 1986. *The Life Course.* Englewood Cliffs, NJ: Prentice-Hall.

———. 1990. "Turning Point as a Life Course Concept." Paper presented at the American Sociological Association. Washington, D.C. August.

CLECAK, PETER. 1983. *America's Quest for the Ideal Self: Dissent and Fulfillment in the 60's and 70's.* New York: Oxford University Press.

COHEN, MARCIA. 1988. *The Sisterhood: The True Story of the Women Who Changed the World,* pp. 149–53. New York: Simon and Schuster.

COLLINS, RANDALL. 1990. *Sociology of the Family.* Chicago: Nelson Hall.

CONGER, J. 1981. "Freedom and Commitment: Families, Youth, and Social Change." *American Psychologist* 36, no. 12: 1475–84.

COOK-GUMPERZ, JENNY. 1973. *Social Control and Socialization: A Study of*

Class Differences in the Language of Material Control. London and Boston: Routledge & Kegan Paul.

COOKINGHAM, MARY E. 1983. "Working After Childbearing in Modern America." *Journal of Interdisciplinary History* 14: 773–92.

COONTZ, STEPHANIE. 1988. *The Social Origins of Private Life: A History of American Families 1600–1900.* London: Verso.

COOPER, ARNOLD M. 1986. "Narcissism." In *Essential Papers on Narcissism.* Edited by Andrew P. Morrison, M.D. New York: New York University Press.

COTT, NANCY. 1987. *The Grounding of Modern Feminism.* New Haven: Yale University Press.

CUBER, J. F., AND P. HARROFF. 1965. *Sex and the Significant Americans.* Baltimore: Penguin.

DANIELS, ROBERT V. 1989. *Year of the Heroic Guerrilla: World Revolution and Counterrevolution in 1968.* New York: Basic Books.

D'ANTONIO, MICHAEL. 1989. *Fall from Grace: The Failed Crusade of the Christian Right.* New York: Farrar, Straus, Giroux.

DAVIS, FRED. 1979. *Yearning for Yesterday: A Sociology of Nostalgia.* New York: Free Press.

DAVIS, KENNETH C. 1984. *Two Bit Culture: The Paperbacking of America.* Boston: Houghton Mifflin.

DAVIS, KINGSLEY. 1988. "Wives and Work: A Theory of the Sex-Role Revolution and Its Consequences." In *Feminism, Children, and the New Families.* Edited by Sanford M. Dornbusch and Myra H. Strober. New York: Guilford Press.

DEGLER, CARL. 1980. *At Odds: Women and the Family in America from the Revolution to the Present.* New York: Oxford University Press.

D'EMILIO, JOHN, AND ESTELLE B. FREEDMAN. 1988. *Intimate Matters: A History of Sexuality in America.* New York: Harper & Row.

DEMOS, JOHN. 1970. *A Little Commonwealth: Family Life in Plymouth Colony.* New York: Oxford University Press.

———. 1976. "Myths and Realities in the History of American Family Life." In *Contemporary Marriage: Structure, Dynamics, and Therapy*, pp. 9–31. Edited by Henry Grunebaum, M.D., and Jacob Christ, M.D. Boston: Little, Brown.

———. 1986. *Past, Present, and Personal: The Family and the Life Course in American History.* New York: Oxford University Press.

DESTEFANO, LINDA, AND DIANE COLESANTO. 1990. "Most Believe U.S. Men Have a Better Life." *San Francisco Chronicle.* 5 February, pp. B3, 5.

DE SWAAN, ABRAM. 1981. "The Politics Of Agoraphobia: On Changes in Emotional and Relational Management." *Theory and Society* 10: 337–58.

DICKSTEIN, M. 1977. *Gates of Eden.* New York: Basic Books.

DIGGINS, JOHN PATRICK. 1988. *The Proud Decades: America in War and Peace, 1941–1960.* New York: Norton.

DI LEONARDO, MICAELA. 1985. "Deindustrialization as a Folk Model." *Urban Anthropology* 14, nos. 1–3: 237–57.

DONALDSON, SCOTT. 1969. *The Suburban Myth.* New York: Columbia University Press.

DORNBUSCH, SANFORD M., AND MYRA STROBER, EDS. 1988. *Feminism, Children, and the New Families.* New York: Guilford Press.

DOUGLAS, MARY. 1970/1973/1982. *Natural Symbols: Explorations in Cosmology.* New York: Pantheon Books.

EASTERLIN, RICHARD. 1980. *Birth and Fortune.* New York: Basic Books.

ECHOLS, ALICE. 1989. *Daring to Be Bad: Radical Feminism in America 1967–1975.* Minneapolis: University of Minnesota Press.

EDWARDS, JOHN N. 1987. "Changing Family Structure and Youthful Well-Being: Assessing the Future." *Journal of Family Issues* 8, no. 4: 355–72. Sage.

EHRENREICH, BARBARA. 1983. *The Hearts of Men: American Dreams and the Flight from Commitment.* Garden City, NY: Anchor Press/Doubleday.

———. 1989. *Fear of Falling: The Inner Life of the Middle Class.* New York: Pantheon Books.

———, ELIZABETH HESS, AND GLORIA JACOBS. 1986. *Re-Making Love: The Feminization of Sex.* New York: Doubleday.

EISENSTADT, S. N. 1956. *From Generation to Generation: Age Groups in Social Structure.* New York: Free Press.

EISLER, BENITA. 1986. *Private Lives: Men and Women of the Fifties.* New York: Franklin Watts.

ELDER, GLEN H. 1974. *Children of the Great Depression.* Chicago: University of Chicago Press.

———. 1981. "History and the Family: The Discovery of Complexity." *Journal of Marriage and the Family* 43: 489–519.

EMERY, R. E. 1982. "Interparental Conflict and the Children of Discord and Divorce." *Psychological Bulletin* 92: 300–330.

———. 1989. "Family Violence." *American Psychologist* 44, no. 2 (February): 321–28.

ERIKSON, E. H. 1963. *Childhood and Society,* 2nd ed. New York: Norton.

ESMAN, AARON. 1990. *Adolescence and Culture.* New York: Columbia University Press.

ESTRICH, SUSAN. 1987. *Real Rape.* Cambridge: Harvard University Press.

EVANS, SARA M. 1989. *Born for Liberty: A History of Women in America.* New York: Free Press.

FARBER, B. 1964. *Family Organization and Interaction.* San Francisco: Chandler.

FARNHAM, M., AND F. LUNDBERG. 1947. *Modern Woman: The Lost Sex.* New York: Harper & Bros.

FASS, PAULA. 1977. *The Damned and the Beautiful: American Youth in the 1920's.* Oxford/New York: Oxford University Press.

FEATHERSTONE, J. 1979. "Family Matters." *Harvard Educational Review* 49: 20–52.

FERRARO, THOMAS J. 1989. "Blood in the Marketplace: The Business of Family in the Godfather Narratives." In *The Invention of Ethnicity*. Edited by Werner Sollors. New York: Oxford University Press.

FIEDLER, LESLIE. 1962. *Love and Death in the American Novel.* New York: Criterion Books.

FIELDS, SUZANNE. 1990. "Wearing Too Many Hats?" *Washington Times.* August 16, p. G1.

FILENE, PETER G. 1986. *Him / Her / Self: Sex Roles in Modern America.* Baltimore: Johns Hopkins University Press.

FINE, BENJAMIN. 1955. *1,000,000 Delinquents.* Cleveland: World Publishing.

FISCHER, CLAUDE S. 1982. *To Dwell Among Friends: Social Networks in Town and City.* Chicago: University of Chicago Press.

FISHMAN, ROBERT. 1987. *Bourgeois Utopias: The Rise and Fall of Suburbia.* New York: Basic Books.

FITZGERALD, FRANCES. 1987. *Cities on a Hill.* New York: Simon & Schuster.

FLEMING, JEANNE J. 1988. "Public Opinion on Change in Women's Rights and Roles." In *Feminism, Children and the New Families.* Edited by Sanford M. Dornbusch and Myra H. Strober. New York: Guilford Press.

FLIEGELMAN, JAY. 1982/1984. *Prodigals and Pilgrims: The American Revolution Against Patriarchal Authority 1750–1800.* New York: Cambridge University Press.

FOOTLICK, JERROLD K. (WITH ELIZABETH LEONARD). 1990. What Happened to the Family? *Newsweek.* Special Edition (Winter/Spring), p. 14.

FRAMO, J. L. 1972. *Family Interaction: A Dialogue Between Family Researchers and Family Therapists.* New York: Springer.

FRASER, RONALD. 1988. *1968: A Student Generation in Revolt: An International Oral History.* New York: Pantheon Books.

FRASER, STEVE, AND GARY GERSTLE, EDS. 1989. *The Rise and Fall of the New Deal Order.* Princeton, NJ: Princeton University Press.

FREEMAN, JO. 1975. *The Politics of Women's Liberation.* New York: McKay.

FREUD, SIGMUND. 1912. "On the Universal Tendency to Debasement in the Sphere of Love," pp. 179–90. *Standard Edition*, vol. 11. New York: Basic Books.

FRIEDAN, B. 1963. *The Feminine Mystique.* New York: Dell.

FRIEDMAN, LAWRENCE M. 1990. *The Republic of Choice: Law, Authority, and Culture.* Cambridge: Harvard University Press.

FRYKMAN, JONAS, AND ORVAR LOFGREN. 1987. *Culture Builders: A Historical Anthropology of Middle-Class Life.* New Brunswick, NJ: Rutgers University Press.

FUCHS, VICTOR R. 1983. *How We Live: An Economic Perspective on Americans from Birth to Death.* Cambridge and London: Harvard University Press.

FURSTENBERG, FRANK F., JR. 1988. "Good Dads—Bad Dads: Two Faces of

Fatherhood." In *The Changing American Family and Public Policy*. Edited by Andrew J. Cherlin. Washington, DC: Urban Institute Press.

———, AND ANDREW J. CHERLIN. 1991. *Divided Families: What Happens to Children When Parents Part*. Cambridge: Harvard University Press.

FURSTENBERG, FRANK F., AND GRETCHEN A. CONDRAN. 1988. "Family Change and Adolescent Well-Being: A Reexamination of U.S. Trends." In *The Changing American Family and Public Policy*. Edited by A. J. Cherlin. Washington, DC: Urban Institute Press.

FURSTENBERG, FRANK F., JR., AND GRAHAM B. SPANIER. 1987. *Recycling the Family: Remarriage After Divorce*. Beverly Hills: Sage.

GADLIN, HOWARD. 1977. "Private Lives and Public Order: A Critical View of the History of Intimate Relations in the United States." In *Close Relationships*, pp. 33–72. Edited by George Levinger and Harold L. Rauch. Amherst: University of Massachusetts Press.

———. 1976. "Child Discipline and the Pursuit of Self: An Historical Interpretation." In *Advances in Child Development and Behavior*, pp. 231–61. Edited by Hayne W. Reese and Lewis P. Lipsitt. New York: Academic Press.

GALLUP, G., JR., AND F. NEWPORT. 1990. "Parenthood—A (Nearly) Universal Desire." *San Francisco Chronicle*. June 4, p. B-3.

GANS, HERBERT J. 1967. *The Levittowners: How People Live and Politic in Suburbia*. New York: Pantheon.

———. 1988. *Middle American Individualism*. New York: Free Press.

GAY, PETER. 1984. *The Bourgeois Experience: Victoria to Freud*. New York: Oxford University Press.

GELLNER, ERNEST. 1985. *The Psychoanalytic Movement or the Coming of Unreason*. London: Paladin Books, Granada Publishing.

GELMAN, AMY. 1990. "Down the Aisle, Surprised." *New York Times*. October 24, p. 25.

GENDLIN, EUGENE T. 1987. "A Philosophical Critique of the Concept of Narcissism: The Significance of the Awareness Movement." In *Pathologies of the Modern Self: Postmodern Studies on Narcissism, Schizophrenia and Depression*. Edited by David M. Levin. New York: Columbia University Press.

GERBER, JERRY, JANET WOLFF, WALTER KLORES, AND GENE BROWN. 1989. *Lifetrends: The Future of Baby Boomers and Other Aging Americans*. New York: Macmillan.

GIDDENS, ANTHONY. 1990. *The Consequences of Modernity*. Stanford, CA: Stanford University Press.

GIELE, JANET ZOLLINGER. 1976. "Changing Sex Roles and the Future of Marriage." In *Contemporary Marriage: Structure, Dynamics, and Therapy*. Edited by Henry Grunebaum, M.D., and Jacob Christ, M.D. Boston: Little, Brown.

GILLIS, JOHN R. 1985. *For Better, For Worse: British Marriages 1600 to the Present*. New York: Oxford University Press.

GITLIN, TODD. 1987. *The Sixties: Years of Hope, Days of Rage.* New York: Bantam Books.

GITTELSON, NATALIE. 1972. *The Erotic Life of the American Wife.* New York: Delacorte Press.

GLENN, NORVAL D. 1987. "Continuity vs. Change, Sanguineness vs. Concern: Views of the American Family in the Late 1980's." *Journal of Family Issues* 8, no. 4: 348–54.

GOETHALS, GEORGE W., ROBERT S. STEELE, AND GWEN J. BROUDE. 1976. "Theories and Research on Marriage: A Review and Some New Directions." In *Contemporary Marriage: Structure, Dynamics, and Therapy.* Edited by Henry Grunebaum, M.D., and Jacob Christ, M.D. Boston: Little, Brown.

GOLDBERG, VICKI. 1987. *Margaret Bourke-White: A Biography.* Reading, MA: Addison-Wesley.

GOLDIN, CLAUDIA. 1983. "The Changing Economic Role of Women: A Cohort Approach." *Journal of Interdisciplinary History* 13: 711.

GOLDTHORPE, J. E. 1987. *Family Life in Western Societies: A Historical Sociology of Family Relationships in Britain and North America.* Cambridge: Cambridge University Press.

GOODE, W. J. 1963. *World Revolution and Family Patterns.* New York: Free Press.

GOODMAN, ELLEN. 1989. *Making Sense.* New York: Atlantic Monthly Press.

GOODMAN, PAUL. 1961. "Why Are There No Alternatives?" *Evergreen Review* 5, no. 16: 1.

GORDON, RICHARD E., KATHERINE K. GORDON, AND MAX GUNTHER. 1961. *The Split Level Trap.* New York: Geis Associates.

GORNICK, VIVIAN. 1978. *Essays in Feminism.* New York: Harper & Row.

GOULART, RON. 1973. *An American Family.* New York: Warner.

GRANT FOUNDATION. 1988. *The Forgotten Half: Pathways to Success for America's Youth and Young Families.* Washington, DC: William T. Grant Foundation Commission on Work, Family and Citizenship.

GREENBERG, DAVID. 1977. "Delinquency and the Age Structure of Society." *Contemporary Crises* 1: 189–223.

GREVEN, PHILIP. 1977. *The Protestant Temperament: Patterns of Childrearing, Religious Experience, and the Self in Early America.* Chicago: University of Chicago Press.

GRISWOLD, ROBERT. 1982. *Family and Divorce in California: Victorian Illusions and Everyday Realities. 1850–1890.* Albany, NY: State University of New York Press.

GROSSBERG, MICHAEL. 1985. *Governing the Hearth: Law and Family in Nineteenth Century America.* Chapel Hill: University of North Carolina Press.

GUTIS, PHILIP S. 1989a. "Court Widens Family Definition to Gay Couples Living Together." *New York Times.* July 7, pp. A1, A13.

———. 1989b. "What Makes a Family? Traditional Limits Are Challenged." *New York Times.* August 31, p. B1.

GUTMANN, AMY. 1989. "Undemocratic Education." In *Liberalism and the*

Moral Life, pp. 71–88. Edited by Nancy L. Rosenblum. Cambridge: Harvard University Press.

HAGESTAD, GUNHILD O. 1986. "The Aging Society as a Context for Family Life." *Daedalus* 115, no. 1: 119–39.

———. 1987. "Families in an Aging Society." *Zeitschrift für Sozialisationsforschung und Erziehungssoziologie* (Spring): 1–8.

HAJNAL, J. 1965. "European Marriage Patterns in Perspective." In *Population in History: Essays in Historical Demography*, pp. 101–43. Edited by D. V. Glass and D. E. C. Eversley. London: Arnold.

HALL, G. 1904. *Adolescence: Its Psychology and Its Relations to Physiology, Anthropology, Sociology, Sex, Crime, Religion, and Education.* New York: Appleton.

HAREVEN, TAMARA K. 1975. "Family Time and Industrial Time: Family and Work in a Planned Corporation Town, 1900–1924." *Journal of Urban History* 1: 365–89.

———. 1982. "American Families in Transition: Historical Perspectives on Change." In *Normal Family Processes*, pp. 446–66. Edited by Froma Walsh. New York: Guilford Press.

HARRINGTON, MICHAEL. 1963. *The Other America. Poverty in the United States.* Baltimore: Penguin Books.

HARRIS, C. C. 1983. *The Family and Industrial Society.* London: George Allen & Unwin.

HARRIS, LOUIS. 1987. *Inside America.* New York: Vintage Books.

HASKELL, MOLLY. 1974. *From Reverence to Rape: The Treatment of Women in the Movies.* New York: Holt, Rinehart and Winston.

HAYDEN, DOLORES. 1984. *Redesigning the American Dream: The Future of Housing, Work and Family Life.* New York: Norton.

HELLER, JOSEPH. 1974. *Something Happened.* New York: Knopf.

HELLERSTEIN, ERNA O., LESLIE P. HUME, AND KAREN M. OFFEN. 1981. *Victorian Women: A Documentary Account of Women's Lives in Nineteenth-Century England, France, and the United States.* Stanford, CA: Stanford University Press.

HETHERINGTON, E. MAVIS, MARGARET STANLEY HAGAN, AND EDWARD R. ANDERSON. 1989. "Marital Transitions: A Child's Perspective." *American Psychologist* 44, no. 2: 303–12.

HEWITT, JOHN P. 1989. *Dilemmas of the American Self.* Philadelphia: Temple University Press.

HEWLETT, SYLVIA ANN. 1986. *A Lesser Life: The Myth of Women's Liberation in America.* New York: Morrow.

———. 1991. *When the Bough Breaks: The Cost of Neglecting Our Children.* New York: Basic Books.

HILL, J., AND F. MONKS. 1977. *Adolescence and Youth in Prospect.* Atlantic Highlands, NJ: Humanities Press.

HINE, THOMAS. 1986. *Populuxe: The Look and Life of America in the 50's and 60's.* New York: Knopf.

HIRSCHMAN, ALBERT O. 1982. *Shifting Involvements: Private Interest and Public Action.* Princeton, NJ: Princeton University Press.

HOCHSCHILD, ARLIE, WITH ANNE MACHUNG. 1989. *The Second Shift: Working Parents and the Revolution at Home.* New York: Viking Penguin.

HODGSON, F. 1976. *America in Our Time.* Garden City, NY: Doubleday.

HOFFMAN, LOIS WLADIS. 1989. "Effects of Maternal Employment in the Two-Parent Family." *American Psychologist* 44, no. 2: 283–97. American Psychological Association.

HOLE, JUDITH, AND ELLEN LEVINE. 1971. *Rebirth of Feminism.* New York: Quadrangle Books.

HOLMES, STEVEN A. 1991. "Unlikely Union Arises to Press Family Issues." *New York Times.* May 1, p. A12.

HONEY, MAUREEN. 1984. *Creating Rosie the Riveter: Class, Gender, and Propaganda During World War II.* Amherst: University of Massachusetts Press.

HOWARD, GERALD, ED. 1982. *The Sixties.* New York: Pocket Books.

HUNT, M. 1974. *Sexual Behavior in the 1970's.* Chicago: Playboy Press.

HUNTER, JAMES DAVISON. 1986. "The Modern Malaise." In *Peter L. Berger and the Vision of Interpretive Sociology.* Edited by James D. Hunter and Stephen C. Ainlay. London and New York: Routledge & Kegan Paul.

———. 1987. *Evangelicalism: The Coming Generation.* Chicago: University of Chicago Press.

IMHOFF, A. E. 1986. "Life Course Patterns of Women and Their Husbands." In *Human Development and the Life Course: Multidisciplinary Perspectives.* Edited by A. B. Sorenson, F. E. Weinert, and L. R. Sherrod. Hillsdale, NJ: Lawrence Erlbaum.

INGLEHART, RONALD. 1977. *The Silent Revolution: Changing Values and Political Styles Among Western Publics.* Princeton, NJ: Princeton University Press.

———. 1990. *Culture Shift.* Princeton, NJ: Princeton University Press.

ISSERMAN, MAURICE, AND MICHAEL KAZIN. 1989. "The New Radicalism." In *The Rise and Fall of the New Deal Order.* Edited by S. Fraser and G. Gerstle. Princeton, NJ: Princeton University Press.

JEFFREY, KIRK. 1972. "The Family as Utopian Retreat from the City: The Nineteeth-Century Contribution." In *The Families, Communes, and Utopian Societies.* Edited by Sallie Teselle. New York: Harper & Row.

JONES, LANDON Y. 1980. *Great Expectations: America and the Baby Boom Generation.* New York: Ballantine Books.

KAGAN, JEROME. 1977. "The Child in the Family." *Daedalus* (Spring): 33–56.

———. 1978. *The Growth of the Child: Reflections on Human Development.* New York: Norton.

KAIN, EDWARD L. 1990. *The Myth of Family Decline: Understanding Families in a World of Rapid Social Change.* Massachusetts/Toronto: Lexington Books.

KAISER, CHARLES. 1988. *1968 in America.* New York: Weidenfeld and Nicholson.

KATZ, MICHAEL, 1989. *The Undeserving Poor: From the War on Poverty to the War on Welfare.* New York: Pantheon Books.

KAY, HERMA HILL. 1989. "Reproductive Technology and Child Custody." In *Family in Transition,* 6th ed. Edited by Arlene S. Skolnick and Jerome H. Skolnick. Glenview, IL: Scott Foresman. (From "Child Custody Litigation Arising From Surrogate Parenting Agreements: A Family Law Perspective on the 'Baby M' Case." Boalt Hall Transcript, vol. 20, no. 2, pp. 405–19.)

KEATS, JOHN. 1956. *The Crack in the Picture Window.* Boston: Houghton Mifflin.

KELLY, DENNIS. 1990. "Man, Are Women Fed Up!" *USA Today.* April 26, p. 1A.

KENISTON, KENNETH 1971. *Youth and Dissent: The Rise of a New Opposition.* New York: Harcourt Brace Jovanovich/Harvest.

KERN, LOUIS J. 1981. *An Ordered Love: Sex Roles and Sexuality in Victorian Utopias—The Shakers, the Mormons, and the Oneida Community.* Chapel Hill: University of North Carolina Press.

KERN, STEPHEN. 1974. "Explosive Intimacy: Psychodynamics of the Victorian Family." *History of Childhood Quarterly* 1: 437–60.

KESSEN, WILLIAM 1965. *The Child.* New York: Wiley.

KESSLER-HARRIS, ALICE. 1982. *Out to Work: A History of Wage-Earning Women in the United States.* New York: Oxford University Press.

———, AND KAREN BRODKIN SACKS. 1987. "The Demise of Domesticity in America." In *Women, Households and the Economy.* Edited by Lourdes Beneria and Catharine R. Stimpson. New Brunswick, NJ: Rutgers University Press.

KILBORN, PETER T. 1990. "Youths Lacking Special Skills Find Jobs Leading Nowhere." *New York Times.* November 27, p. 1.

KIMMEL, MICHAEL S. 1987. "The Contemporary 'Crisis of Masculinity' in Historical Perspective." In *The Making of Masculinities.* Edited by Harry Brod. Boston: Allen and Unwin.

KING, MARY. 1987. *Freedom Song: A Personal Story of the 1960s Civil Rights Movement.* New York: Quill/William Morrow.

KINSEY, ALFRED S., WARDELL B. POMEROY, AND CLYDE E. MARTIN. 1948. *Sexual Behavior in the Human Male.* Philadelphia: Saunders.

———. 1953. *Sexual Behavior in the Human Female.* Philadelphia: Saunders.

KITSON, G. C., K. B. BABRI, AND M. J. ROACH. 1985. "Who Divorces and Why: A Review." *Journal of Family Issues* 6, no. 3 (September): pp. 255–93.

KLATCH, REBECCA E. 1987. *Women of the New Right.* Philadelphia: Temple University Press.

KLINEBERG, STEPHEN L. 1984. "Social Change, World Views, and Cohort Succession: The United States in the 1980s." In *Life-Span Developmental Psychology: Historical and Generational Effects*. Edited by Kathleen A. McCluskey and Hayne W. Reese. Orlando, FL: Academic Press.

KOHLI, MARTIN. 1986. "The World We Forgot: A Historical Review of the Life Course." In *Later Life: The Social Psychology of Aging*, pp. 271–303. Edited by V. M. Marshall. Beverly Hills: Sage.

KOHN, MELVIN M. 1959. "Social Class and Parental Values." *American Journal of Sociology* 64: 337–51.

KNAPP, RONALD J. 1987. *Beyond Endurance: When a Child Dies*. New York: Schocken Books.

KOMAROVSKY, MIRRA. 1990. Speech reported in *Footnotes* 18 (September): 1. American Sociological Association.

KRANTZ, DAVID L. 1988. "The Anti-Psychiatric Film in the New Age." *Readings: A Journal of Reviews and Commentary in Mental Health* 3 (December): 16–19. American Orthopsychiatric Association.

LABARRE, WESTON. 1954. *The Human Animal*. Chicago: University of Chicago Press.

LANDIS, P. H. 1955. *Making the Most of Your Marriage*. Englewood Cliffs, NJ: Prentice-Hall.

LANGER, W. L. 1972. *"Checks on Population Growth: 1750–1850."* Scientific American 226: 93–100.

LASCH, CHRISTOPHER. 1975. "The Family and History." *New York Review of Books*. November 13, pp. 33–38.

———. 1976. "The Narcissist Society." *New York Review of Books*. September 30, pp. 5–8, 10–13.

———. 1977. *Haven in a Heartless World*. New York: Basic Books.

———. 1979. *The Culture of Narcissism*. New York: Norton.

LASLETT, B. 1973. "The Family as a Public and Private Institution." *Journal of Marriage and the Family* 35 (August): 480–94.

LASLETT, PETER. 1965. *The World We Have Lost: England Before the Industrial Age*. New York: Scribners.

———. 1976. "Societal Development and Aging." In *Handbook of Aging and the Social Sciences*, pp. 87–116. Edited by R. H. Binstock and E. Shanas. New York: Van Nostrand Reinhold.

———. 1989. *A Fresh Map of Life: The Emergence of the Third Age*. London: Weidenfeld and Nicolson.

LAWSON, ANNETTE. 1988. *Adultery: An Analysis of Love and Betrayal*. New York: Basic Books.

LEAR, MARTHA W. 1988. "The New Marital Therapy." *New York Times*. March 6, p. 63.

LEARS, JACKSON. 1989. "A Matter of Taste: Corporate Cultural Hegemony in a Mass-Consumption Society." In *Recasting America: Culture and Politics in the Age of Cold War.* Edited by Lary May. Chicago: University of Chicago Press.

LENNARD, HENRY L., AND A. BERNSTEIN. 1969. *Patterns in Human Interaction.* San Francisco: Jossey-Bass.

LEKACHMAN, ROBERT. 1966. *The Age of Keynes.* New York: Random House.

LEUCHTENBURG, WILLIAM E. 1958. *The Perils of Prosperity 1914–32.* Chicago: University of Chicago Press.

LEVENSON, E. A. 1972. *The Fallacy of Understanding: An Inquiry into the Changing Structure of Psychoanalysis.* New York: Basic Books.

LEVINE, ROBERT A. 1965. "Intergenerational Tensions and Extended Family Structures in Africa." In *Social Structure and the Family: Generational Relations,* pp. 188–204. Edited by E. Shanas and G. F. Streib. Englewood Cliffs, NJ: Prentice-Hall.

———, AND MERRY WHITE. 1987. "Parenthood in Social Transformation." In *Parenting Across the Life Span: Biosocial Dimensions.* Edited by Jane B. Lancaster, Jeanne Altmann, Alice S. Rossi, and Lonnie R. Sherrod. New York: Aldine De Gruyter.

LEVITAN, SAR A., RICHARD S. BELOUS, AND FRANK GALLO. 1981/1988. *What's Happening to the American Family? Tension, Hopes, Realities,* rev. ed. Baltimore: Johns Hopkins University Press.

LEVY, FRANK. 1987. *Dollars and Dreams: The Changing American Income Distribution.* New York: Russell Sage Foundation.

———, AND RICHARD C. MICHEL. 1985. "Are Baby Boomers Selfish?" *American Demographics.* 17: 38–41.

LEWIN, TAMAR. 1990. "Suit over Death Benefits Asks, What Is a Family?" *New York Times.* September 21.

LHAMON, W. T. 1990. *Deliberate Speed: The Origins of a Cultural Style in the American 1950's.* Washington, DC: Smithsonian Institution Press.

LIPSET, SEYMOUR MARTIN. 1982. "Failures of Extremism." *Transaction/Society* 20, no. 1: 48–58.

LIPSITZ, GEORGE. 1990. "Why Remember Mama? The Changing Face of a Woman's Narrative." In *Time Passages: Collective Memory and American Popular Culture.* Minneapolis: University of Minnesota Press.

LONG, ELIZABETH. 1985. *The American Dream and the Popular Novel.* Boston: Routledge & Kegan Paul.

LUEDKE, LUTHER S. 1986. "From Fission to Fusion: Sam Shepard's Nuclear Families." Unpublished manuscript. University of Southern California.

LUKER, KRISTIN. 1984. *Abortion and the Politics of Motherhood.* Berkeley: University of California Press.

LYKSTRA, KAREN. 1989. *Searching the Heart: Women, Men, and Romantic Love in Nineteenth Century America.* New York: Oxford University Press.

LYND, ROBERT S., AND HELEN M. LYND. 1929/1956. *Middletown: A Study in American Culture.* New York: Harcourt Brace Jovanovich.

LYNES, RUSSELL. 1953. *A Surfeit of Honey.* New York: Harper & Bros.

MacDonald, Dwight. 1957. "A Theory of Mass Culture." In *Mass Culture: The Popular Arts in America*, pp. 59–73. Edited by Bernard Rosenberg and David M. White. Glencoe, IL: Free Press.

MacFarlane, Alan. 1986. *Marriage and Love in England 1300–1840*. New York: Basil Blackwell.

McKendrick, Neil, John Brewer, and J. H. Plumb. 1982. *The Birth of Consumer Society: The Commercialization of Eighteenth-Century England*. Bloomington: Indiana University Press.

McLaughlin, Steven D., Barbara D. Melber, John O. G. Billy, Denise M. Zimmerle, Linda D. Winges, and Terry R. Johnson. 1988. *The Changing Lives of American Women*. Chapel Hill: University of North Carolina Press.

McLoughlin, William. 1978. *Revivals, Awakenings, and Reform*. Chicago: University of Chicago Press.

Mandel, Bill. 1987. "Back to the Future: How We Thought We'd Live in 1987." *San Francisco Examiner*, August 9.

Mander, J. 1969. "In Defense of the 50's." *Commentary* (September).

Mansbridge, Jane. 1986. *Why We Lost the ERA*. Chicago: University of Chicago Press.

Marcus, Steven. 1984. *Freud and the Culture of Psychoanalysis*. Boston: George Allen & Unwin.

Margolis, Maxine L. 1984/1985. *Mothers and Such: Views of American Women and Why They Changed*. Berkeley: University of California Press.

Masnick, George, and Mary Jo Bane. 1980. *The Nation's Families: 1960–1990*. Boston: Auburn House.

Mathews, Jane De Hart. 1982. "The New Feminism and the Dynamics of Social Change." In *Women's America: Refocusing the Past*, pp. 397–421. Edited by Linda K. Kerber and Jane De Hart Mathews. New York: Oxford University Press.

May, Elaine Tyler. 1988. *Homeward Bound: American Families in the Cold War Era*. New York: Basic Books.

———. 1989. "Explosive Issues: Sex, Women, and the Bomb." In *Recasting America: Culture and Politics in the Age of Cold War*. Edited by Lary May. Chicago: University of Chicago Press.

May, Lary, ed. 1989. *Recasting America: Culture and Politics in the Age of Cold War*. Chicago: University of Chicago Press.

Mead, Walter Russell. 1987. *Mortal Splendor: The American Empire in Transition*. Boston: Houghton Mifflin.

Mellman, Mark, Edward Lazarus, and Allan Rivlin. 1990. "Family Time, Family Values." In *Rebuilding the Nest: A New Commitment to the American Family*. Edited by D. Blankenhorn, Steven Bayme, and Jean Bethke Elshtain. Milwaukee, WI: Family Service America.

Melucci, Alberto. 1989. *Nomads of the Present: Social Movements and Individual Needs in Contemporary Society*. Edited by John Keane and Paul Mier. Philadelphia: Temple University Press.

MERRITT, SHARYNE, AND LINDA STEINER. 1984. *And Baby Makes Two: Motherhood Without Marriage.* New York: Franklin Watts.

MILLER, DANIEL, AND GUY SWANSON. 1958. *The Changing American Parent.* New York: Wiley.

MINTZ, STEVEN, AND SUSAN KELLOGG. 1988. *Domestic Revolutions: A Social History of American Family Life.* New York: Free Press.

MODELL, JOHN. 1980. "Normative Aspects of Marital Timing Since World War II." *Journal of Family History* 5: 210–34.

————. 1989. *Into One's Own: From Youth to Adulthood in the United States 1920–1975.* Berkeley: University of California Press.

MODELL, JOHN, FRANK F. FURSTENBERG, AND DOUGLAS STRONG. 1978. "The Timing of Marriage in the Transition to Adulthood: Continuity and Change 1860–1975." In *Turning Points.* Edited by John Demos and Saranne S. Boocock. *American Journal of Sociology* 84 (supp. S120–S150).

MODELL, JOHN, AND TAMARA K. HAREVEN. 1973. "Urbanization and the Malleable Household: An Examination of Boarding and Lodging in American Families." *Journal of Marriage and the Family* 35: 467–79.

MOORE, HENRIETTA L. 1988. *Feminism and Anthropology.* Minneapolis: University of Minnesota Press.

MOORMAN, JEAN E. 1987. "The History and Future of the Relationship Between Education and First Marriage." (Unpublished paper.) Washington, DC: U.S. Bureau of the Census.

MORGAN, ROBIN. 1975/1987. "Rights of Passage." In *A History of Our Time: Readings on Postwar America,* pp. 229–30. Edited by William H. Chafe and Harvard Sitkoff. New York: Oxford University Press. (Originally published in *Ms.* magazine, November 1975.)

MORONEY, R. 1980. *Families, Social Services and Social Policy.* Washington, DC: U.S. Department of Health and Human Services.

MOYNIHAN, DANIEL P. 1965. *The Negro Family: The Case for National Action.* Washington, D.C.: U.S. Government Printing Office.

————. 1986. *Family and Nation.* San Diego, CA: Harcourt Brace Jovanovich.

MUUSS, R. E. 1962. *Theories of Adolescence.* New York: Random House.

NAISBETT, JOHN. 1982. *Megatrends: Ten New Directions Transforming Our Lives.* New York: Warner Books.

NEWMAN, KATHERINE S. 1988. *Falling from Grace: The Experience of Downward Mobility in the American Middle Class.* New York: Free Press.

NORTON, MARY B., DAVID M. KATZMAN, PAUL D. ESCOTT, HOWARD P. CHUDACOFF, THOMAS G. PATERSON, AND WILLIAM M. TUTTLE, JR. 1986. *A People and a Nation: A History of the United States.* Boston: Houghton Mifflin.

OAKLEY, J. RONALD. 1986. *God's Country: America in the Fifties.* New York: Dembner Books.

OGBURN, WILLIAM F. 1950. *Social Change.* New York: Viking.

OGDEN, ANNEGRET. 1986. *The Great American Housewife: From Helpmate to Wage Earner, 1776–1986.* Westport, CT: Greenwood Press.

OGILVY, JAY, AND HEATHER OGILVY. 1972. "Communes and the Reconstruction of Reality." In *The Family, Communes, and Utopian Societies.* Edited by Sallie Teselle. New York: Harper & Row.

OLDENBURG, RAY. 1989. *The Great Good Place: Cafes, Coffee Shops, Community Centers, Beauty Parlors, General Stores, Bars, Hangouts, and How They Get You Through the Day.* New York: Paragon House.

O'NEILL, NENA. 1977. *The Marriage Premise.* New York: Evans.

———, AND G. O'NEILL. 1972. *Open Marriage.* New York: Evans.

O'NEILL, WILLIAM L. 1986. *American High: The Years of Confidence, 1945–1960.* New York: Free Press.

O'REILLY, JANE. 1972. "The Housewife's Moment of Truth." *Ms.* magazine (Spring): 54–59.

ORTHNER, DENNIS K. 1990. "The Family in Transition." In *Rebuilding the Nest: A New Commitment to the American Family.* Edited by David Blankenhorn, Steven Bayme, and Jean Bethke Elshtain. Milwaukee: Family Service America.

OXFORD ANALYTICA. 1986. *America in Perspective: The Social, Economic, Political, Fiscal, and Psychological Trends That Will Shape American Society for the Next Ten Years and Beyond.* Boston: Houghton Mifflin.

PARSONS, T. 1955. "The American Family: Its Relations to Personality and the Social Structure." In *Family Socialization and Interaction Process*, pp. 3–21. Edited by T. Parsons and R. F. Bales. Glencoe, IL: Free Press.

PERUN, P. J., AND D. D. BIELBY. 1979. "Midlife: A Discussion of Competing Models." *Research on Aging* 1: 275–300.

PETCHESKY, ROSALIND POLLACK. 1984. *Abortion and Woman's Choice: The State, Sexuality, and Reproductive Freedom.* Boston: Northeastern University Press.

PHILLIPS, KEVIN P. 1982. *Post-Conservative America: People, Politics and Ideology in a Time of Crisis.* New York: Random House.

———. 1990. *The Politics of Rich and Poor: Wealth and the American Electorate in the Reagan Aftermath.* New York: Harper Perennial.

PHILLIPS, R. 1988. *Putting Asunder: A History of Divorce in Western Society.* New York: Cambridge University Press.

PLATH, DAVID W. 1980. *Long Engagements: Maturity in Modern Japan.* Stanford, CA: Stanford University Press.

PLECK, J. H. 1985. *Working Wives/Working Husbands.* Beverly Hills, CA: Sage.

POLLOCK, LINDA. 1983. *Forgotten Children: Parent–Child Relations from 1500–1900.* Cambridge: Cambridge University Press.

POOVEY, MARY. 1988. *Uneven Developments: The Ideological Work of Gender in Mid-Victorian England.* Chicago: University of Chicago Press.

POPENOE, DAVID. 1988/1989. *Disturbing the Nest: Family Change and Decline in Modern Societies.* New York: Aldine De Gruyter.

PRESTON, S. J. 1976. *Mortality Patterns in National Population: With Special References to Recorded Causes of Death.* New York: Academic Press.

PULVER, SYDNEY E. 1986. "Narcissism: The Term and the Concept." In *Essential Papers on Narcissism.* Edited by Andrew P. Morrison, M.D. New York: New York University Press.

RAFFERTY, C., AND M. K. POWELSON. 1988. "Love in the Nineties." *San Francisco Focus.* March, pp. 46ff.

REED, JAMES. 1978. *From Private Vice to Public Virtue: The Birth Control Movement and American Society Since 1830.* New York: Basic Books.

REICH, CHARLES. 1970. *The Greening of America.* New York: Random House.

REISS, IRA L. 1960. *Premarital Sexual Standards in America.* Glencoe, IL: Free Press.

———. 1966. "The Sexual Renaissance: A Summary and Analysis." *Journal of Social Issues* 22: 126.

———, AND GARY R. LEE. 1988. *Family Systems in America,* 4th ed. New York: Holt Rinehart & Winston.

REISSMAN, C. K. 1990. *Divorce Talk: Women and Men Make Sense of Personal Relationships.* New Brunswick, NJ: Rutgers University Press.

RICHMAN, LOUIS S., WITH JULIENNE SLOVAK. 1990. "The New Middle Class: How It Lives." *Fortune Magazine.* August 13, p. 104.

RIESMAN, DAVID, IN COLLABORATION WITH RUELL DENNY AND NATHAN GLAZER. 1950. *The Lonely Crowd. A Study of the Changing American Character.* New Haven, CT: Yale University Press.

ROBINSON, P. 1976. *The Modernization of Sex.* New York: Harper & Row.

ROIPHE, ANNE. 1973. "Things Are Keen But Could Be Keener." In *An American Family,* text prepared by Ron Goulart. New York: Warner Books.

ROSEN, RUTH. 1987. "The Need for Memory." *Tikkun* 2, no. 3 (July–August): 53.

ROSENFELT, DEBORAH, AND JUDITH STACEY. 1987. "Second Thoughts on the Second Wave." *Feminist Studies* 13, no. 2 (Summer): 341–61.

ROTHMAN, ELLEN K. 1984. *Hands and Hearts: A History of Courtship in America.* New York: Basic Books.

RUBIN, LILLIAN B. 1976. *Worlds of Pain: Life in the Working Class Family.* New York: Basic Books.

———. 1979. *Women of a Certain Age: The Midlife Search for Self.* New York: Harper & Row.

———. 1990. *Erotic Wars: What Happened to the Sexual Revolution?* New York: Farrar, Straus & Giroux.

RUPP, LEILA. 1978. *Mobilizing Women for War: German and American Propaganda, 1939–1945.* Princeton, NJ: Princeton University Press.

RYAN, MARY. 1981. *Cradle of the Middle Class: The Family in Oneida County, New York, 1790–1865.* New York: Cambridge University Press.

RYCROFT, CHARLES. 1968. *A Critical Dictionary of Psycho-Analysis.* New York: Basic Books.

SCARR, S., D. PHILLIPS, AND K. MCCARTNEY. 1989. "Working Mothers and Their Families." *American Psychologist* 44, no. 11: 1402–9.

SCHEPER-HUGHES, N. 1985. "Culture, Scarcity, and Maternal Thinking: Maternal Detachment and Infant Survival in a Brazilian Shanty-town." *Ethos: Journal of the Society for Psychological Anthropology* 13, no. 4 (Winter): 291–317.

SCHLESINGER, ARTHUR, JR. 1960. "The New Mood in Politics." Reprinted in Gerald Howard, ed. *The Sixties: The Art, Attitudes, Politics, and Media of Our Most Explosive Decade*, pp. 44–55. New York: Washington Square Press.

SCHLOSSMAN, STEVEN L. 1980. "The Multiple Possibilities of Decency: Family and Society in American History." Paper presented at a conference on "The American Family: Moving Towards the 21st Century." Columbus, GA, May 13.

SCHNAIBERG, ALLAN, AND SHELDON GOLDENBERG. 1989. "From Empty Nest to Crowded Nest: The Dynamics of Incompletely-Launched Young Adults." *Social Problems* 36, no. 3 (June): 251–69.

SCHNEIDER, DAVID M., AND RAYMOND T. SMITH. 1973. *Class Differences and Sex Roles in American Kinship and Family Structure*. Englewood Cliffs, NJ: Prentice-Hall.

SEARS, R. R., E. E. MACCOBY, AND H. LEVIN. 1957. *Patterns of Child Rearing*. Evanston, IL: Row, Peterson.

SEIGEL, JERROLD. 1986. *Bohemian Paris: Culture, Politics, and the Boundaries of Bourgeois Life, 1830–1930*. New York: Viking Penguin.

SHAMMAS, C. 1980. "The Domestic Environment in Early Modern England and America." *Journal of Social History* 14, no. 1: 3–24.

SHEEHY, GAIL. 1976. *Passages*. New York: Bantam.

SHEFF, DAVID. 1988. "Portrait of a Generation." *Rolling Stone*. May 5, p. 62.

SHORTER, E. 1975. *The Making of the Modern Family*. New York: Basic Books.

SIDEL, RUTH. 1990. *On Her Own: Growing Up in the Shadow of the American Dream*. New York: Viking Penguin.

SKOLNICK, ARLENE. 1981. "Married Lives: Longitudinal Perspectives on Marriage." In *Present and Past in Middle Life*, pp. 269–98. Edited by D. H. Eichorn, J. A. Clausen, N. Haan, M. P. Honzik, and P. H. Mussen. New York: Academic Press.

SKOLNICK, JEROME H. 1969. *The Politics of Protest. A Task Force Report to the National Commission on the Causes and Prevention of Violence*. New York: Ballantine.

SLUZKI, C. E., AND V. ELISEO. 1971. "The Double Bind as a Universal Pathogenic Situation." *Family Process* 10, no. 4: 397–410.

SMELSER, NEIL J., AND SYDNEY HALPERN. 1978. "The Historical Triangulation of Family, Economy, and Education." *American Journal of Sociology* 84. University of Chicago Press.

SMITH-ROSENBERG, CARROLL. 1978. "Sex as Symbol in Victorian Purity:

An Ethnohistorical Analysis of Jacksonian America." In *Turning Points: Historical and Sociological Essays on the Family*, pp. S212–S247. Edited by John Demos and Sarane Spence Boocock. Chicago: University of Chicago Press.

———. 1985. *Disorderly Conduct: Visions of Gender in Victorian America.* New York: Knopf.

SOLOMON, DEBORAH. 1991. "New and Improved?" Review of *Ms.* Magazine. *Women's Review of Books* 8: 9–10.

SORENSON, R. C. 1973. *Adolescent Sexuality in Contemporary America.* New York: World.

SPACKS, PATRICIA. 1981. *The Adolescent Idea: Myths of Youth and the Adult Imagination.* New York: Basic Books.

SPANIER, G. 1989. "Bequeathing Family Continuity." *Journal of Marriage and the Family* 51 (February): 3–13.

SPECK, R. V., ET AL. 1972. *The New Families: Youth, Communes and the Politics of Drugs.* New York: Basic Books.

SPIEGEL, JOHN. 1971. *Transactions: The Interplay Between Individual, Family, and Society.* New York: Science House.

STACEY, JUDITH. 1990. *Brave New Families: Stories of Domestic Upheaval in Late Twentieth Century America.* New York: Basic Books.

STEARNS, CAROL ZISOWITZ, AND PETER N. STEARNS. 1986. *Anger: The Struggle for Emotional Control in America's History.* Chicago: University of Chicago Press.

STEINER, GILBERT. 1981. *The Futility of Family Policy.* Washington, D.C.: Brookings Institution.

STEINMETZ, SUZANNE K., AND MURRAY S. STRAUS. 1974. *Violence in the Family.* New York: Dodd, Mead.

STEWART, THOMAS J., OLIVER J. BJORKSTEN, AND IRA D. GLICK. 1985. "Sociodemographic Aspects of Contemporary American Marriage." In *New Clinical Concepts in Marital Therapy.* Edited by Oliver J. Bjorksten. Washington, DC: American Psychiatric Press.

STIPEK, DEBORAH, AND JACQUELYN McCROSKEY. 1989. "Investing in Children: Government and Workplace Policies for Parents." *American Psychologist* 44, no. 2: 416–23. American Psychological Association.

STONE, LAWRENCE. 1977. *The Family, Sex, and Marriage in England, 1500–1800.* New York: Harper & Row.

———. 1989. "The Road to Polygamy." *New York Review of Books* 36, no. 3 (March 2): 12–15.

———. 1990. *Road to Divorce: England 1530–1987.* Oxford: Oxford University Press.

SULLIVAN, ANDREW, 1989. "Here Comes the Groom: The Case for Gay Marriage." *The New Republic.* August 28, p. 201.

SUSMAN, WARREN I. 1984. *Culture as History: The Transformation of American Society in the Twentieth Century.* New York: Pantheon Books.

———, WITH THE ASSISTANCE OF EDWARD GRIFFIN. 1989. "Did Success Spoil the United States? Dual Representations in Postwar America." In *Re-*

casting America: Culture and Politics in the Age of Cold War. Edited by Lary May. Chicago: University of Chicago Press.

SWIDLER, ANN. 1985. "Still the Same Old Story." In *Talk of Love.* Manuscript in process.

TAFT, HORACE. 1922. Letter to William Howard Taft, then Chief Justice of the United States (formerly president). December 31. In Taft Papers, Library of Congress. Discovered by Robert Post and reported in personal communication, May 2, 1991.

TAYLOR, CHARLES. 1989. *Sources of the Self: The Making of the Modern Identity.* Cambridge: Harvard University Press.

TAYLOR, ELLA. 1989. *Prime-Time Families: Television Culture in Postwar America.* Berkeley: University of California Press.

TERMAN, L. 1938. *Psychological Factors in Marital Happiness.* New York: McGraw-Hill.

THORNTON, ARLAND, AND THOMAS E. FRICK. 1987. "Social Changes and the Family: Comparative Perspectives from the West, China and South Asia." *Sociological Forum* 2: 746–74.

TIGER, LIONEL. 1989. "A Tribe's Tone and Texture." In *America Worked: The 1950's Photographs of Dan Weiner.* Edited by William A. Ewing. New York: Abrams.

TOCQUEVILLE, ALEXIS DE. 1835/1966. *Democracy in America.* Translated by George Lawrence. New York: Harper & Row.

TREXLER, R. C. 1973. "Infanticide in Florence: New Sources and First Results." *History of Childhood Quarterly* 1, no. 1: 98–116.

TRIBE, LAWRENCE. 1978. *American Constitutional Law.* Mineola, NY: Foundation Press.

TRILLING, LIONEL. 1972. *Sincerity and Authenticity.* Cambridge: Harvard University Press.

TRUMBACH, J. 1978. *The Rise of the Egalitarian Family: Aristocratic Kinship and Domestic Relations in 18th Century England.* New York: Academic Press.

TURNER, VICTOR. 1974. *Dramas, Fields, and Metaphors: Symbolic Action in Human Society.* Ithaca, NY: Cornell University Press.

UHLENBERG, PETER. 1980. "Death and the Family." *Journal of Family History* 5, no. 3: 313–20.

———, AND DAVID EGGEBEEN. 1986. "The Declining Well-Being of American Adolescents." *The Public Interest* 82: 25–38.

VAN HORN, SUSAN HOUSEHOLDER. 1988. *Women, Work, and Fertility, 1900–1986.* 1988. New York: New York University Press.

VEROFF, J., G. DOUVAN, AND R. A. KULKA. 1981. *The Inner American: A Self-Portrait from 1957–1976.* New York: Basic Books.

WACHTEL, PAUL L. 1983. *The Poverty of Affluence: A Psychological Portrait of the American Way of Life.* New York: Free Press.

WALL, HELENA M. 1990. *Fierce Communion: Family and Community in Early America.* Cambridge: Harvard University Press.

WALLACE, ANTHONY F. C. 1956. "Revitalization Movements." *American Anthropology* 58: 264–81.

———. 1970. *The Death and Rebirth of the Seneca.* New York: Knopf.

WALLERSTEIN, JUDITH S., AND SANDRA BLAKESLEE. 1989. *Second Chances: Men, Women and Children a Decade After Divorce.* New York: Ticknor & Fields.

WEEKS, JEFFREY. 1985. *Sexuality and Its Discontents: Meanings, Myths and Modern Sexualities.* London: Routledge & Kegan Paul.

WEINER, LYNN Y. 1985. *From Working Girl to Working Mother: The Female Labor Force in the United States, 1820–1980.* Chapel Hill: University of North Carolina Press.

WEIR, MARGARET, ANN S. ORLOFF, AND THEDA SKOCPOL, EDS. 1988. *The Politics of Social Policy in the United States.* Princeton, NJ: Princeton University Press.

WEISS, MICHAEL J. 1988. *The Clustering of America.* New York: Harper & Row..

WEISS, NANCY P. 1977. "Mother, the Invention of Necessity: Dr. Benjamin Spock's Baby and Child Care." *American Quarterly* 29.

WEISS, ROBERT. 1979. "A New Marital Form: The Marriage of Uncertain Duration." In *On the Making of Americans: Essays in Honor of David Riesman,* pp. 221–34. Edited by Herbert J. Gans, Nathan Glazer, Joseph R. Gusfield, and Christopher Jencks. Philadelphia: University of Pennsylvania Press.

WEITZMAN, LENORE. 1985. *The Divorce Revolution: The Unexpected Social and Economic Consequences for Women and Children in America.* New York: Free Press.

WELLS, ROBERT V. 1982. *Revolutions in Americans' Lives: A Demographic Perspective on the History of Americans, Their Families, Their Society.* Westport, CT: Greenwood.

WELTER, BARBARA. 1966/1973. "The Cult of True Womanhood: 1820–1860." In *The American Family in Social–Historical Perspective,* pp. 224–51. Edited by Michael Gordon. New York: St. Martin's Press. (Reprinted from *The American Quarterly* 18, no. 2, pt. 1: 151–74.)

WESTKOTT, MARCIA. 1986. *The Feminist Legacy of Karen Horney.* New Haven, CT: Yale University Press.

WHITE, JOHN KENNETH. 1988. *The New Politics of Old Values.* Hanover and London: University Press of New England.

WHITE, L. 1978. "Science and the Sense of Self: The Medieval Background of a Modern Confrontation." *Daedalus* 107, no. 2: 47–59.

WHYTE, WILLIAM F. 1956. *The Organization Man.* New York: Simon & Schuster.

WILENSKY, HAROLD L. 1990. "Common Problems, Divergent Policies: An 18-Nation Study of Family Policy." In *Public Affairs Report* 31, no. 3: 1–

3. Institute of Governmental Studies, University of California, Berke-
ley.
WILKES, PAUL 1975. *Trying Out the Dream: A Year in the Life of an American
Family.* Philadelphia: Lippincott.
WILKINSON, RUPERT. 1983. "American Character Revisited." *American
Studies* 17: 165–87.
———. 1988. *The Pursuit of American Character.* New York: Harper &
Row.
WILLIAMS, RAYMOND. 1961. *The Long Revolution.* New York: Columbia
University Press.
WILLIS, ELLEN, 1981. *Beginning to See the Light.* New York: Knopf.
WILSON, WILLIAM J. 1987. *The Truly Disadvantaged: The Inner City, the Un-
derclass and Public Policy.* Chicago: University of Chicago Press.
WOLFE, TOM. 1976/1982. "The Me Decade and the Third Great Awaken-
ing." In *Tom Wolfe: The Purple Decades,* pp. 265–93. New York: Berkeley
Books. (First published in *New York Magazine* and *New West Magazine,*
August 23, 1976.)
WOLFENSTEIN, MARTHA. 1955. "Fun Morality: An Analysis of Recent
American Child-training Literature." In *Childhood in Contemporary Cul-
tures,* pp. 169–78. Edited by M. Mead and M. Wolfenstein. Chicago:
University of Chicago Press.
WOLOCH, NANCY. 1984. *Women and the American Experience.* New York:
Knopf.
WRONG, DENNIS. 1976. "Identity: Problem and Catchword." In *Skeptical
Sociology,* pp. 81–94. New York: Columbia University Press.
WYLIE, PHILIP. 1942/1955. *Generation of Vipers.* New York: Holt, Rinehart
& Winston.

YANKELOVICH, DANIEL. 1981. *New Rules: Searching for Self-Fulfillment in a
World Turned Upside Down.* New York: Random House.
YOUNG, M., AND P. WILLMOTT. 1973. *The Symmetrical Family.* New York:
Random House/Pantheon.

ZABLOCKI, B. 1971. *The Joyful Community: An Account of the Bruderhof, A
Communal Movement Now in Its Third Generation.* Baltimore: Penguin.
———. 1980. *Alienation and Charisma. A Study of Contemporary American
Communes.* New York: Free Press.
ZARETSKY, E. 1976. *Capitalism, the Family and Personal Life.* New York:
Harper & Row/Colophon.
ZELDITCH, M., JR. 1964. "Cross-Cultural Analyses of Family Structure." In
Handbook of Marriage and the Family, pp. 462–500. Edited by H. T. Chris-
tensen. Chicago: Rand McNally.
ZELIZER, VIVIANA A. 1985. *Pricing the Priceless Child: The Changing Social
Value of Children.* New York: Basic Books.
ZILL, NICHOLAS, AND CAROLYN G. ROGERS. 1988. "Recent Trends in the
Well-Being of Children in the United States and Their Implications

for Public Policy." In *The Changing American Family and Public Policy*, pp. 31–98. Edited by Andrew J. Cherlin. Washington, DC: Urban Institute Press.

ZUCKERMAN, MICHAEL. 1975. "Dr. Spock: The Confidence Man." In *The Family in History*, pp. 179–207. Edited by Charles E. Rosenberg. Philadelphia: University of Pennsylvania Press.

ZWEIG, PAUL. 1980. *The Heresy of Self-Love*. Princeton, NJ: Princeton University Press.

INDEX